THE ECONOMIC BASIS
OF POLITICS
AND RELATED WRITINGS

THE ECONOMIC

BASIS

OF POLITICS

AND

RELATED WRITINGS

BY CHARLES A. BEARD

———

COMPILED AND ANNOTATED BY

WILLIAM BEARD, PH.D.

FORMERLY ASSISTANT PROFESSOR OF POLITICAL SCIENCE
UNIVERSITY OF WISCONSIN

———

VINTAGE BOOKS

NEW YORK 1958

CONTENTS

PART III

TWO SPECIFIC EXAMPLES OF THE INTERPLAY OF ECONOMICS
AND POLITICS IN EUROPEAN HISTORY

PART IV

SOME ECONOMIC ASPECTS OF AMERICAN POLITICAL HISTORY

COMPILER'S INTRODUCTION

IT IS COMPARATIVELY safe and easy to describe the past
in terms of the surface manifestations of politics—such
as the provisions of the Constitution of the United States
as presented to the states for adoption in 1787, or the
official wording of papers traded among diplomats during
major disputes over foreign policy. Charles A. Beard was
much too outspoken, however, and far too inquisitive to
be satisfied with a limited program of this nature. In the
course of a long, active, and often stormy career as a
writer and university professor, he probed deeply behind
the scenes in quest of basic economic explanations for
major political developments. What was the alignment of
commercial interests during the writing of the Constitution
of the United States? What business motives found expression in the messages dispatched by the government of
one nation to that of another, in periods of tension over
faraway places? Questions such as these he did not hesitate to discuss openly in print.

Researches in this vein gave rise to a wealth of argument,
some of it very heated. "Idealists" who denied that economics had exerted anything like the influence on political
affairs Beard was said to have claimed, lashed out at him
as a "materialist"—one who sought to undermine human-
kind's claim to disinterested nobility of character. Marxians
complained that his labors neglected to provide that
special brand of economic insight into events which, in
their judgment, alone afforded a "correct" understanding
of political history. Some took a more neutral position,
recognizing fundamental value in Beard's work yet differing with him as to certain details and emphases. Still others

were enthusiastic followers, hailing him as one who had dared to open valuable new areas to research.

Publicized not only by a host of friends but by foes as well—who felt his work was much too challenging to be ignored—Beard's labors exerted tremendous influence. Over ten million copies of histories bearing his name have been sold, many of them stressing economic considerations in political history. He attained the Presidency of both the American Historical Association and the American Political Science Association. His *The Economic Basis of Politics* was translated into German, supplied with a special introduction by a member of the American Military Government, and then employed in the "re-education" of Germans in their homeland, following the Second World War.[1] To cite another example, the Columbia network devoted a half-hour nation-wide broadcast, on October 24, 1954, to a discussion by Norman Thomas, David Denker, and Lyman Bryson on the lasting importance of Beard's *An Economic Interpretation of the Constitution of the United States*. Further evidence of the vitality of Beard's ideas is afforded by a recent bibliography of published comments on them.[2]

Yet inquirers seeking a convenient cross-section of Beard's thinking on the subject of the impact of economics on political history have long found it difficult to obtain a representative sampling of his labors. Not only were his contributions to the topic widely scattered and aimed at diverse objectives, but numerous of his works have been out of print for years—and could ordinarily be inspected only after making special arrangements with a few major libraries or eliciting the sympathetic help of secondhand-book sellers. The present volume was undertaken in an effort to provide easier access to his passages on the subject. Following a preliminary sketch of his familiarity with pioneers in this field, and his manifold personal contacts with the everyday economic life about him, it offers selections from his writings which, it is hoped, will give greater understanding of the breadth of his interest in, and

[1] *Die Wirtschaftliche Grundlage der Politik* (1949).
[2] Beale, Howard K., ed., *Charles A. Beard*, University of Kentucky Press (1954), pp. 284–6.

knowledge of, the interplay of economics and politics through many centuries of Western history.[3]

The great bulk of the material offered here is from volumes or periodicals now otherwise completely out of print. Those wishing to supplement the text with books still readily available directly from publishers' stocks are advised that at this writing (August, 1956) The Macmillan Co. had on hand Beard's *An Economic Interpretation of the Constitution of the United States* (1913) and *Economic Origins of Jeffersonian Democracy* (1915). It is the opinion of the compiler of the present volume that to have inserted sizable passages from either or both of these treatises here would have markedly reduced the availability of Beard's writings by forcing compensating omissions of hard-to-get material and would have seriously diminished the space devoted to a much broader consideration of historiography and of the economic features of political history than these two specialized studies provide.

While the passages bound within these covers are representative of much of Beard's thinking on the subject at hand, they fall somewhat short of finality. The one prime task he felt he had left undone when, in the words of Johannes von Müller, "he stepped down to join the shadows he had depicted," was the preparation of a popularly written volume on history which would clarify still further the nature of his labors—and those of others in the "historical guild." That it would have commented on the "economic interpretation" of history seems highly probable. At least, in talks about "unfinished business," he discussed the tendency of one side in a political dispute to overemphasize the "low" economic motives of the opposition, thus affording a specious explanation of events, and the question whether an economic interpretation is more acceptable to a society in the midst of an economic de-

[3] Material for this venture has been largely drawn from a reservoir of literary property rights accumulated by Charles A. Beard's heirs, and released for this project with their consent. However, a few supplementary passages have been included with the express permission of their original publishers—*The American Historical Review, Harper's Magazine, The New Republic,* the *Political Science Quarterly,* and *The Southern Economic Journal.*

pression, and an idealistic one more welcome in days of
prosperity. Certain ages and periods, he said, might lend
themselves more precisely to an economic interpretation
than others. In the former category might come the time
when Marx lived and wrote, while to the latter might be
assigned the years immediately preceding the American
Civil War. Hence it seems likely that Beard, had he had
the opportunity, would have altered and rearranged the
ideas forming the bulk of this volume, to bring them
abreast of his more mature thinking at the close of his
life.

From whence came Beard's deep and abiding interest,
up to the very end, in economic factors underlying past
political events? As he has indicated, it was derived in
part from the study of the printed works of others who had
engaged in such explorations long ago.

Included in the great mine of ideas on economics and
politics from which he drew were the thoughts of Aristotle
(384–322 B.C.) who: "When he approaches . . . causes
of variations in the forms of the state . . . immediately relates economics and politics" (below, p. 27). Of a later
contributor, Beard remarks that: "In advising the prince,
once established, how best to maintain his power, Machiavelli [1469–1527] warns him to take account of the conflict of classes out of which political power springs. . . ."
(Below, p. 31.) Beard also notes that: "Both the origin
and end of the state Locke [1632–1704] finds in the roots
of property." (Below, p. 33.) Discussing a more recent
period, Beard declares that Barnave, in writing about the
French Revolution: "displayed a remarkable insight into
the economic causes of the struggle. Long before Marx,
Barnave had written 'as soon as industry and commerce
have entered into the life of a nation and have created a
new source of wealth for the support of the working
class, a revolution in political institutions begins. A new
distribution of wealth produces a new distribution of
power. . . .' " [4] Of the Marxians Beard wrote: "In the
field of history Marx and his followers undoubtedly helped
to turn the attention of historians from purely political

[4] Book Review, *Political Science Quarterly,* March, 1906,
pp. 111 ff., quoted by permission.

and diplomatic affairs to the more permanent and fundamental forces in the development and conflict of nations. . . ." [5] A careful study of numerous other citations
given by Beard would permit lengthy expansion of the
above list.

Less well-known, perhaps, than his debt to his literary
predecessors is the fact that Beard, unlike many historians
whose activities have been more largely confined to academic circles, was in unusually close and stimulating contact with the everyday economic life about him, and with
its varied political ramifications. These personal experiences
supplemented the impetus for economic analysis provided
by quiet reading.

Beard's direct insight into the stern realities of agriculture, for example, began as soon as he was old enough
to shoulder his share of the hard work required to keep
his parents' large Indiana farm operating properly. Though
he "escaped" from this routine in early manhood to devote himself to study, writing, and teaching, his interest in
the soil remained very much alive. In 1929, he acquired
a farm covering some three hundred rolling acres in Connecticut, about ten miles from his own residence at New
Milford. On this new tract he housed a farm family and
through it entered commercial dairying on an extensive
scale. True, others performed the physical labor, but
Beard made frequent visits to this enterprise and took an
active part in its management. For a time, he even ran a
second major dairy farm in Connecticut, but mounting
burdens finally induced him to shrink his undertakings to
the confines of his earlier farm, which was still in full
swing at the moment of his death, in 1948.

Busy as he was with writing, he still did not shirk his
responsibilities as a citizen-farmer. During a threatened
strike of Connecticut dairy farmers in 1933, in co-operation with another "scholar in politics," Governor Wilbur
Cross, he took a hand in meeting the emergency. Important gatherings were held in the Beard residence at this
juncture and Beard not only helped to develop plans to
cope with the crisis but advised fellow farmers as to how to
present their problems to the public for appropriate political action. When, therefore, Beard examined the writings

[5] *Idem.*

of such thinkers as Aristotle and Jefferson on the subject of the place of the farmer in the economic and political life of the community, he had a better than average comprehension of the substance of their remarks.

Beard was also closely associated with capital and labor in commerce and industry. As a boy, he observed his father carrying on a successful contracting and building business in Indiana and otherwise participating in the economic life of the community. As Beard described this formative period: "My early memories are filled with the stories of log-cabin days—of community helpfulness, of co-operation in building houses and barns, in harvesting crops, in building schools, in constructing roads and bridges, in nursing the sick, in caring for widows, orphans and the aged. Of individuals I heard much, of individualism little. I doubt whether anywhere in the United States there was more community spirit, more mutual aid in all times of need, so little expectation of material reward for services rendered to neighbors." [6]

To fill the interlude between high school and college, the father devoted some of his funds to the purchase of the *Knightstown Banner* for his two sons, Charles and Clarence. They proceeded to write, manage, and in emergencies apparently set type for this small-town journal, thus receiving valuable training in the expression of ideas, community service, and the management of funds.

After leaving the *Banner* and graduating from De Pauw University, Beard went to England for graduate study. There he traveled extensively through the "black country," so named from its many smoking chimneys, witnessing at first hand the stark realism of the English factory system. Greatly stirred by these sights, he studied the history of the industrial revolution in the British Isles and undertook to put his knowledge to practical use by helping to found and operate a workingmen's college at Oxford. Moreover, he lectured for the English co-operative societies which were then trying to find a practical way to reduce the ordinary worker's cost of living.

Following his return to the United States, the success of his writing ventures ultimately made it possible for him

[6] Book review in *The New Republic*, Feb. 1, 1939, p. 361, reprinted with the magazine's permission.

to invest in a variety of American corporations. One of his possessions consisted of a block of Missouri Pacific Railway bonds. When a group of bankers sought to reorganize that carrier in a manner Beard deemed inimical to the welfare of the purchasers of these underlying securities, he organized a bondholders' committee and challenged the might not only of the Van Sweringens but of J. P. Morgan and Company as well. His outspoken comments on the bankers' operations received wide publicity in the press and produced important political repercussions in the halls of Congress.

Through his services with the Bureau of Municipal Research in New York City, Beard participated directly in the struggle among economic interests that forms much of the substance of state and local politics. For example, he played an important part in Governor Alfred E. Smith's drive to reorganize the administration of New York State to reduce waste, inefficiency, and bungling, and, at the municipal level, Beard tackled the likewise difficult task of reviewing the conflicting opinions of powerful groups, during the serious traction crisis of 1919 in New York City, in an effort to arrive at some practical solution for the emergency.

Beard's understanding of economic issues in politics was further enhanced by extensive foreign travels. He saw the breakdown in European economy following World War I, in England, France and Italy, and the diverse reactions of the public thereto—including a large street riot associated with Mussolini's rise to power. Later, he journeyed far and wide in the Orient—traversing China from port cities along the coast to the far interior, incidentally getting a glimpse of an American naval patrol, anchored several hundred miles up the Yangtze Kiang River. He visited England's imperial outpost at Hong Kong and Japan's colonial enterprises in Manchuria and Korea. Through the courtesy of a former Japanese governor of the Island, he penetrated deep into the jungles of Formosa, to reach a region where efforts were being made to adapt former head-hunting savages to the requirements of the camphor industry.

As an adviser to the Tokyo Institute for Municipal Research, both before and after the disastrous earthquake of 1923, Beard was drawn into the contest among economic groups over broad plans for the more effective reconstruction of the metropolis. A few years later, in 1927 and 1928, he was back in Europe, this time laboring in Yugoslavia for the American-Yugoslav Society, examining the special economic and political problems of that newborn and struggling nation.

Being deeply aware of the vitality and importance of the economic drive in politics, by reading and by direct personal contact, Beard undertook to describe the linkage fearlessly and at length, in print.

Scottsdale, Arizona   WILLIAM BEARD
Aug. 20, 1956

PART I

THE BROAD PROBLEM OF DISCUSSING HUMAN AFFAIRS

THIS VOLUME PROCEEDS FROM THE
GENERAL TO THE PARTICULAR

COMPILER'S NOTE: In organizing selections from Beard's writings for this enterprise, the plan was adopted of proceeding from the general to the particular—from a broad analysis of the whole business of discussing human affairs to detailed studies of the economic factors affecting specific political events.

The initial selection is Chapter I—Beard's comprehensive warning to readers against swallowing too avidly any offerings now available in the vast realm of the social studies. Here he points out certain specific weaknesses common to all human discussions in this area. Being universal in scope, this portion of the text by implication serves notice on the public that it should approach not only the works of Beard, but those of his critics and friends as well, with some degree of circumspection if it is to see matters in their "true light."

From a frank analysis of the problems common to discussions of human affairs generally, the theme turns in the second chapter to a consideration of the special difficulties confronting those engaged in the writing of history. Here Beard comments on the numerous obstacles encountered by anyone who seeks to provide an accurate and full account of the past, and on the advantages and disadvantages of certain prime methods employed in tying together historical events. In the process, he deals concretely with efforts to analyze the long course of human affairs in economic terms, dwelling in the large on their usefulness as well as their shortcomings. Thus readers receive a picture of the great "seamless web" of history, as Beard visualized it, before struggling with those particular threads of economics and politics which form the substance of the remainder of this volume.

CHAPTER I

WHAT IS OCCURRING WHEN
HUMAN AFFAIRS ARE
BEING DISCUSSED? [1]

COMMITTING OURSELVES to a simple or common sense realism, we inquire: What is occurring when human affairs are being discussed? And we answer provisionally: Whatever else may be involved, six features enter into consideration.

In the first place some person or persons are engaged in speaking or writing or making symbols of one kind or another. . . . But few essays, editorials, orations, dissertations, and serious volumes open with the confession: "I am speaking, in fact, making a statement of the things which I have found true, or of good report, and worthy of discussion."

For various reasons the confession is avoided. Obvious as the fact is, it sounds conceited. Humility, true or mock, suggests the impersonal, the avoidance of the ego. Was it not once the sport of critics to count the number of times the pronoun "I" occurs in Theodore Roosevelt's papers and messages, and employ the result in ridiculing the author? Yet, after all, those papers and messages were Theodore Roosevelt's papers and messages. No one claimed that God or Nature wrote them. The constant use of the "I" added nothing to the truth, falsity, value, or utility of the facts and ideas contained in them. . . .

It is not probable . . . that there will be any material

[1] From *The Discussion of Human Affairs,* The Macmillan Co. (1936).

change in the dislike of the writings liberally sprinkled with "I's." Nor would there be any advantage in the universal use of the first person singular, beyond emphasizing the fact that in every discussion some "I" is speaking,[2] and thus putting readers or participants on their guard against cloaked pretensions to omniscience and infallible authority.

In cold truth impersonal discourse, as perhaps in the case of Cæsar, may represent the puffed-up conceit of false humility. It may be a mere subterfuge, designed to give weight or compulsion to statements that would seem negligible if made on mere personal authority. . . .

Although there is no way of knowing, the avoidance of the confessional style and the resort to the impersonal are doubtless due to another temper rather than that of humility, true or false. Human beings seem to be so constituted that they love to speak with an authority not their own—the authority of God, Nature, Science, the System, or some other absolute. Authority is often an effective instrument for stopping the mouths and filling the ears of opponents.

After all, if it is a case of "I" against "I," what chance does the expositor have against an opposition possessing a majority? Besides, who is he to set himself up, to mount his pulpit, or thump his tub? Only by clothing himself in the garment of impersonal power can he hope to attain weight in the councils of discussion. . . .

Not only is some person speaking. Every discussion is occurring at a given period in time. . . . And at each given period the ideas in circulation and the interests prevailing are marked by certain characteristics that have features of uniqueness. As we say, they "belong to the age."

Since this seems to be true, each person taking part in a discussion reflects in some manner ideas and interests uppermost in his time, and they are ever-changing ideas and interests, however strong the perdurance of formalities. No doubt, many who discourse on human affairs seek to be

[2] COMPILER'S NOTE: For an account of the "I" that was finding expression when Beard wrote, see the Introduction to the present volume.

"timeless," but few if any attain that "perfection of wisdom." All discussions are timed and dated. This would appear to be an obvious maxim of common sense.

The person. The time. The discussion of human affairs always occurs at some place—Shanghai, Tokyo, Chicago, London, Berlin, Prague, Belgrade. Ideas may be gathered from the literature and practices of the wide earth, and sent forth broadcast by modern agencies of dissemination. But each participant in a discussion is at the moment in some place.

The place, of course, is not a mere geographical spot. It is a point in a particular social and traditional milieu, with its own peculiarities, loyalties, interests, and values. Though the time may be the same in many widely separated places, the ideas and interests are divergent. This, too, is obvious. Yet who is willing to confess: "It is I speaking, at this fleeting moment, in this place with its intellectual and social peculiarities"?

This is a dreadful thought. It places man far below the angels. He speaks or writes at a time and at a place—a fleeting moment [in] a small corner of the great earth. No wonder that he resorts to God, Nature, Science, the System, or some other universal, toward which his aspirations reach.

. . . Usually the discussion is directed to some end or purpose. Possible ends are numerous. The purpose may be to earn a penny a line or the fee paid by the auditors. It may be to amuse, entertain, convince, confirm, convert. It may be to prevent impending change, to promote change, to effect a compromise between the past and the future, to do good, to wreak vengeance, to discomfit an opponent. . . . That end may not be openly avowed, consciously clarified and rationalized, but it is present, giving some direction to discussion.

. . . Do not speakers on the right discount opinions tendered by labor leaders and socialists, as anchored in their prejudices? Do not speakers on the left discount opinions tendered by "capitalist" speakers, as anchored in their prejudices?

For such queries there is good reason. It is possible for

any competent historian familiar with the forms, phrases, and creeds of groups, classes, and organizations to classify them into types that appear with almost wearisome re-iteration. Such a historian can predict, with a high degree of certainty, the formulas, slogans, clichés, and positions that will be disclosed by the editors of the New York *Tribune,* and the editors of the *Daily Worker,* for example, when some strikers are shot or beaten in a labor disturb-ance.

Indeed many of the formulas used by writers and speakers are so well worn and so well known that they are like ancient and familiar songs which can be sung to a harp. The moment the name of the speaker or writer is announced, the general tenor of the tune can be guessed with a high degree of assurance. The moment the first notes of the tune are heard, the singer can be placed in his category of social affiliation with a considerable amount of assurance.

The person. The time. The place. The purpose. The fifth feature of discussion is the preliminary assumptions. All discussion of human affairs proceeds upon some as-sumption or assumptions respecting the nature of things or upon the assumption that no assumption has been made. An assumption, like a purpose, may be sublimated, hid-den in the subconscious self, or open, avowed, clarified, and confessed.

Ordinarily we are controlled by what John R. Commons calls our "habitual assumptions." They are made up of our early ideas hardened into dogmas, our customary *mores* rationalized, our cosmogonies and cosmologies acquired in childhood, or/and our more or less consciously explored acceptances.

The existence of preliminary assumptions may be de-nied; indeed, is hotly denied by many persons who claim to discuss human affairs "scientifically." They pretend to assume nothing, to take nothing for granted, not even private property, sex, qualities of human nature, and many other considerations that enter into discussion. But unless some things are taken for granted, assumed, and some common principles are accepted, discussion cannot pro-ceed at all.

Moreover common sense reveals man to himself as a bundle of habitual assumptions, of things he takes for granted when he begins to discourse on human affairs. He cannot think of his mind as a bottomless pit, containing nothing, out of which come timeless, placeless, purposeless words beyond his control. Before a person is old enough to enter into discussions, his mind has some things in it. And among them is a great collection of ideas taken for granted, seldom if ever re-examined, and never to be explored into that dark ultimate beyond his grasp.

The person. The time. The place. The purpose. The preliminary assumptions. These enter into all discussions of human affairs. It seems impossible to conceive of any discussion without these features.

A sixth feature is the form of statement. Analyzed down to its irreducible elements every statement respecting human affairs asserts facts or opinions or both. . . .

CHAPTER II

WHAT IS HAPPENING WHEN
HISTORY IS BEING WRITTEN?[1]

. . . ALL INDIVIDUALS DO, certainly, come upon many
facts by direct contact as life proceeds—in industry, labor,
enterprise, and social intercourse—without looking for
them purposefully. . . . [The historian, however,] can
observe only a few of them at first hand. . . . [The] major portion of facts employed in the discussion of human
affairs in any comprehensive way are not facts that come
more or less fortuitously into the range of direct observation. . . . Unlike the physicist or chemist, the historian is not a personal observer of events that lie beyond
his own time. He cannot see historical occurrences with
his own eyes, as the chemist sees compounds in his test
tubes and retorts. The historian must "see" the actuality
of history through the medium of records, documents,
memoirs, papers, and monuments. That is his sole recourse
for the events beyond his own time. . . . Such sources are
multitudinous. They vary in correctness of statement, reporting, and authenticity. . . .

[In the presence of these sources, almost] any literate
person can write some history, of a kind, can tell a story,
compile a narrative, describe an adventure. While no one
would think of writing seriously on physics or chemistry
without preliminary training, there is nothing to estop the
merest amateur from taking a few documents, letters, and
memoirs, and preparing "a history" of this or that, without
fear and without thought. Indeed scholars who devote a

[1] From *The Discussion of Human Affairs,* The Macmillan
Co. (1936).

lifetime to the critical analysis of historical sources frequently write huge works on history without ever asking themselves just what they are doing. Accordingly, there is some reason for treating written history lightly, as dull, unilluminating, and meaningless for life—for practical affairs.

But the scope and achievements of historical writing must not be judged by random examples. . . . [History] must be judged by the more critical and comprehensive thought that has been given to the subject.

Doubtless it would be startling news to the overwhelming majority of those who take part in discussing human affairs to learn that there exists in the field of historiography a body of highly technical literature dealing with the subject: "What is history?" It is not to be read casually by laymen any more than the technical literature on higher physics.

None of these works on historiography, to be sure, is as exact as an engineer's handbook on highway construction, and for this reason some men of natural science are inclined to ascribe to historians a lack of the power to analyze, establish fixed sequences, and disclose laws. In other words, historians suffer from some deficiency of mental capacity. Yet other reasons may account for their difficulties, especially the complexity of their subject, the paucity of the data available, and the intricate problems of thought involved. After all, physics, complex as it may be, is relatively simple as compared to a subject which includes physicists and physics, and everything else mankind has said and done on earth since it began its checkered career here. . . .

Yet heroic efforts have been made by competent thinkers to answer the question: What are we doing when we are writing history—selecting and organizing facts of history? They have not succeeded in making a final answer, but they have produced an immense amount of fairly exact knowledge pertaining to it. To run through a few thousand pages of this analytical and critical literature is a lesson in humility for those who fain would discourse sagely on human affairs.

There was a time, in the proud age of scientific assurance, when many historians imagined that "the scientific method" enabled them to describe history as it actually was. Leopold von Ranke, the founder of this school, introduced the idea that history could be written as it actually had been (*Wie es eigentlich gewesen ist*).

How was this feat to be accomplished? The documents, letters, memoirs, papers, and monuments of the period or nation chosen were to be assembled, scrutinized for authenticity, collated, sifted, and checked. The historian was to divest himself of all religious, political, philosophical, social, economic, sex, moral, and esthetic interests, and from the "sources" describe personalities and events as they had been in reality.

. . . Under the spell of this idea an enormous amount of invaluable work was done in history. The collection and preservation of historical sources were stimulated and made systematic. An immense body of exact knowledge concerning past personalities and events was accumulated. Every phase of history was illuminated by recourse to authentic evidence. A thousand historical myths and rumors were exploded, as in the field of exact science. History written for purposes obviously partisan was discredited, and made suspect among adepts, if not among readers at large. As a result the twentieth century possesses far more precise and authentic knowledge of the past than did the eighteenth century.

As work was carried forward under this ideal, some historians cherished the hope that by the scientific method the laws of history could be revealed, and history as actuality reduced to an exact science. Near the end of the nineteenth century, Henry Adams declared that every historical scholar with high ambition thought that he almost had the science "in his inkstand."

About that time the dream exploded. . . . Criticism was turned upon critical history. The result was a series of conclusions which may be summarized in the following manner:

. . . The materials from which the historian must derive his knowledge cover merely a portion of the events and personalities in question. In other words, most of them escaped recording. . . . [Moreover,] pages and volumes have disappeared amid the ravages of time. . . . Concerning the nature of the unrecorded [or permanently lost] no knowledge is available or ever can be available.

. . . Not only are the records partial at the outset. In very few cases can the historian be sure that he has assembled all the existing records that pertain to the age, theme, or period with which he is concerned. As a rule he makes a partial selection from the incomplete records of the events and personalities involved in the actuality which he is attempting to describe.

. . . Since the actual history of any period embraces all the events and personalities and since the records of these events and personalities are scanty at best, it follows that the total actuality of the period cannot be known, can never be known, no matter how zealous and laborious the historical searcher.

. . . Since the known or knowable facts relative to any large period and to world history run into the millions, if not billions, it follows that any written history is a *selection* and *organization* of facts—a selection and organization made by a given person at a given time and place.

. . . Although many relationships among past events and personalities, immediate, proximate, and remote, have been established by historical research, paucity of knowledge, for reasons cited, does not permit the attainment of an exact and complete structure of relationships, if indeed such be assumed to have existed.

. . . Into the selection of topics, the choice and arrangement of facts, the historian's "me" will enter, no matter what efforts he makes to be neutral. He cannot be otherwise than he is. This "me" will enter with a conscious clarification of philosophy and purpose or, as Croce says, surreptitiously, without confession, knowledge, and acknowledgement. The philosophy may be grand and universal in its reach, or small, provincial, class, and national in form and nature. . . .

How could it be otherwise? When he is mature enough to begin work, the historian has already gathered impressions and conceptions in the process of study and experience—rearing and training in some place or places, and social order. If it be said that the historian may put out of mind all conceptions, then the question arises: By what criteria does he choose a theme to be studied or select facts from among the millions or billions available?

The proposition seems inescapable: some conception or assumption respecting the nature of all things exists in the historian's mind and acts more or less as a controlling force in the selection of facts, in the creation of what purports to be descriptions of past situations in development. Such, at least, is the conclusion at which contemporary historiography has arrived. Whoever challenges it is called upon to produce counterevidence as powerful as that upon which it now rests.

Having reached the conclusion that some conception of the nature of things controls the selection and organization of recorded facts into written history, contemporary historians inquire: What conceptions that have been employed in the past are now available to us?

Long and patient analysis of written discussions of human affairs, whether professedly historical or economic or political or cultural, has disclosed numerous conceptions. But these have been reduced to a small number, each enclosing turns or nuances of its own. The following, if not all-embracing, are now deemed primary in Western usage.

1. The Jewish-Christian conception of the world and mankind, with history as a kind of divine drama in which God's will or providence is revealed or illustrated by personalities and events. The conflicts, antagonisms, and oppositions of real life are to be explained by reference to some divine overruling purpose—a synthesis that reconciles them in one all-embracing totality.

History of this type is now seldom written in its pure form, even by Jewish, Protestant, or Catholic writers. The problems and difficulties involved in assigning such matters as the outcome of the last presidential election or the last war to divine plan and will make the cautious hesitate. Just what place did the election of Herbert Hoover and the defeat of Alfred E. Smith in 1928 occupy in God's providence? . . . Just what position in the drama of the West's God is to be assigned to peoples that never heard of it or Him? . . .

2. The second conception of the nature of human affairs is that of man as *Homo sapiens,* without reference to any divine origins or purposes. This conception takes man as

he seems to be, a more or less rational animal whose history consists of thought and activities in relation to human purposes. In fact, and to some extent in theory, it discards all efforts to relate human conduct to an overarching divine scheme. It seeks to "explain" history in terms of human intelligence used in the attainment of human ends.

In application this conception also encounters difficulties. . . . Innumerable activities ranging from individual deeds to mass conflicts and wars often seem to spring from distempers wholly irrational, . . . and even when activities are directed ostensibly to ends they are as likely as not to be utterly defeated, either immediately or in the long run.

3. Equally earthy but more special is the third conception of history founded on the idea of *homo faber*—men and women busy continuing biological life, sustaining it, and doing innumerable things, often without respect to clear ends, perhaps for the pleasure or pain of doing them. . . .

The difficulties of applying the conception of *homo faber* are not immediate. In fact we have large bodies of literature—anthropological and historical—which do describe with a high degree of accuracy particular behaviors and types of behavior. But apparently insuperable obstacles appear when efforts are made to "explain" such behaviors and types and to relate them to the surrounding totality of history in development. . . .

Among the variations is the still more specialized conception of *homo economicus*, employed by such writers as Adam Smith and Karl Marx; human beings . . . rational enough to know and attain economic interests and ends. Indeed it may be justly said that *homo economicus* implies *Homo sapiens*. . . .

The theory of *homo economicus* is more effective in "explaining" particular institutions and events. But it is baffled in many places by the fact that a considerable portion of human ideas and activities, if conditioned by economic practices, seem not to arise out of economic interests and to have only a remote, if any, relation to such concerns. It encounters the same troubles as the theory of *Homo sapiens;* human beings do not always know their economic interests and constantly engage in activities that are adverse to these interests.

4. In efforts to escape some of the dilemmas presented

by other conceptions, or without employing much thought at all, a few writers have introduced the *Superman,* a kind of *deus ex machina,* that "makes history." The history of the world, says Carlyle, is at bottom merely the history of the great men who have worked here. Heroes are everything; masses, despite all their interests, activities, ideas, and distempers, are as nothing, save pawns in the game of heroes. The past history of masses may be ignored; it neither conditions nor determines the work which the hero, the captain, the leader, the dictator, does. The leader creates the myth; the masses goose-step into line and obey the hero's will.

Although this conception denies the inevitability of things as created by centuries of past thought and practice, there is some element of truth in it. For example, the liberal conception of democracy and the Marxian conception of social democracy made headway in Europe between 1789 and 1920 and seemed to present signs of inevitable advance. Yet Mussolini in Italy and Hitler in Germany reversed the whole trend, for the time being at least, by raising up symbols and organizing force as force.

Nevertheless they did not work in a vacuum, and it must be admitted that certain conditions of life and labor in Italy and Germany favored their designs. Their rise to power was conditioned and their exercise of power is still conditioned [1936], in part determined, by the operations of the economic system and by their relations to other countries over which their power does not [1936] extend. The Superman theory does not correspond to reality.

It also encounters contradictions in its emphasis on masculinity. It fails to reckon with "the women of the Cæsars," and such women as Joan of Arc, Elizabeth of England, Catherine of Russia, and Maria Theresa of Austria. It can only escape this dilemma by saying that they were more masculine than feminine, which opens the door for declaring that the bodily forms of sex do not in fact mark men as men or women as women. If that is maintained, then how do we know that the Superman is not merely the embodiment of "feminine force and intuition," denying the rationality of history?

There is something in the power of "great" personalities, but to found a theory of history on it is to deny the demonstrated existence of surrounding circumstances which condition and/or determine the conduct of leaders, heroes, and dictators. They can scarcely be regarded as independent gods operating under their own will and creating the world in their image, unless we throw overboard all that is known about masses, institutions, continuing traditions, and changing economies.

5. Stemming out of the conception of *homo economicus,* and of the Superman, is the class conception of history. All history is the history of class struggles and the leader is a class hero. Each class has its interests, its conceptions of itself and history, its myths, and its symbolic figures. There is no such thing as "general" interests or "general" history. Everything is enclosed in classes and their conflicts.

All we can have then is the theory of a particular class— the Prussian Junker, the British aristocracy, the freehold peasant or farmer, the petty capitalist, the great finance capitalist, or the industrial worker possessing little or no property. Theories of society, economics, politics, history, and literature are class theories.[2]

This conception of history is very old and very persistent. Many of the world's great secular thinkers have entertained it in some form—Aristotle, Polybius, Harrington, Locke, Alexander Hamilton, James Madison, Daniel Webster, and Karl Marx, for example. It has behind it the weight of high authority and the testimony of many historic struggles. That it comes into close correspondence with many known and established realities cannot be denied by historians of competence.

More than two thousand years ago, Aristotle made a close study of Greek history, society, politics, government, and culture. Out of his researches and personal experience, he came to three basic conclusions: (1) the conflicts that shake society and make history turn on the pursuit of interests by classes in society. (2) There are two broad theories of society, namely, individualism and communism, and all other theories are modifications of these opposites. (3)

---

[2] COMPILER'S NOTE: Beard does not here point to the shortcomings of the class conception of history, but its limitations are indicated in quotations made later from another of his works. See Chapter VII of the present volume.

Since society itself implies more than a mere aggregation of individuals, the eternal question is: What goods shall be community goods and to what extent shall obligations be imposed on the use of individual goods?

6. Wider than any other positive formulations of history, and not necessarily in direct conflict with the other conceptions, is the idea of progress.[3] According to this hypothesis, humanity in its long and zigzag march from barbarism is conquering its environment and itself, and may make the nobler aspirations of mankind prevail over material circumstances and the passions of acquisitive conflict. This is both an interpretation of the past and a projection for the future.

The application of the idea of progress to history as actuality has been mercilessly attacked, often by critics not familiar with its most rigid formulations. This is no place to review the criticisms or consider their validity. It is sufficient to say that the proponents of the idea have emerged with two contentions: (1) unless all history is a senseless *faux pas,* some advances have been made, if painfully, since the stone age; and (2) if there has been no progress in the past, mankind by awareness and by taking thought can *make* it in the future.

In any case the idea is not easily disposed of completely. Whatever goal may be set up for the future, it is reasonably certain that it will not be attained overnight. The achievement will take time and will involve innumerable events and personalities—stages in development. Hence it will be in the nature of progress. Unless we assume chaos and meaninglessness in the time unfoldment of human affairs, unless we accept the present state of things as perfection, we seem bound to accept progress of some kind in some form. And from past experience we may infer that at no time in the future will the movement of ideas and interests, which is history as actuality, cease. In other words there are grounds for inferring that history will not be closed at any given date in the future by some unchangeable and unchanging utopia of perfection or a disaster of dissolution.

. . . [If the selection and arrangement of facts, and the

[3] J. B. Bury, *The Idea of Progress.* American edition with an Introduction by Charles A. Beard.

"deductions" made from them, often represent opinion, and to this are added the frank opinions of the writers, then many] if not most of the statements appearing in discussions of human affairs are at bottom simply expressions of opinions advanced by the proponents. Even when having the garb of profundity and decorated by numerous citations of fact, true or alleged, they are merely assertions of things cherished by the writer or speaker—his good wishes or good will. . . . Hence we seem driven to the conclusion that all general discussions of human affairs are in truth assertions of opinions, good, bad, and indifferent. . . .

One truth rising above the conflicts and distempers of time does emerge, and it is a truth important for practice. This truth may be formulated as follows: it is possible for all who discuss human affairs to distinguish somewhat effectively between fact and opinion and to have extensive knowledge of the various positions or points of view (tacit or admitted) from which any expression of opinion proceeds or takes direction. As knowledge of these positions or points of view is widened by persistent inquiry, their overlapping or interpenetrating nature enters into human consciousness, with the result that sharpness of division is softened and the way prepared for resolving conflicts by the magic of thought projected into the forum of practice. For whatever it is worth, this is the supreme contribution of contemporary historiography to the process of coping with present perplexities and making a civilization in which humanity can possess the beautiful and the good.

PART II

THE DISCUSSION NARROWS
—TO BASIC ECONOMIC
CONSIDERATIONS IN THE
ANALYSIS OF WESTERN
POLITICAL HISTORY

BEARD'S QUEST FOR FUNDAMENTALS IN THE AMHERST COLLEGE LECTURE SERIES

COMPILER'S NOTE: In the preceding chapter, Beard called brief attention to certain special efforts that had been made to interpret history in terms of the economic interests of the human race. It was his frank opinion that this field had not been explored as fully and vigorously as circumstances warranted. In an article published years ago he said: ". . . a cursory examination of economic journals in the Library of Congress discloses no considerable interest in the theory and practice of historical composition. . . . This indifference is doubtless reciprocated by most historians. It would be interesting to know how many American students of history have read the great classics in economics from Adam Smith through Marx to Marshall and John Bates Clark. Not many, it may be guessed. Some historians have given a little thought to economic matters. In dealing with Hamilton, Webster, Calhoun, and Andrew Jackson, they can scarcely escape seeing banks, tariffs, currency, and slavery. Yet historians seldom deal with these topics in the coherent manner that characterizes economic thought. Either they do not have the requisite training, or, having training, they find it impossible to bring the stubborn facts of the historical uproar into any consistent and meaningful whole."

Beard attributed this, in large measure, "to the growth of specialization." In reality, he held: "Political facts, economic facts, ethical facts are not isolated particularities; they are phases or aspects of events and personalities. . . . An economic fact . . . may be at the same time a political or ethical or military fact." [1]

[1] "History and Economics," *The Southern Economic Journal,* July, 1936, pp. 1–8, reprinted with the magazine's permission.

Undaunted, himself, by the formal boundaries erected by the specialists, Beard ultimately undertook a comprehensive study of the economic forces affecting the political history of the Western world to see if he could, by tackling what he had once termed "the stubborn facts of the historical uproar," bring them into some "consistent and meaningful whole." In 1916, he embodied the results of this inquiry in four lectures delivered at Amherst College, under the auspices of the Clark Foundation. With some revision, this material was published by Alfred A. Knopf in 1922 as *The Economic Basis of Politics*. In 1945, hesitating to obscure his early work, Beard added some footnotes in brackets and included a new fifth chapter, to bring the account abreast of more recent developments. Finally, the compiler of the present volume has integrated the new material of the last chapter of the 1945 edition with the old material in the last chapter of the 1922 edition—to smooth the flow for easier use today—in a manner carefully described by footnotes for the convenience of anyone wishing to distinguish between passages written in different years. Thus overhauled, *The Economic Basis of Politics* is reprinted here as Chapters III through VII.

As should logically be expected of the author of the presentation in Part I on the shortcomings of historians and of the conventional methods of organizing historical data, Beard qualifies his basic economic analyses of political history in the pages that follow, an operation deserving the close scrutiny of the critical reader.

CHAPTER III

THE DOCTRINES OF THE PHILOSOPHERS

THE FOUNDERS of this lectureship desire to help carry forward the eternal quest of mankind for ways and means with which to control its social destiny for noble ends. Some of the most splendid traditions of the race are associated with this search. The mystic Plato, the sagacious Aristotle, the gentle Sir Thomas More, and the courageous Condorcet, to mention none nearer our time, sought far and wide for the key to the great mystery. The fruits of their labors are a priceless heritage.

The imperious Burke likewise thought the theme worthy of his talents, but he soon gave it up, confessing defeat. "I doubt," he says, "whether the history of mankind is yet complete enough, if it ever can be so, to furnish ground for a sure theory on the internal causes which necessarily affect the fortune of a state. I am far from denying the operation of such causes: but they are infinitely uncertain, and much more obscure and much more difficult to trace than the foreign causes that tend to raise, to depress, and sometimes to overwhelm a community. It is often impossible, in these political inquiries, to find any proportion between the apparent force of any moral causes we may assign and their known operation. We are therefore obliged to deliver up that operation to mere chance, or, more piously (perhaps, more rationally), to the occasional interposition and irresistible hand of the Great Disposer." In short, confronted by the complex and bewildering facts of social life, Burke cries aloud, with the mediæval priest overwhelmed by the horror of the Black Death: *"Deus vult."*

In the field of natural science, such a confession is a plea of intellectual bankruptcy. In that sphere persistent and penetrating research, relentless and unafraid, brings about the progressive conquest and subjugation of the material world. Indeed the very research in mechanics and chemistry that produced the machine age has torn asunder the foundations of the old social order, released new and terrifying forces, and now threatens the dissolution of society itself. The present plight of the world seems to show that mankind is in the grip of inexorable forces which may destroy civilization if not subdued to humane purposes. It may be that in the end we must, with Burke, confess the futility of our quest. Even then we shall say with Heine:

> *Also fragen wir beständig*
> *Bis man uns mit einer Handvoll*
> *Erde endlich stopft die Maüler,*
> *Aber ist das eine Antwort?*[1]

So the eternal search goes on. At the very outset the seekers are confronted by two conflicting theories concerning the problem itself. These are summed up by John Stuart Mill at the opening of his famous work on representative government. According to one of them, government, namely, human control, is merely a problem in invention, of determining what is best and adapting our means to the desired end. According to the other theory, government is not a matter of human choice at all but an inevitable, natural growth in which the purposes of man have no part.

Each of these doctrines, we must admit with Mill, is untenable if pushed to an exclusive and logical conclusion; yet somewhere between them lies important truth. Long the victim of material forces, man has, by taking thought, made himself master of wind and wave and storm. May he not, by taking thought, lift himself above the social con-

---

[1] COMPILER'S NOTE: Translated, the passage reads as follows:
  And so we ask, and ask again
  Without rest, until at last,
  With a handful of earth they stop up our mouths.
  But is that an answer?

flicts that destroy civilizations and make himself master of his social destiny? Perhaps not; but as the human mind is greater than the waterfall which it compels or the lightning's flash which it confines, so the control of human destiny is a nobler object of inquiry than the search for material power. Even though every door be slammed in our faces, still must we knock.

As the theme is old, we, as humble students, must, of necessity, first survey the conclusions of the great masters who have gone on before. We must first find out what they thought about the nature of the forces which are responsible for the origins, forms, and changes of political institutions.

At the beginning of such an inquiry we face, of course, the mighty Aristotle,[2] "the master of all them that know." He rightly deserves to be called "the father of political science" because he took it out of the sphere of utopian idealism where Plato left it and placed it on the strong foundation of natural history. As Oncken rightly says, it was the use of the methods of natural science in his inductive studies that enabled Aristotle to make his great contribution to Greek thought. He was the son of a doctor who had written many books on medicine and physiology and he was himself no mean student of morphology and anatomy. Moreover he combined practical experience in politics with long and wide-reaching researches in the history of human institutions. It is for these reasons, perhaps, that Aristotle stood midway between those who thought that human society was a mechanism to be refashioned at will and those who accepted good and ill as fatalities of the gods. At all events we know that he sought to combine the idealism of ethics with the realism of historical research.

The most striking thing about Aristotle's *Politics* is the sharp contrast which it presents to most modern books on the same subject. The latter deal mainly with the structure and forms of government, the machinery and methods of elections, the powers and duties of public officers. The texture of society itself is left to the sociologist. The pro-

[2] COMPILER'S NOTE: Aristotle (384–322 B.C.), philosopher of Ancient Greece.

duction and distribution of wealth, the foundations of human life, are assigned to the economist.

The reasons for this somewhat arbitrary carving up of the social organism for the purposes of study are not difficult to discover. Adam Smith and the older writers spoke of "political economy." About the middle of the nineteenth century, thinkers in that field were mainly concerned with formulating a millowner's philosophy of society; and millowners resented every form of state interference with their "natural rights." So "political economy" became "economics." [3] The state was regarded as a badge of original sin, not to be mentioned in economic circles. Of course, it was absurd for men to write of the production and distribution of wealth apart from the state which defines, upholds, taxes, and regulates property, the very basis of economic operations; but absurdity does not restrain the hand of the apologist.

To this simple historical explanation must be added another. This is an age of intense specialization. Every field of human knowledge is so vast that the workers therein are driven, in their endeavor to see things as they really are, further and further into the details of their subject. They then easily forget the profound truth enunciated by Buckle that the science of any subject is not at its center but at its periphery where it impinges upon all other sciences. So the living organism of human society as a subject of inquiry has been torn apart and parceled out among specialists.

Aristotle, in contrast, combines economics, politics, and ethics. He considers the nature and function of the family before he takes up the forms of state. He then moves to the subject of property in its human relationships and considers the limits of communism and individualism. He rejects the former as impossible but he tells us that "poverty is the parent of revolution and crime." At no time does he lose sight of ethics. The aim of the family and of property, as of the state, is the best life. Property as a means of getting more property or as an end in itself is inconceivable to him as a philosopher. Its aim is to en-

---

[3] [The history of the transition from "political economy" to "economics" has not yet been written. It is, of course, far more complex than my summary statements indicate.]

able man to live temperately and well, and this aim should determine the amount which each citizen ought to hold.

Having surveyed the family and property and the production and distribution of wealth—the texture of society—Aristotle proceeds to the consideration of the forms and nature of government, the causes of revolutions, and the conditions which favor the best society of which human nature is capable. How sound is this, how wise, how much more scientific than our modern practice of dissection and distribution among specialists! So the first conclusion to be drawn from Aristotle is that he never for an instant dreamed that ethics, politics, and economics could be torn apart and treated as separate subjects. He would have said of such pseudo-sciences with Ruskin: "I simply am uninterested in them as I should be in a science of gymnastics which assumed that men had no skeletons. It might be shown on that supposition that it would be advantageous to roll students up into pellets, flatten them into cakes, or stretch them into cables; and that when these results were effected the re-insertion of the skeleton would be attended with various inconveniences to their constitutions." Aristotle simply could not imagine a treatise on the state that did not consider the whole man rather than a highly hypothetical man—man as a mere political animal. This is apparent in his treatment of every phase of his subject.

When he approaches the heart of the matter, namely, the causes of variations in the forms of the state, he immediately relates economics and politics. He declares that there must "necessarily be as many different forms of government as there are ranks in the society, arising from the superiority of some over others and their different situations. And these seem to be two, as they say of the winds: namely, the north and the south; and all the others are declinations from these. And thus in politics, there is the government of the many and the government of the few; or a democracy and an oligarchy. . . . A democracy is a state where the freemen and the poor, being the majority, are invested with the power of the state. An oligarchy is a state where the rich and those of noble families, being few, possess it." In commenting on this laconic explanation of the differences in the form of the state by reference to differences in wealth, Aristotle's distinguished editor, Jowett, remarks in an equally laconic fashion: "As the poor or the middle class, or the notables predominate, they divide the government among themselves."

As economic classes depend upon the character and distribution of property, and as the forms of state turn upon the predominance of classes, it would follow logically that alterations in the form of state must have some connection with the changing fortunes of classes. This is exactly the conclusion Aristotle reached after he had considered the forces and conditions which produce revolutions in the affairs of nations. "Political revolutions," he says, "spring from a disproportionate increase in any part of the state. . . . When the rich grow numerous or properties increase, the form of government changes into an oligarchy or a government of families. . . . Revolutions break out when opposite parties, e.g. the rich and poor, are equally balanced and there is little or nothing between them. . . . Revolutions in democracies are generally caused by the intemperance of demagogues who either in their private capacity lay information against rich men until they compel them to combine (for a common danger unites even the bitterest enemies) or, coming forward in public, stir up the people against them. The truth of this remark is proved by a variety of examples. At Cos the democracy was overthrown because wicked demagogues arose and the notables combined. . . . The democracy at Heraclea was overthrown shortly after the foundation of the colony by the injustice of the demagogues which drove out the notables, who came back in a body and put an end to the democracy." There are collateral and incidental causes of revolutions, but "the universal and chief cause" of revolutionary feeling is "the desire of equality, when men think they are equal to others who have more than themselves; or again, the desire of inequality and superiority when, conceiving themselves to be superior, they think they have not more but the same or less than their inferiors; pretensions which may or may not be just."

It can hardly be doubted that Aristotle, in spite of some confusion of thought, looks upon the character and distribution of wealth in society as the chief determining factors in fixing the form of state. It is equally clear that he finds the causes of revolutions in states in contests among those who have much, those who have little, and those who have no, property. This disparity in fortune is the fundamental condition of which the demagogue avails himself in order to stir up strife and overturn established orders. Another commentator, Mr. A. D. Lindsay, observes: "When we come to Aristotle's analysis of existing constitutions we find that while he regards them as imperfect approximations to the ideal, he also thinks of them as the result of struggles between classes. . . . And each class is thought of, not as trying to express an ideal, but as struggling to acquire power to maintain its position. . . . His analysis of the facts forces him to look upon them [the Greek states] as the scene of struggling factions. The causes of revolutions are not described as primarily changes in the conception of the common good, but changes in the military or economic power of the several classes in the state."

Having come, by an inductive study, to the conclusion that there is a fundamental relation between the form and fortunes of the state and the character and distribution of property among the population, Aristotle applies the doctrine in his inquiry into "what is the best constitution for most states and the best life for most men, neither assuming a standard of virtue which is above ordinary persons, nor an education which is exceptionally favored by nature and circumstances, nor yet an ideal state which is an aspiration only."

His opinion touching this point is clear and simple: "Now in all states there are three elements; one class is very rich, another very poor, and a third is a mean. It is admitted that moderation and the mean are best, and therefore it will clearly be best to possess the gifts of fortune in moderation; for in that condition of life men are most ready to listen to reason. . . . Those who have too much of the goods of fortune, strength, wealth, friends, and the like are neither willing nor able to submit to authority. . . . On the other hand, the very poor, who are in the opposite extreme, are too degraded. So that the one class cannot obey and can only rule despotically; the other knows not how to command and must be ruled like slaves. Thus arises a city not of freemen but of masters and slaves, the one despising, the other envying. . . . A city ought to be composed, as far as possible, of equals and similars; and these are generally the middle classes. Wherefore a city which is composed of middle class citizens is necessarily best governed; they are, as we say, the natural elements of a state. And this is the class of citizens which is most secure in a state, for they do not, like the poor, covet their neighbour's goods; nor do others covet theirs, as the poor covet the goods of the rich; and as they neither plot against others, nor are themselves plotted against, they pass through life safely."

When Aristotle takes up the problem of finding the best material for a democracy he is no less insistent upon the economic element as the fundamental factor. The safest and most enduring form of democracy is, in his opinion, that based upon agriculture. In such a state the people are compelled to work hard for a livelihood, they have little time for political intrigue and combinations, they do not covet the property of others, and they will endure in patience oligarchies or tyrannies if they are allowed to work and are not deprived of their lands or cattle. Next to an agricultural democracy, that of a pastoral people is best, for those who live by their flocks are in many ways similar to husbandmen and they are well fitted for war. The worst and most dangerous democracy of all is that founded on commerce, for there is no moral excellence in the employments of traders, mechanics, and laborers. By virtue of their economic occupations, they are turbulent, instable, and easily the prey of demagogues.[4]

[4] "The best material of democracy is an agricultural population; there is no difficulty in forming a democracy where the mass of the people live by agriculture or tending of cattle. Being poor, they have no leisure and therefore do not often attend the assembly, and not having the necessaries of life they are always at work, and do not covet the property of others. . . . Next best to an agricultural and in many respects similar are a pastoral people, who live by their flocks; they are the best trained of any for war, robust in body, and able to camp out. The people of whom other democracies consist are far inferior to them, for their life is inferior; there is no room for moral excellence in any of their employments, whether they be mechanics, traders, or labourers . . . The last form of democracy, that in which all share alike, is one which cannot be

As Aristotle, first among the ancients, commands the attention of every student of politics, so Machiavelli,[5] first among the moderns, arrests our interest. Like his Greek predecessor, he was a man of affairs and a painstaking searcher into the history of political institutions. During most of his active life he was in the public service of Florence. He was familiar with the inner politics of the turbulent Italian states. To experience in domestic politics he added a knowledge of foreign affairs gathered from many difficult diplomatic negotiations and missions. As his voluminous writings attest, he was a profound student of history, politics, and diplomacy.

When he writes of states founded upon the sword, his task is simple. He has merely to reckon with military forces and devices. When he deals with the origins of civil principalities he follows in the path cut by Aristotle. "A principality," he says, "results either from the will of the people or that of the nobles according as one or the other prevails. For the nobles, seeing that they cannot resist the people, begin to have recourse to the influence and reputation of one of their own class, and make him a prince, so that under the shadow of his power they may give free scope to their desires. The people also seeing that they cannot resist the nobles, have recourse to the influence and reputation of one man and make him a prince so as to be protected by his authority."

In advising the prince, once established, how best to maintain his power, Machiavelli warns him to take account of the conflict of classes out of which political power springs and to balance one over against the other, leaning to the right or to the left as occasion demands. By this shifting of affections the prince can cause the passions and ambitions of each class to nullify those of the other and so keep himself secure in power. In times of peace, even,

---

borne by all states, and will not last long unless well regulated by laws and customs. The most general causes which tend to destroy this or other kinds of government have now been pretty fully considered." Here Aristotle evidently refers to Bk. V. ch. 5 where he ascribes revolutions in democracies to hatred stirred by demagogues against the rich.

[5] COMPILER'S NOTE: Machiavelli (A.D. 1469–1527), Italian statesman.

the prince should give attention to the balance of classes. "As cities are generally divided into guilds and classes, he should keep account of these bodies and occasionally be present at their assemblies, and should set an example of his affability and magnificence; preserving, however always the majesty of his dignity."

If time permitted it would be interesting to survey the political philosophies of Bacon, Raleigh, Harrington,[6] Montesquieu, Burke, and a score of other great men who have speculated upon the origin, nature, and fortunes of the state; but there is a limit to our enterprise. Students familiar with their writings know how deep is the impress of economics upon them.

Still there is one more philosopher of the Old World who cannot be neglected. As we have, of necessity, examined the opinions of Aristotle and Machiavelli, so must we, of equal necessity, look into the writings of John Locke.[7] He was, in a serious way, the forerunner of the American and French revolutions as well as the supreme apologist for the English revolution of 1688. All the great

[6] More than a century after Machiavelli's death an English writer, James Harrington, in constructing his model commonwealth, *Oceana,* gave to idealists the same advice that Machiavelli gave to the prince, namely that they should take into account the fact that the forms and distribution of property in society determine the nature of the state. "Dominion," he wrote, "is property, real or personal; that is to say, in lands, or in money and goods. Lands or the parts and parcels of a territory are held by the proprietor or proprietors, lord or lords of it, in some proportion; and such (except it be in a city that has little or no land and whose revenue is in trade) as is the proportion or balance or dominion or property in land, such is the nature of the empire. If one man be sole landlord or own three parts in four, the state is an absolute monarchy. If a few or a nobility with a clergy be the landlords and overbalance the people to a like proportion, the state is an oligarchy or a mixed monarchy. If the whole people be landlords or the lands are so divided among them that no man or aristocracy of men overbalance the many then the state is a commonwealth or anarchy." In short, political power follows property and it is the function of the statesman to see that property is not too narrowly concentrated, that a substantial landed class be maintained as the basis or stabilizer of the state.

[7] COMPILER'S NOTE: John Locke (1632–1704).

French critics of the old régime from Voltaire to Condorcet were familiar with their Locke. His works were translated into French for the benefit of those not familiar with his native tongue. Everywhere in the English colonies in America, students of politics were also acquainted with the philosopher of the Glorious Revolution. From him Jefferson drew both inspiration and guidance. Parts of the Declaration of Independence are merely paraphrases of passages in Locke's *Two Treatises on Government*. Like Aristotle and Machiavelli, this English thinker combined literary pursuits with practical affairs, although it must be said that his first-hand experience with politics is not to be compared with that of the Greek or the Italian.

Both the origin and end of the state Locke finds in the roots of property. "To avoid these inconveniences which disorder men's property in the state of nature," he writes, "men unite into societies, that they may have the united strength of the whole society to secure and defend their properties and may have standing rules to bound it, by which every one may know what is his. . . . The reason why men enter into society is the preservation of their property, and the end why they choose and authorize a legislature is that there may be laws made and rules set as guards and fences to the properties of all the members of the society." As the origin of the state is to be found in the requirements of property owners, so is the end of the state to be sought in the same source. "The great and chief end, therefore, of men's uniting into commonwealths and putting themselves under government is the preservation of their property."

As the preservation of property is the origin and end of the state, so it gives the right of revolution against any government or authority that invades property. Such is the economic foundation of the ethics of revolt. "The supreme power cannot take from any man part of his property without his consent." If perchance this is done, the owners of property, the people, have the right to cast off the old form of government and to establish a new one that will observe the ends of civil society. This will not be undertaken, of course, for light and transient reasons, but when a long train of abuses menaces the privileges of property and person, the right of revolution may be exercised.

So far we have considered only Old World writers, and according to methods of thinking cherished in many quarters we might easily conclude that European philosophy has no application to us—a favored people who live in a new dispensation of our own making. It cannot be denied that the social and economic conditions of Athens, feudal Europe, or the Stuart age were in many respects different from those prevailing in the United States. Still, mankind here, as in the Old World, must struggle for existence and, allowing for the divergences in circumstances, we have no reason for assuming that the economic laws which governed in other times and other lands are without effect in this fortunate country. Certainly the founders of the American republic did not assume that in shaping our political institutions they could break with the experience and philosophy of the past.[8] That will be discovered by any one who takes the trouble to read the records of the convention assembled at Philadelphia in 1787 to frame the Constitution of the United States.

Time does not permit even a casual survey of those voluminous documents. Nor is such a general inquiry necessary. By common consent it is recognized that James Madison was "the Father of the Constitution." He was a profound student of history and government. He kept the most complete record of the debates in the federal convention that has come down to us. He spent his long life in public service and political activities. He was twice President of the American union, and was intimately acquainted with nearly all the great statesmen of his time. He was the adviser of Washington and the confidant of Jefferson. He knew at first hand the stuff of which governments are made. To a study such as we are now making his views are simply indispensable and he may speak for his contemporaries.

In a powerful essay written in defense of the Constitution of the United States—Number Ten of *The Federalist*

---

[8] COMPILER'S NOTE: For specific consideration of this topic, see below, Chapters X and XI, dealing with economic influences affecting the preparation and adoption of the Constitution of the United States.

—Madison sums up his political science in such a clear and concise form that no one can mistake his meaning. The prime function of government, he says, is the protection of the different and unequal faculties of man for acquiring property. "From the protection of different and unequal faculties of acquiring property, the possession of different degrees and kinds of property immediately results." This inexorable economic fact is the basis of political fact. Madison goes on: "From the influence of these [different degrees and kinds of property] on the sentiments and views of the respective proprietors ensues a division of society into different interests and parties. The latent causes of faction are thus sown in the nature of man; and we see them everywhere brought into different degrees of activity, according to the different circumstances of civil society." Thus, in the opinion of the Father of the American Constitution, politics springs inevitably, relentlessly, out of economics. The *sentiments* and *views* which arise from the possession of different degrees and kinds of property form the stuff of so-called "political psychology."

After this statement of controlling principle, Madison moves to his next fundamental problem, namely, the effect of these differences in economic condition and in political psychology on the government and its operation. Here too he has no doubts. He admits that there are occasionally fanciful and frivolous causes of internal disturbances but he is quick to add that "the most common and durable source of factions[9] has been the various and unequal distribution of property. Those who hold and those who are without property have ever formed distinct interests in society. Those who are creditors and those who are debtors fall under a like distinction. A landed interest, a manufacturing interest, a mercantile interest, with many lesser interests grow up of necessity in civilized nations and divide them into different classes actuated by different sentiments and views. The regulation of these various and interfering interests forms the principal task of modern legislation, and involves the spirit of party and faction in the necessary and ordinary operations of the government. . . . The

[9] "Faction" was the common term in the eighteenth century for "political party."

causes of faction cannot be removed. . . . We well know that neither moral nor religious motives can be relied on as an adequate control."

Thus Madison holds that, owing to the nature of men, unequal distribution of property is unavoidable; that in every civilized society, there will be persons holding different kinds and amounts of property; that from their holdings will arise special sentiments and views; that from these differing sentiments will arise contending political parties; and that political parties will seek to accumulate a majority and control the state. This danger, majority rule, Madison said in the constitutional convention, was especially grave in view of the inevitable rise of a landless proletariat—a vast class of propertyless persons likely to be actuated by the same sentiments and therefore certain to assault the rights of the propertied classes. To secure the public good and private rights against the dangers of such a majority party bent on attacking the property of the minority, and at the same time preserve the spirit and form of popular government, he concluded, was the object toward which the framers of the Constitution of the United States directed their skill and their energies.

In short, the fundamental purposes and ideals of a free government in the New World, by the iron necessity of circumstances could not be essentially different from those of the Old World or the Ancient World. If government here is different from government in other times and places it is mainly because the forms and distribution of property are different.

But it may be said that Madison was from a slave state where political power did in fact result from the possession of land and slaves and that he was reading into universal politics the conclusions drawn from local accidents. Such a conclusion would of course be unjust to the great Virginian because all through his works there are the evidences of erudition which mark him out as one of the most learned men of his day. For a moment we may let the objection stand and inquire what were the views of some leading statesman and philosopher in the free North. Surely none will object if I choose a man who long and honorably represented the Commonwealth of Massachusetts in the Senate of the United States and who found imperishable fame in the annals of his country, Daniel Webster. In a speech of great cogency and learning, delivered in the constitutional convention of his state in 1820, he defended the distribution of representation in the Senate on the basis of property. The principle of representing property, he said, was well established by writers of the greatest authority. Then he went on to expound his views with a show of learning and philosophy not often displayed in the American constitutional discussions.

"Those who have treated of natural law have maintained," he said, "as a principle of that law, that, as far as the object of society is the protection of something in which the members possess unequal shares, it is just that the weight of each person in the common councils should bear a relation and proportion to his interest. Such is the sentiment of Grotius, and he refers, in support of it, to several institutions among the ancient states.

"Those authors who have written more particularly on the subject of political institutions have, many of them, maintained similar sentiments. Not, indeed, that every man's power should be in exact proportion to his property, but that, in a general sense, and in a general form, property, as such, should have its weight and influence in political arrangements. Montesquieu speaks with approbation of the early Roman regulation, made by Servius Tullius, by which the people were distributed into classes, according to their property, and the public burdens apportioned to each individual according to the degree of power which he possessed in the government. By this regulation, he observes, some bore with the greatness of their tax because of their proportionable participation in power and credit; others consoled themselves for the smallness of their power and credit by the smallness of their tax.

"One of the most ingenious of political writers is Mr. Harrington, an author not now read as much as he deserves. It is his leading object, in his *Oceana*, to prove, that power *naturally* and *necessarily* follows property. He maintains that a government founded on property is legitimately founded; and that a government founded on the disregard of property is founded in injustice, and can only be maintained by military force. 'If one man,' says he, 'be sole landlord, like the Grand Seignior, his empire is absolute. If a few possess the land, this makes the Gothic or feudal constitution. If the *whole people* be landlords, then it is a commonwealth.' 'It is strange,' says an ingenious person in the last century, 'that Harrington should be the first man to find out so evident and demonstrable a truth as that of property being the true basis and *measure* of power.' In truth, he was not the first. The idea is as old as political science itself. It may be found in Aristotle, Lord Bacon, Sir Walter Raleigh, and other writers. Harrington seems, however, to be the first writer who has illustrated and expanded the principle, and given to it the effect and prominence which justly belong to it. To this sentiment, Sir, I entirely agree. It seems to me to be plain, that, in the absence of military force, political power naturally and necessarily goes into the hands which hold the property. In my judgment, therefore, a republican form of government rests, not more on political constitutions, than on those laws which regulate the descent and transmission of property. . . .

"If the nature of our institutions be to found government on property, and that it should look to those who hold property for its protection, it is entirely just that property should have its due weight and consideration in political arrangements. Life and personal liberty are no doubt to be protected by law; but property is also to be protected by law, and is the fund out of which the means for protecting life and liberty are usually furnished. We have no experience that teaches us that any other rights are safe where property is not safe. Confiscation and plunder are generally, in revolutionary commotions, not far before banishment, imprisonment, and death. It would be monstrous to give even the name of government to any association in which the rights of property should not be completely secured. The disastrous revolutions which the world has witnessed, those political thunderstorms and earthquakes which have shaken the pillars of society to their very deepest foundations, have been revolutions against property.

"The English Revolution of 1688 was a revolution in favor of property, as well as of other rights. It was brought about by men of property for their security; and our own immortal Revolution was undertaken, not to shake or plunder property, but to protect it. The acts which the country complained of were such as violated the rights of property. An immense majority of all those who had an interest in the soil were in favor of the Revolution; and they carried it through, looking to its results for the security of their possessions."

In another address, equally cogent, delivered on the anniversary of the landing of the Pilgrims, Webster applied the economic interpretation of politics directly to American institutions. "Our New England ancestors," he said, "brought thither no great capitals from Europe; and if they had, there was nothing productive in which they could have been invested. They left behind them the whole feudal policy of the other continent. . . . They came to a new country. There were as yet no lands yielding rent, and no tenants rendering service. The whole soil was unreclaimed from barbarism. They were themselves either from their original condition, or from the necessity of their common interest, nearly on a general level in respect to property. Their situation demanded a parcelling out and division of the lands, and it may be fairly said that this necessary act *fixed the future frame and form of their government*.[1] The character of their political institutions was determined by the fundamental laws respecting property. . . . The consequence of all these causes has been a great subdivision of the soil and a great equality of condition; the true basis, most certainly, of popular government."

Having thus laid the foundations of politics in economics, Webster went on to give a warning and a prophecy. "The freest government," he said, "if it could exist, would not be long acceptable, if the tendency of the laws were to create a rapid accumulation of property in few hands and to render the great mass of the population dependent and penniless. In such a case, the popular power must break in upon the rights of property, or else the influence of property must limit and control the exercise of popular power. Universal suffrage, for example, could not long exist in a community where there was great inequality of property. The holders of estates would be obliged in such case either in some way to restrain the

[1] Italics are Webster's own.

right of suffrage, or else such right of suffrage would ere long divide the property."

It is to be regretted that time does not permit the reading of these remarkable speeches in full, but we may summarize all of Webster's conclusions in the following manner:

1. The form of a government is determined (except where the sword rules) by the nature and distribution of property.

2. Republican government rests upon a wide distribution of property, particularly in land.

3. Government to be stable must be founded on men's interest.

4. Property to be secure must have a direct interest, representation, and check in the government.

5. Disturbances in countries arise principally from the conflict of groups resulting from variations in the form and distribution of property.

6. Universal suffrage is incompatible with great inequality of wealth.

7. Political wisdom requires the establishment of government on property and the control of its distribution through the regulation of alienage and transmission.

Far away in South Carolina, one of Webster's distinguished contemporaries, John C. Calhoun, reached substantially the same conclusions as he pondered upon the rise and fall of states and the problems of statecraft. Like his antagonist in the forum, he had his mind fixed upon the instant need of things—the defense of the special interest for which he was the leading spokesman; but in his quest for power he also sought for the inherent nature of things. Quickly his penetrating glance shot through the texture of political rhetoric to the underlying economic facts.

"If the whole community had the same interests," he declared, "so that the interests of each and every portion would be so affected by the action of the government, that the laws which oppressed or impoverished one portion, would necessarily oppress and impoverish all others,—or the reverse,—then the right of suffrage, of itself, would be all-sufficient to counteract the tendency of the government to oppression and abuse of its powers; and, of course, would form, of itself, a perfect constitutional government. The interest of all being the same, by supposition, as far as the action of the government was concerned, all would have like interests as to what laws should be made, and how they should be executed. All strife and struggle would cease as to who should be elected to make and execute them. The only question would be, who was most fit; who the wisest and most capable of understanding the common interest of the whole. This decided, the election would pass off quietly, and without party discord; as no one portion could advance its own peculiar interest without regard to the rest, by electing a favourite candidate.

"But such is not the case. On the contrary, nothing is more difficult than to equalize the action of the government, in reference to the various and diversified interests of the community; and nothing more easy than to pervert its powers into instruments to aggrandize and enrich one or more interests by oppressing and impoverishing the others; and this too, under the operation of laws, couched in general terms;—and which, on their face, appear fair and equal. Nor is this the case in some particular communities only. It is so in all; the small and the great,—the poor and the rich,—irrespective of pursuits, productions, or degrees of civilization;—with, however, this difference, that the more extensive and populous the country, the more diversified the condition and pursuits of its population, and the richer, more luxurious, and dissimilar the people, the more difficult is it to equalize the actions of the government,—and the more easy for one portion of the community to pervert its powers to oppress, and plunder the other.

"Such being the case, it necessarily results, that the right of suffrage, by placing the control of the government in the community must, from the same constitution of our nature which makes government necessary to preserve society, lead to conflict among its different interests, —each striving to obtain possession of its powers, as the means of protecting itself against the others;—or of advancing its respective interests, regardless of the interests of others. For this purpose, a struggle will take place between the various interests to obtain a majority, in order to control the government. If no one interest be strong enough, of itself, to obtain it, a combination will be formed between those whose interests are most alike;—each conceding something to the others, until a sufficient number is obtained to make a majority. The process may be slow, and much time may be required before a compact, organized majority can be thus formed; but formed it will be in time, even without preconcert or design, by the sure workings of that principle or constitution of our nature in which government itself originates. When once formed, the community will be divided into great parties,—a major and a minor,—between which there will be incessant struggles on the one side to retain, and on the other to obtain the majority,—and, thereby, the control of the government and the advantages it confers.

"So deeply seated, indeed, is this tendency to conflict between the different interests or portions of the community, that it would result from the action of the government itself, even though it were possible to find a community, where the people were all of the same pursuits, placed in the same condition of life, and in every respect, so situated, as to be without inequality of condition or diversity of interests. The advantages of possessing the control of the powers of the government, and, thereby, of its honours and emoluments, are, of themselves, exclusive of all other consideration, ample to divide even such a community into two great hostile parties."

It is evident from this review that the six great thinkers we have brought under consideration were in substantial agreement on the subject in hand. They believed that the fundamental factors with which the statesman has to deal are the forms and distribution of property and the sentiments and views arising from the possession of different degrees and kinds of property. Upon this generalization, we rest one of two conclusions. We may, upon reflection, decide that the distribution of property is the result of changeless forces inherent in the nature of man, and that the statesman is not a maker but an observer of destiny. Or we may hold that once the forces of social evolution are widely understood man may subdue them to his purposes. He may so control the distribution of wealth as to establish an ideal form of society and prevent the eternal struggle of classes that has shaken so many nations to their foundations. Man, the servant of fate, may become the master. But here we pause. Can the spirit of man be permanently enclosed in any system?

CHAPTER IV

ECONOMIC GROUPS AND THE
STRUCTURE OF THE STATE

HAVING SURVEYED the theories of our six political philosophers, it is fitting and proper that we should inquire
whether there has been in fact a close relation between the
structure of the state and the economic composition of
society. It would be interesting, if time permitted, to examine the constitution of Athens and to consider such
matters as Draco's legislation and Solon's reforms or to
analyze the illuminating pages in which Polybius describes
the balance of powers in Rome. The results of such a
study, pondered in connection with the theories we have
just reviewed, could not fail to set in train a fascinating
line of speculation. There are, however, limits to this
undertaking, and we must confine our scrutiny to the
modern state in its historical growth.

In reviewing the history of government in Western
Europe, from the disintegration of the Roman Empire to
the opening years of the nineteenth century, we discover
that wherever the simple sword-won despotism of the
war leader, prince or king, is supplemented or superseded
by some form of representation, it is not the people, considered as abstract equal personalities, who are represented, but it is propertied groups, estates. We are told
by that profound student of mediæval law, Dr. Stubbs,
that the ideal toward which Europe was slowly working
in the middle ages, was a constitution under which each
class was admitted to a share of power and control, and
national action determined by the balance of forces thus
combined.

This was not, as he admits, a conscious design by which statesmen shaped their policies. Many forces and circumstances contributed to the making of the representative system of estates. Sometimes it was the resistance of a particular economic group to royal despotism that won for it a recognized share in the government. An example of this is afforded by the contest which ended in the grant of *Magna Carta*.[1] The barons wrote their interest into the public law of England, and secured it by obtaining the right of actual participation as a class in the control of government. At other times kings, especially during wars of conquest or defense, found themselves straitened for funds, and they called upon certain classes or groups of men to fill their treasury. Such, for instance, was the origin of the English House of Commons. To the continued financial necessity of English kings, particularly during the long war with France, was due the extraordinary development in the power of the English Parliament. Whatever the circumstances in each particular case, the striking fact is that we find all over mediæval Europe what Dr. Stubbs calls "National assemblies composed of properly arranged and organized classes."

If we examine the constitution of England in the middle ages we find, in fact whatever the theory, four estates: the clergy, the baronage, the landed gentry, and the burgesses. Of these, the first three were founded, in the main, upon landed property. The first or spiritual estate in the English constitution comprised the whole body of the clergy. The clergy were invited to form a part of Parliament for two reasons. Their spiritual power was great, and even the boldest kings did not dare to defy them until the days of the mighty Henry VIII. But it is hardly to be doubted that it was as holders of property of immense value that the clergy came to a large share of the sovereign power. The bishops and the abbots, who were summoned to Parliament by name, were tenants-in-chief of the crown; in other words, they were great landed barons. As such they sat in the House of Lords. The inferior clergy in England, unlike their French brethren, though duly summoned to take their place in the great council of the realm, refused to obey the summons and remained for centuries in a

[1] COMPILER'S NOTE: by King John, in A.D. 1215.

convocation of their own, voting taxes on their property independent of the Parliaments of the realm. Though the clerical order was thus divided, the high authorities of the church sitting in the House of Lords and the inferior clergy dealing with the crown directly, it was mainly as a body of landed proprietors that the spiritual estate shared in the government.

The second English estate was the lay baronage, the members of which sat by their own right in the House of Lords along with the spiritual peers from the clerical estate. It is not necessary to inquire here into the historical circumstances which resulted in drawing a line between the richer barons and the untitled landed gentry, nor into those vainly disputed points of law which have been raised in the search for the origin and exact nature of the property rights which entitled a peer to a seat in the upper House. Whatever the cause may have been, the fact clearly stands forth, as Dr. Stubbs says, that in the middle ages the great land owners, tenants-in-chief, or titled lords, who appeared in person at the Parliament, were separated by a broad line from the freeholders who were represented by the knights of the shire.

According to a custom consecrated by time, it is the fashion to speak of the House of Commons as representing a sort of third estate, the commonalty of the realm. A little antiquarian inquiry, however, shows that the term "Commons" does not derive its meaning, as is often erroneously supposed, from any connection with "the common people." On the contrary it comes from the vague word *communitas* which was used in the middle ages to describe a political organism such as a county or chartered town. The House of Commons, therefore, was in reality the house of the *communitates*, composed of representatives of the gentry of the counties and the burgesses of the towns considered as collective bodies within their respective geographical areas. Strictly speaking, we find in the lower house of Parliament the spokesmen of two estates: the smaller landowners and the burgesses. In the early stages of parliamentary evolution, the agents sent by the burgesses were even treated as a separate house or estate, although the way in which they voted on measures is obscure. Later they were combined with the gentry.

It was one of the peculiarities of the English system that the Parliament was not constituted of three or four distinct orders. In France, as we shall see, there were three separate estates—clergy, nobility, and third estate. In Sweden there were four orders—clergy, nobility, burghers, and peasants. In both of these countries each order formed a separate chamber and acted as a collective body. In England, on the other hand, there were only two chambers in the political system, unless we treat the separate convocation of the clergy as a part of the political organism. The House of Lords combined the great landed lay barons with the great landed clerical barons. The House of Commons included burgesses from the towns and representatives of the landed gentry below the baronial line. Still, it is quite apparent, in spite of these combinations, that the English constitution of the middle ages was a group system, resting upon a foundation of economic classes.[2]

The principles underlying this mediæval system of class representation have never been entirely abandoned in England in favor of the theory of abstract individual equality. They were well understood by Harrington, Locke, and Burke. Indeed the British constitution of mediæval origin remained substantially unchanged until 1832, when the first of the great series of parliamentary reform bills was enacted. Although nearly half a century had elapsed since the French Revolution let loose its flood of liberty and equality doctrines, English reformers, even in 1832, remained unmoved. They widened the suffrage, it is true, but what they did in effect was to enfranchise, by a set of ingenious qualifications, another "estate" which had grown up with the advance of industry and commerce, namely, a body of middle-class manufacturers and shopkeepers. In vain did the English Chartists talk of "one man one vote," and universal manhood suffrage.

When the next generation of English reformers "shot Niagara," in 1867, they merely enfranchised another "es-

[2] It must not be forgotten that the mediæval clergy had a large vested interest in the profession. In addition to the huge landed estates given by pious benefactors for religious purposes, the clergy as a class had a large revenue from fees of various kinds. Much of the opposition of the middle classes to the Catholic Church was economic in origin.

tate"—the working classes of the great industrial centers. And when again in 1884 a new addition was made to the British constitution, another "estate" was enfranchised, the agricultural laborers. At no point was the tax-paying or property notion abandoned by the English in favor of the rule that a man should be allowed to vote simply because he is what Carlyle called "an unfeathered biped."

After the era of individualism set in it was more difficult to trace the line between economic groups than it had been in the middle ages, but whoever reads the debates over the great reform bills in England can see that statesmen, at each period, had in mind not abstract human equality, but what Dr. Stubbs characterized as a constitution in which each class of society should be admitted to a share of power and control. The significance of this story for the political future of England, in view of the changed position of women in industry, particularly since the outbreak of the Great War,[3] can readily be seen by one who has eyes to see.[4]

Everywhere in mediæval Europe, as in England, we find constitutions resting upon estates, assemblies representing various orders, classes, and conditions of men, except the rightless serf at the bottom of society. In the Cortes of Aragon sat the clergy, the great barons (*ricos hombres*), the minor barons or knights, and the burgesses of the towns. The old parliament of Scotland was composed of prelates, barons, and the smaller townsmen. In the representative assemblies which sprang up in some German principalities and in Russia, the same idea of class representation prevailed.

In the economic foundations of her constitution, mediæval France differed in no fundamental way from the neighboring countries. The history of the French estates, local and general, offers to the student of political science an abundance of group phenomena for analysis and interpretation. The records of more than three hundred years copiously illustrate the operation of the group process; an added and very significant interest is given to the study by

---

[3] COMPILER'S NOTE: i.e. World War I.

[4] This sentence may stand as written in 1916. Not until 1917, during the great "War for Democracy," did England establish a practically universal suffrage.

the role of the Estates General on the eve of the great Revolution.

As early as 1212, Simon de Montfort called a parliament to which he summoned bishops, nobles, and distinguished bourgeois. A few years later, there was held at Beziers an assembly of the three orders (*des trois ordres*) to give advice relative to provincial administrative organization. In 1254, by royal ordinance, the Seneschal Beaucaire was instructed to take counsel with the prelates, the barons, the knights, and the representatives of the towns (*hominibus bonarum villarum*).

The first Estates General, or National Parliament, was held in France in 1303. This was speedily followed by other parliaments. Speaking of the session of 1308, a chronicler said that the king wished to have the advice and consent of men "of every condition in the realm."

Like all early national assemblies, the French Estates General met only on the call of the king, and the methods of election depended naturally upon the terms of the royal orders. Complicated and varying practices were adopted at different times and places, but the following general principles were commonly observed. The members of the two privileged classes, the high clergy and the nobility, were summoned in person. The important convents and chapters were invited to send delegates. Occasionally the regular and secular clergy of a diocese united to elect their deputies. The nobility of the lower order usually chose their representatives, but sometimes members of this group appeared in person. In the towns the delegates were elected —often under a widely extended suffrage, including, on some occasions, women voters. These orders of society were known collectively as the clergy, the nobility, and the third estate.

It was not thought necessary, however, that each order should be represented only by members of the group. In mediæval practice, on the contrary, clerks, nobles, curates, and canons were sometimes chosen to represent townsmen. Often laymen were selected to speak for the clergy. Again, we see farmers (*roturiers*) and clergy standing as the spokesmen for men of noble order. Again it happened, perhaps to save expense, that the same deputies represented clergy, nobility, and third estate. Whatever the process of selection, however, each class acted separately and developed a certain consciousness of identical interest. When, in 1543, the king sought to unite the three groups in a common election, he found that instead of mitigating the group conflicts he only sharpened them. In a little while he restored the old practice of separate elections.

The French Estates General continued to meet from time to time until 1614, when the last grand session previous to the eve of the Revolution was held. At this memorable meeting there broke out a conflict between the nobility and the third estate which foreshadowed the struggle that was destined, more than one hundred and fifty years later, to destroy the whole system. The violence of this session, and perhaps the conflict then raging in England between the Parliament and James I, served as a warning that the monarch should beware of nourishing a dangerous hostility among the national estates.

Whatever may have been the cause—with that we are not now concerned—no session of the Estates General was again called until 1788. In that year the king, being in desperate financial straits, once more summoned the representatives of the different economic groups, that could give him relief, to consider the state of the realm. Immediately the antiquarians busied themselves with historical researches in order to restore the ancient and honorable institution of class government in its old form.

To the Estates General of 1789, each estate—clergy, nobility, and third estate—sent its members and representatives. Then arose, as every one knows, a fateful struggle for power. The clergy and nobility, bent on preserving their dominion, insisted that the vote on measures should be taken by the houses, as three distinct orders. Thus they hoped to prevent the upper classes from being overwhelmed by the numerical majority of the third estate, which had twice as many representatives in the assembly as the other two estates combined. Every school history tells us of the deadlock which ensued, of Mirabeau's eloquence, of the Tennis Court Oath, and of the National Assembly which, by firm action, was substituted for the old three-class system. Had the clergy and the nobility been willing earlier to surrender some of their privileges, and concede to the third estate a fair portion of political power, the history of the desperate years that followed the peaceful revolution of 1789 might have been far different. By resisting to the breaking point, the clergy and the nobility were conquered and almost destroyed by the third estate.

Less significant for the history of the world, but by no means less interesting in itself, is the parliamentary development of Sweden. From very early times the constitution of that kingdom recognized and provided for the representation of four distinct classes, clergy, nobility, burghers, and peasants. In the constitutional reorganization which followed the disturbances of the French Revolution and the Revolutionary Wars, this system was kept intact. Each class was not only distinctly represented, but each class had a house of its own through which the interests of the group were expressed in the government. The great landlords appeared in person. The spiritual house included the bishops and a number of other persons chosen by the clergy, the universities, and the academy of sciences, respectively. The representatives of the middle class were elected by the properly qualified burghers of the towns and the mineowners. The representatives of the peasants were chosen by the landowning farmers and certain other members of the soil-tilling population. Each of the four houses of parliament deliberated alone and acted in the name of and for the class which it represented. Ingenious provisions were devised for obviating deadlocks. This four-class parliament was retained until 1866 when two houses took the place of the old system.

The principle of class representation, which had been adopted in the development of mediæval governments, was taken over entirely by Austria in her constitutional reconstruction shortly after the middle of the nineteenth century. The Austrian upper house consisted, of course, of the nobility, whose economic foundation was the land. In the formation of the lower house, in 1860–1, representation was distributed among the several provinces of the realm and it was provided that the quota to which each province was entitled should be selected by the local legislatures from definite economic groups.

It was stipulated that the total number of deputies to be chosen should be distributed among four distinct "estates," namely: (1) the great landlords (except in Trieste and Vorarlberg where no such class existed, and in Dalmatia where the highest taxpayers were put into this group); (2) the burghers of the cities, markets, and industrial places; (3) the peasants of the rural communes; and (4) the chambers of commerce. In 1873 indirect election was abandoned for direct election by popular vote, but the system of class representation remained intact. Twenty-three years later, that is, in 1896, the non-taxpayers and industrial proletariat were admitted to a share in the government. It was provided that seventy-two deputies, now added to the parliament, should be chosen by the voters in general, including those already members of other classes. This system of group representation remained in force until 1907 when manhood suffrage was adopted.

In formulating a constitution after the Revolution of 1848, the king of Prussia deliberately founded his government upon a class system, as you all know from your study of comparative politics. The voters of Prussia are divided into three classes: those who pay one-third of the income taxes elect indirectly one-third of the delegates to the Prussian Diet; those who pay a second third of the income taxes likewise elect a third of the delegates; and finally, all the rest of the voters, who constitute almost the entire electorate, choose the remaining third of the deputies. Thus the Prussian Parliament is made up of a House of Lords, representing the landed interests, and a House of Commons or Diet, representing in two-thirds of its membership the wealth of the kingdom, and in one-third the propertyless. Years of agitation and a threatened revolt on the part of the masses have failed to shake the foundations of this strongly knit system of class government.[5]

All this, you may think, is interesting enough, but without bearing upon American conditions. It may be said that whatever were the practices of mediæval France, England, Sweden, and Aragon, they have no meaning for the United States founded under another dispensation. There stands

[5] So things stood in 1916 when these lectures were given. This system was overthrown in the German Revolution of 1918. [After the advent of Hitler in 1933 the equalitarian political regime substituted for the old Prussian class government was extinguished by force.]

the Declaration of Independence with its immortal statement that all men are created free and equal and that
governments derive their just powers from the consent of
the governed. Here is what seems to be a repudiation of
the whole notion of class or group interest in the process
of government; but when we turn from theory to fact
we find ourselves in the midst of mediæval forms and institutions.

An examination of the first American state constitutions
reveals no abandonment of the Old World notion that
government rests upon property. Take, for instance, the
Massachusetts constitution of 1780 drawn by John Adams
and adopted after long and serious deliberation. In this
document we discover that no man could vote for members
of the legislature or for governor, unless he had a freehold estate of the annual value of three pounds, or some
estate of the value of sixty pounds. Here is a distinct
recognition of two classes of property interests in the
government—real property and personalty. To add further security to the two orders or "estates" the constitution provided that no one could be elected governor who
did not possess a freehold of the value of one thousand
pounds, and furthermore, that the senators should be distributed among the respective districts of the state on the
score of the amount of taxes paid in each of them. It was
in defense of this last provision that Daniel Webster made
his famous speech in the Massachusetts convention of
1820, defending the economic basis of government. If
the Massachusetts constitution proved to be rather democratic in its operations, that was, as Webster pointed out,
due to the wide distribution of property, not to any desire
of the Massachusetts Fathers to sacrifice the security of
property to a political shibboleth.

If we take a great middle state like New York, we find
that the constitution drafted in 1777 distinctly recognized
the existence of classes by establishing the predominance
of the farmers. It provided that the senate should be composed of freeholders, and that none but freeholders possessing one hundred pounds' worth of land could vote for
the senators or for governor. A slighter property qualification was placed upon voters for the lower house—a
qualification which admitted freemen of the incorporated

towns, renters, and a few others, but kept out the lower
levels of the proletariat. This class system remained in
vogue until 1821. It was abolished then only against the
violent protests of many intellectual leaders of the time,
such as Chancellor Kent, who maintained that the rights
of property could be protected only when property was
frankly represented in the government, and that those
"without a stake in the country" should have no voice in
its politics.

The Fathers of the South did not differ from those of
the North. In the agricultural state of Virginia, where there
were few merchants and capitalists, the predominance
which the landed classes possessed in fact was also established in right. Only freeholders could vote in that
state under the constitution of 1776, and this restriction
was kept in force for more than half a century. When a
vigorous but vain attempt was made, in the constitutional
convention of 1829, to abolish it, the freehold suffrage was
defended on the ground that the landed group was the
only secure foundation for government because all other
classes were variable and transitory in character, while the
possession of land furnished the strongest evidence of
permanent, common interest with, and attachment to, the
community.

Admitting the plain evidence of the first state constitutions, that the wise founders of this Republic recognized
the place of property interests in political processes, it may
be said that the Constitution of the United States, drawn in
that period, nowhere takes into account the existence of
economic divisions. This is true, if we read merely the
language of the instrument and not the records of the
convention which drafted it. In the document itself there
are no provisions similar to those which appear in the
first state constitutions, placing landed- and personal-
property qualifications on the suffrage and officeholding;
but the omission was not made because the framers of that
immortal instrument were indifferent to the rights of property or unaware of the influence wielded by economic
groups upon the course of government. Neither was it
because they disapproved of property qualifications, for
such existed in nearly every state in the Union. In fact,

property qualifications for officers and for voters were proposed in the convention, but it was impossible to agree on their precise form. Inasmuch as many of the troubles under the Articles of the Confederation had arisen from attacks on capital by state legislatures elected by free-holders, and inasmuch as the convention was especially eager to safeguard the rights of personal property, a free-hold qualification did not seem to offer an adequate remedy. On the other hand, to impose a large personal-property qualification on voters would have meant the defeat of the Constitution by the farmers who were, of necessity, called upon to ratify it. Under the circum-stances the framers of the Constitution relied, not upon direct economic qualifications, but upon checks and bal-ances to secure the rights of property—particularly per-sonal property—against the assaults of the farmers and the proletariat.[6]

At this point we may summarize. Our six political phi-losophers regarded property, in its various forms and distri-bution, and the social groups which arise out of economic processes, as the fundamental materials for the science of government. We have seen also that the constitutions of government of great nations were, for centuries, deliber-ately fitted to the division of society into separate orders, groups, and estates, each of which pursued a separate calling and cherished its own sentiments about economic interests.

This great fact stands out clearly, that through the cen-turies—down until our own day—group interests were recognized as forming the very essence of politics both in theory and practice. Statesmen spoke of them, negoti-ated with them, placated them, legislated for them, and sought generally to secure the predominance of one or the other or the balance of several against one or another. At all events, statesmen spoke not of abstract men and abstract rights, but of real men and real rights. What has

---

[6] This subject is covered at length in Beard's *An Economic Interpretation of the Constitution of the United States,* pp. 152–68. COMPILER'S NOTE: For a discussion of the economic factors affecting the writing and adoption of the Constitution, see Chap-ters X and XI of the present text.

happened to sweep away the practices of centuries, to challenge the philosophy of the world's greatest political thinkers, and to introduce the rule of "the people" instead of the rule of estates? Have the economic conditions of the world been revolutionized, the estates and orders abolished?

CHAPTER V

THE DOCTRINE OF POLITICAL EQUALITY

THE GREAT POLITICAL PHILOSOPHERS, with few exceptions, have regarded property as the fundamental element in political power, and have looked upon a constitution as a balance of economic groups. The governments founded and developed before the nineteenth century were in fact complexes of group interests. Nowhere was the representative system, in its origin, designed to reflect the opinions of mere numerical aggregations of human beings considered in the abstract apart from property and employment. On the contrary, it reflected the sentiments and views of different sorts and conditions of men, estates or orders: clergy, nobility, burghers, and minor landowners.

In the United States where there was no clerical estate or established nobility to be represented in the government, the existence of the two fundamental property groups—the owners of realty and the owners of personalty—was taken into account either in positive constitutional law, or in the check and balance system provided by the separation of powers.[1] If the first American constitutions were more democratic than those of Europe, the fact is not to be at-

---

[1] Much ingenuity has been spent by American lawyers in elaborating the theoretical fictions of Montesquieu. The real significance of the separation of powers and its relation to the balance of class interests in society was appreciated by eighteenth-century writers, but if more modern statesmen have understood them they have seldom been frank in setting forth their views.

tributed to radical changes in human nature, induced by a voyage across the Atlantic, but, as the great Webster pointed out, to a very wide distribution of property, due mainly to cheap land.

So things stood in the closing years of the old régime. Then suddenly came two great revolutions, one in economic fact, and the other in political theory. The first was brought about by the invention of the steam engine and machinery, creating an immense amount of property which had hitherto existed only as a minor element in economic life, namely, industrial and mercantile capital. So rapidly did this new form of property accumulate that even in the United States, by the middle of the nineteenth century, it exceeded in value the agricultural land of the country.

Being more mobile and more easily concentrated than land, a vast portion of it quickly fell into the hands of, relatively speaking, a small portion of society. As land was the great stabilizer of the old order, so capital became the great disturber in the new order. Like a mighty giant tossing to and fro in a fever, in its quest for profits, it tore masses of men from the land, from their sleepy villages and hamlets, and hurled them here and there all over the globe. Under its influence the old sharp class differences were disarranged. The peasant might become a successful cotton spinner, a financial magnate, a contributor to party war-chests, a peer of the realm. The Manchester individualists, Cobden and Bright, looking upon the new order which they had helped to create, pronounced it good and declared that because any hustling individual might rise from poverty to wealth, the era of *individual* equality had arrived. Instead of studying the new groups, the new class divisions, more subtle and complex than ever before, they proclaimed the glad day of equality. While James Watt was experimenting in Glasgow with the steam engine, and thus preparing to blow up the old economic order in the realm of fact, a French philosopher, Jean Jacques Rousseau, was experimenting with ideas scarcely less dangerous to the *ancien régime* than the operations of the Scotch mechanic. Unlike his distinguished predecessor in political science, Montesquieu, Rousseau did not search assiduously among the institutions and habits of mankind to find a basis for his political philosophy.[2] Rousseau was not a man of science or a detached scholar. He was a passionate propagandist. He formulated the sentiments and views for the third estate in France then beginning to thunder against the monarchy, which was buttressed by the special privileges of the clergy and the nobility. In his *Social Contract* he set forth the moral and philosophic justification for the revolt of the third estate.

In his system of political thought, Rousseau, in effect, advanced several negative propositions. He denied that there was any inherent and essential connection between economics and politics. He repudiated the idea that the nature and amount of men's material possessions and the character of their occupations could have any substantial influence on their political sentiments and their political actions. He rejected the age-long view that the transmission, alienation, accumulation, and distribution of wealth bore a fundamental relation to the form and practices of the government. He denied the doctrine that society is a complex of more or less conscious groups and interests.

[2] Montesquieu recognized the place of economic groups in his system of political economy:

"In a popular state the inhabitants are divided into certain classes. It is in the manner of making this division that great legislators have signalized themselves; and it is on this the duration and prosperity of democracy have ever depended. Servius Tullius followed the spirit of aristocracy in the distribution of his classes. We find in Livy and in Dionysius Halicarnassus, in what manner he lodged the right of suffrage in the hands of the principal citizens. He had divided the people of Rome into a hundred and ninety-three centuries, which formed six classes; and ranking the rich, who were in smaller numbers, in the first centuries; and those in middling circumstances, who were more numerous, in the next, he flung the indigent multitude into the last; and as each century had but one vote, it was property rather than numbers that decided the elections. Solon divided the people of Athens into four classes. In this he was directed by the spirit of democracy, his intention not being to fix those who were to choose, but such as were eligible: therefore, leaving to every citizen the right of election, he made the judges eligible from each of those four classes; but the magistrates he ordered to be chosen only out of the first three, consisting of persons of easy fortunes."— Montesquieu, *The Spirit of the Laws*, Vol. I, p. 10.

For the group- or class-man he substituted the abstract, the cosmopolitan, the universal man.

In order that we may get the essence of this new political philosophy, let us make a somewhat close examination of the doctrines laid down by Rousseau. He simply cannot be ignored, for his *Social Contract* became the textbook of the French Revolution and of that world-wide equalizing movement which has in our day penetrated even the heart of China, preparing the way for the overthrow of absolutism and the triumph of the third estate. (See footnote 6.)

The origin of the state Rousseau finds not in a divine command that one should rule over others, or in the fusion of estates, but in a voluntary union of free men. Of course Rousseau knows that this was not true in point of fact, and respect for the truth compels him to admit it. But he cannot allow the matter of historicity to interfere with the foundations of his system of political ethics.

In Book I of his *Social Contract,* he says: "If, then, we remove from the social contract all that is not of its essence, it will be reduced to the following terms: Each of us gives in common his person and all his force under the supreme direction of the general will; and in return we receive each member as an indivisible part of the whole.

"Immediately, this act of association produces, instead of the individual person of each contracting party, a moral and collective body, composed of as many members as the assembly has votes, which receives from the same act its utility,—its common being, its life and its will. This public personage, thus formed by the union of all the others, formerly took the name of city, and now takes that of republic or body politic. This is called the *state* by its members when it is passive; the *sovereign* when it is active; and a *power* when comparing it to its equals. With regard to the associates, they take collectively the name *people,* and call themselves individually *citizens,* as participating in the sovereign authority, and *subjects,* as submitted to the laws of the state. But these terms are often confounded and are taken one for the other. It is enough to know how to distinguish them when they are employed with all precision."

Having found the origin of society in a general agreement of free and equal men, Rousseau naturally places sovereign power by moral right in "the people"—a collectivity of all the individual members of the state. The law of the state is therefore not the will of some class (like the landed gentry) imposed upon all the others, or a compromise rule produced by a balance of conflicting group interests, but is, according to Rousseau, an expression of "the general will." This alone is its justification.

Even if it destroys the rights and property of the individual, still he must abide by it. "In order then that the social contract may not be an idle formula, it includes tacitly this engagement, which alone can give force to the others, that whoever shall refuse to obey the general will, shall be compelled to it by the whole body. This signifies nothing if not that he will be forced to be free; for it is this condition which, giving each citizen to the country, guarantees him from all personal dependence—a condition which forms the device and working of the political machine, and alone renders legitimate civil engagements which without that would be absurd, tyrannical, and subject to great abuse."

In the formulation of this general will, all individuals share alike. Here Rousseau proclaims the doctrine of absolute political equality with a vengeance. If the state, he says, is composed of ten thousand citizens, then each member of the state has one ten-thousandth part of the sovereign authority. If the people is composed of one hundred thousand men, then the citizen's suffrage is reduced to a hundred-thousandth part, and he has obviously ten times less influence in the formation of the laws. Hence it follows, declares the philosopher, "that the larger the state becomes, the less liberty there is."

But Rousseau is face to face with the fact that unanimity among citizens is impossible and that the general will cannot be the will of the whole ten thousand or the whole hundred thousand, as the case may be, but must, perforce, be the will of a certain fraction of the citizens. He boldly meets the problem, and following the old philosophers he holds that the exercise of sovereignty is by the majority. The *general will* of which he makes so much, is in practice, the will of a majority. With fine confidence he contends that the will of the majority is right and works for the good of the state. The minority is wrong; it is nothing, because it follows from the nature of the social contract that the minority must accept the decrees of the majority. With the courage of his convictions, he says: "When, however, the opinion contrary to mine prevails, it only shows that I was mistaken, and that what I had supposed to be the general will was not general. If my individual opinion had prevailed, I should have done something other than I had intended, and then I should not have been free."

As he contemplates the consequences of this bold doctrine Rousseau shrinks a bit. There is a limit even to the self-abnegation of the reformer. In Chapter VI of the Fourth Book Rousseau safeguards the oppressed minority in certain fundamental matters by requiring an extraordinary majority of two-thirds—even three-fourths in some cases. But this is rather an afterthought, though a very serious one. It does not vitally affect his extreme doctrines of individualization. Neither did it check materially the fateful consequences of his general doctrine of universal male equality. Rousseau is aware of the dangers of mere numerical majorities, but he cannot escape altogether the results of his general leveling down. There is simply a limit to which he can allow the logic of his argument to carry him. Just as he excludes women from his "people" so he sets some metes and bounds to the doings of the mere majority.[3]

Nothing further need be said to show how revolutionary was Rousseau's doctrine for the old order, or for any order. Under it the rights and property of all groups and all classes become subject to the will of the numerical majority. Any system of government founded on a compromise, or a balance of interest, in defiance of mere numbers on the one side or the other, thus becomes not only indefensible, but immoral and undemocratic. Written to exalt the individual, it subjects him to a new tyranny—the will of a temporary majority. For his sufferings in

[3] Aulard contends that Rousseau was a *bourgeois* and in reality wished to exclude the propertyless as well as the women from his "people." Whether this is true or not, Rousseau's disciples, in the earlier stages of the Revolution, were not ready to throw away all property qualifications on the suffrage.

conscience or in property, it offers him the consoling information that his individual will, being contrary to the general will, is wrong, and, in fact, not his intention at all or in keeping with his own freedom!

Indeed, as we look at this system, it seems so unreal, so ill-adapted to the world of industry and trade, commerce and agriculture, that its implications are astounding. We can hardly imagine how it could become the philosophy of any people. An examination into the course of events, however, makes the explanation clear.

Naturally enough Rousseau's philosophy did not appeal to the French clergy and nobility, who were aware of their class interests and of their numerical inferiority. To them the social contract was poisonous and impious anarchy.

To the bourgeois, on the other hand, it presented a different aspect. They had grown powerful in numbers and wealth, and they felt keenly the oppressive privileges enjoyed by the clergy and nobility. They were determined to sweep away the discriminations against them, and to control the government in their own interests. If they did not contemplate the destruction of the clergy and the nobility as classes, they did contemplate leveling them down in their political and economic privileges. The clergy and the nobility had a monopoly of the philosophy of divine right—the moral support of their power. The bourgeois had to look elsewhere for a philosophy to justify such leveling as they contemplated. They found it in Rousseau's *Social Contract*. Searching for an ethical support for their attack upon two powerful groups, they exalted "the people" as against all special privileges. They were playing with fire and they knew it, but there seemed no other philosophy at hand to serve as a foil for their enterprise. Unwittingly they started a conflict, the consequences of which will last until the end of time.

In the shock of the French Revolution the bourgeois overthrew the nobility and the clergy. They abolished the feudal rights of the former and seized the property of the latter. In their fear of the privileged orders they established a legislature of one chamber and sought to safeguard their property by a tax-paying qualification on the right to vote; but the logic of their position was fatal. They had proclaimed the rights of man as the moral justification for the destruction of the rights of two classes, and they had at the same time coolly repudiated the rights of man by limiting the application of the doctrine to members of their own class who had certain property qualifications.

Then followed the Revolution of violence and terror in which radical leaders inflamed the disfranchised by appeals to the gospel of Rousseau and to the proclamations of the bourgeois. To save themselves the latter had to resort to that other great source of authority, the sword. This instrument was wielded by Napoleon Bonaparte, a man who understood the relation of property to political power, and who, through his constitutions based on checks and balances, gave stability to bourgeois institutions. Even Napoleon, the Bourbons, and the Orleanists, however, could not stay the onward march of Rousseau and his legions.[4]

But it may be asked, how did this leveling doctrine of universal political equality find a foothold in the United States where there were no official clergy and nobility to be overthrown by the third estate? Well, some writers have labored hard to show that it is a French creation utterly at variance with Anglo-Saxon tradition—whatever that may mean. In the interest of truth, however, it should be said that the free-and-equal doctrine is not French, but English in origin. Its beginnings among English-speaking peoples may be traced to the flood of speculation that broke loose in England during the seventeenth century when the merchants and gentry were engaged in a revolt against the crown and aristocracy—the clergy having been broken a century earlier by the bluff king, Henry VIII, who confiscated much of their property. It was from

[4] In the Declaration of the Rights of Man—August 1789—the French National Assembly proclaimed in theory the political philosophy of Rousseau: "men are born and remain equal in rights," and "law is the expression of the general will." In the National Assembly it appears that only five deputies, however, asked for universal manhood suffrage—among them Robespierre, who was destined to ride the storm of the proletarian revolution which he fain would have tempered with a pale and sickly piety. It is estimated that under the first French constitution about three-fifths of the adult males were deprived of the suffrage by the property qualifications established. Thus did the bourgeois mutilate the doctrines of Jean Jacques.

English defenders of revolution, like John Locke, rather than from French authors, that Jefferson derived the gospel of the Declaration of Independence. Moreover, the economic circumstances in the United States were on the whole favorable to the propaganda of that word. There was no established clergy here. There was no titled aristocracy. There was no such proletariat as formed the "mob" of Paris. Land was the chief form of property and its wide distribution among the whites (leaving the slaves out of account) brought about in fact a considerable economic equality to correspond to the theory of political equality.

Moreover, at the time that America was committed to the theory of political equality, the people were engaged in a revolt against the government imposed on them under the authority of Great Britain. Like the third estate in France they needed some effective and compelling justification for their extraordinary conduct. Of course the leaders of the American Revolution could have said coldly: "We are fighting for the plantation owners of the South, the merchants and landed gentry of the North, and the free farmers in both sections, in order that they may govern themselves."

Obviously, such a chilly declaration of fact would not have thrilled the masses, especially the mechanics of the towns who enjoyed no political rights under either system, the old or the new. It was necessary to have something that would ring throughout the country. Hence the grand words of the Declaration of Independence: "All men are created equal" and "governments derive their just powers from the consent of the governed." There were critics ready to point out that these high principles did not square with slavery, indentured servitude, and political disfranchisement, but they did not prevail. In the fervor of the moment, Jefferson, while bent on justifying the revolt against George III, in fact challenged the rule of property which was guaranteed by the state constitutions drafted by his fellow revolutionists in that very epoch. Even Jeffersonians, when confronted, like Rousseau's followers, with the logical consequences of their doctrine, shrank from applying it. Nevertheless the grand words stood for all time, and advocates of manhood suffrage and woman suffrage afterward appealed to them with great effect in attacking property and sex qualifications on the right to vote.

When once the free-and-equal doctrine had been let loose in the New World and the Old, it was impossible to check its course. Steadily it made headway against governments founded upon a class basis. Steadily it supplanted the old philosophy of politics which gave to property and to estates a place in the process of government. Within seventy years after the Declaration of Independence the battle for white manhood suffrage was virtually won in the United States. Some remnants of the old system of class privilege in politics remained, but they were regarded as anachronisms. Time was to dispose of them. America was committed to the great doctrine that in politics all heads are equal and all are entitled to the same share of power in the government.

In Europe also political equalitarianism has done deadly work in the old order. In England it has not been carried to the same degree as in the United States, but the Lords' Veto Act, leveling down the power of the ancient and honorable Chamber of Peers, is an echo of it, full of significance for the future.[5] In Sweden, in 1866, the four-class system was swept away in favor of a general suffrage. Austria abandoned group representation in 1907. The third French republic abolished the Chamber of Peers and substituted a Senate, now chosen by indirect election. At this moment China is in the throes of a Revolution due to the struggle between those who would establish a stable gov-

[5] The suffrage act of 1917, passed after this was written, carried England into Rousseau's camp. The revolution that followed the German defeat in 1918 swept Germany and the new continental states into the main current. Russia, however, went back to the class system while attempting to abolish the clergy, the nobility, and the bourgeois as classes. [Nearly all the democratic governments set up in Europe after the First World War were destroyed by dictators within a brief span of years. See below, pp. 92–6. The Bolshevik class system of councils representing workers, peasants, and soldiers underwent many changes before a final constitution was adopted in 1936. Under that constitution, the All-Union Congress represents population and nationalities. Theoretically there are now no classes in Russia. See below, p. 74.]

ernment on the foundations of effective economic and military interests, and those fired with a passion for "the rights of man." [6]

The logical application of Rousseau's doctrine of complete and abstract human equality is clear. It means that the number of members in any legislature shall be apportioned among geographical districts approximately according to the number of inhabitants without reference to their wealth, occupations, or interests. It means that all high public officers shall be elected by majorities or pluralities. Man is to be regarded as a "political" animal. No account is to be taken of those sentiments and views which, as Madison says, arise from the possession of different degrees and kinds of property. All heads are equal and, from the point of view of politics, alike. The statesman is a mathematician concerned with counting heads. The rule of numbers is enthroned. The homage once paid to kings is to be paid to the statistics of election returns. Surely, in all the history of thought, there is nothing more wonderful than this "logic of democracy."

While this political revolution has been going on, have the economic groups once recognized by statesmen and political philosophers disappeared? The answer is emphatic. It is to be found in the census returns, which, as certainly as the doomsday book of William the Conqueror, record the perdurance of group and class interests despite the rhetoric of political equality. It is to be found in practical politics day by day. Does anyone think that a thousand farmers or laborers, going on about their tasks, have the same influence in the formation of a protective-tariff bill as a thousand manufacturers represented by spokesmen in the lobbies and committee rooms of the Congress of the United States? Does anyone suppose that the exemption of trade unions from the provisions of the Sherman Anti-Trust Law was the result of the platonic wishes of "the people," rather than the determined and persistent activity of the American Federation of Labor?

We are therefore confronted by an inherent antagonism between our generally accepted political doctrines, and the

---

[6] COMPILER'S NOTE: Since this paragraph was written the mainland of China has become a communist state.

actual facts of political life. In the world of natural science men do not tarry long with hypotheses that will not square with observed phenomena. Shall we in the field of political science cling to a delusion that we have to deal only with an abstract man divorced from all economic interests and group sentiments?

CHAPTER VI

THE CONTRADICTION AND
THE OUTCOME [1]

THREE GENERAL CONCLUSIONS were reached in the preceding chapters. A survey of six great systems of political philosophy supports the proposition that there is a vital relation between the forms of state and the distribution of property, revolutions in the state being, usually, the results of contests over property. A study of the evolution of government in Western civilization during many centuries shows the recognition of economic classes in the creation of political organisms. Finally, modern equalitarian democracy, which reckons all heads as equal and alike, cuts sharply athwart the philosophy and practice of the past centuries.

Nevertheless, the democratic device of universal suffrage does not destroy economic classes or economic inequalities. It ignores them. Herein lies the paradox, the

[1] COMPILER'S NOTE: This chapter is primarily the 1922 revision of one of Beard's 1916 lectures, dealing among other things with Russian developments. When Beard reprinted the chapter during 1945 in the last edition of *The Economic Basis of Politics,* he added a footnote to the Russian passages of 1922, referring to a modernized, amplified, and clarified account of the Russian story appearing in the next chapter, just added. To save the reader the bother of inspecting the obsolete parts of the 1922 passage, then flipping the pages to reach the 1945 presentation, the two versions have been consolidated within the confines of the present Chapter VI. Since the integration improves the illustrations without altering the original theme or one single word of the conclusions, the compiler believes the operation to have been fully justified.

most astounding political contradiction that the world has ever witnessed. Hence the question arises: Has political democracy solved the problem of the ages, wrung the answer from the sphinx? Is it a guarantee against the storms of revolution? Does it make impossible such social conflicts as those which tore ancient societies asunder? Does it afford to mankind a mastery over its social destiny?

To ask these questions is to answer them. Nothing was more obvious in the thinking of Western civilization before the outbreak of [World War I] than dissatisfaction with political democracy. Equally obvious was the discontent with representative government based on the doctrine of abstract numbers and civic equality. Whether one went into the countryside of Oregon or strolled along Quai d'Orsay, one heard lively debates over "the failure of representative government." The initiative and referendum and recall—direct government—more head-counting on the theory of numbers and abstract equality, such was the answer of the Far West to the riddle. Europe had another answer, or rather many other answers.

Indeed, John Stuart Mill, in his work on representative government published in 1859, nearly ten years before the radical suffrage measure of 1867, sensed grave dangers ahead. He utterly rejected the theory that political democracy would inevitably avoid those acts of selfishness and arbitrary power that had characterized monarchies and oligarchies and aristocracies. "Looking at democracy in the way in which it is commonly conceived," he said, "as the rule of the numerical majority, it is surely possible that the ruling power may be under the dominion of sectional or class interests pointing to conduct different from that which would be dictated by impartial regard for the interest of all. . . . In all countries there is a majority of poor, a minority who, in contradistinction, may be called rich. Between these two classes, on many questions, there is a complete opposition of interest. We will suppose the majority sufficiently intelligent to be aware that it is not to their advantage to weaken the security of property, and that it would be weakened by any act of arbitrary spoliation. But is there not considerable danger lest they should throw upon the possessors of what is called realizable property and upon larger incomes, an unfair share, or even the whole of the burden of taxation; and having done so, add to the amount without scruple, expending the proceeds in modes supposed to conduce to the profit and advantage of the labouring class?" Mill then goes on to cite other examples of the possible abuse of political power in the interests of the economic classes.

His solution of the problem was a balance of classes and the introduction of minority or proportional representation. "If the representative system could be made ideally perfect," he said, "and if it were possible to maintain it in that state, its organization should be such that these two classes, manual labourers and their affinities on one side, employers of labour and their affinities on the other, should be, in the arrangement of the representative system, equally balanced, each influencing about an equal number of votes in Parliament." The more rational minority in each class should then hold the balance. "Assuming that the majority of each class, in any differences between them, would be mainly governed by their class interests, there would be a minority of each in whom that consideration would be subordinate to reason, justice, and the good of the whole; and this minority of either joining with the whole of the other, would turn the scale against any demands of their own majority which were not such as ought to prevail."

Whether this solution is fanciful or sound need not detain us now. The point is that this learned and sincere friend of democracy, writing at the middle of the nineteenth century, believed that the introduction of "numerical democracy" had not solved and could not resolve the most fundamental of all contradictions: namely the contests over property and the distribution of wealth that accompany the development of civilization. Indeed Mill's very solution, minority representation, in effect was designed to reintroduce, without rigid legal divisions, the scheme of class representation which had been for centuries the basis of all parliamentary systems. On the significance of this it is not necessary to comment.

Long after Mill's day a group of continental writers, Leon Duguit, Charles Benoist, and Albert Schaeffle, for example, declared the system of artificial territorial divisions and numerical majorities to be a sham and a delusion, and advocated the frank and legal recognition of commerce, industry, property, professions, and crafts in the constitution of the representative system. They held that the doctrine of abstract equality was essentially false and in plain contradiction to the facts of modern social life. They declared that it made the politician a sort of broker (hardly an honest one at that) mediating between conflicting groups and slipping into parliament by deluding electors with phrases, promises, and rhetoric. Thus, in their opinion, the state had passed from the hands of practical and informed men of affairs into the control of the "politicians" —men without any business qualifications whose stock in trade was oratory. Thus they could only see disaster ahead, unless the rhetoricians were expelled and representation restored to the basis of economic realities.

Even more savage in their criticism of numerical democracy and abstract political equality were the socialists. They also declared that the idea of political equality and economic inequality contained an inherent contradiction. They offered, however, a drastic solution—the ownership of all productive property by society and the consequent destruction of both the capitalist class and the working class. The guild socialists, as another school was called, proposed to substitute for the system of numerical and territorial representation a congress composed of delegates from the various craft or trade unions. Still other socialists, fearing the disruptive effects of craft jealousies, insisted that at least one branch of the parliament should represent the people considered as a national unity as distinguished from the people divided into crafts and unions. These last reformers argued that man was a civic and patriotic animal and that his whole nature was not expressed or exhausted in his capacity as an engineer, machinist, or farmer.

All these schemes, however, remained devices on paper until the communist upheaval in Russia in November, 1917. Then . . . the idea of political democracy was denounced and cast aside as a mere "bourgeois" device calculated to delude the working class. In the place of a congress of representatives chosen by equal suffrage from territorial districts having substantially the same number of inhabitants, there was established a soviet or council representing economic groups as such . . . a simple and drastic attempt to dispose of the contradiction between political theory and economic facts. . . .

[The early councils representing workers, peasants, and soldiers were transitional in nature. Under communist theory all classes, including the proletariat, were to disappear. When the new Russian constitution was drawn up in 1936 representation in the All-Union Congress was based on two principles. For one chamber delegates are apportioned according to population—one delegate per 300,000 inhabitants. In the second chamber, called the Council of Nationalities, the republics constituting the Union are represented. Thus the Russian constitution of 1936 bears no traces of the class-system such as appeared in the early councils representing workers, peasants, and soldiers. . . .][2]

[Meanwhile, the capitalist class has been eliminated through the seizure of commerce and industry by the state.][3] What had appeared in 1919 to be an insuperable obstacle to a complete nationalization of agriculture . . . —the tenacity with which the small peasants clung to their lands—was finally overcome, subject to minor concessions. Lenin had opposed the use of violence against the peasant. After he died, however, the Soviet government adopted a policy of extreme land nationalization and carried it out by forcible methods—including the "liquidation" and deportation of recalcitrant peasants by the millions. Thus a propertied class numerically large was exterminated, and communism, or collectivization, was established even in agriculture.[4] By 1939 the small landowners of the old régime

[2] COMPILER'S NOTE: This bracketed paragraph, originally inserted by Beard in 1945 as a footnote, has been elevated to the body of the text to clarify the theme.

[3] COMPILER'S NOTE: Immediately after this bracketed sentence of mine, there begins the new material on the Russian situation prepared by Beard in 1945, shifted ahead here from its former place on pp. 77–87 of Chapter V of the 1945 edition of *The Economic Basis of Politics.*

[4] "In 1940 almost all the agricultural production in the [Soviet] Union came from the 240,000 consolidated collective farms that had taken the place of the 25,000,000 separate peasant holdings that had existed in 1928." B. H. Sumner, *A Short History of Russia* (1943), p. 115. Only a certain number

had gone the way of the great landlords, bureaucrats, and middle classes of the Tsarist days. Former class barriers had been leveled.

According to communist theory Russia was now supposed to be "classless," for the distinctions founded on landed and other forms of material property had been extinguished, at least as far as direct ownership was concerned. But other important kinds of social distinction rapidly developed. The introduction of technology into socialized agriculture was attended by gradations of technical competence among the millions nominally called "workers on the land." In connection with this transformation appeared large numbers of agronomists, engineers, skilled farm mechanics, managers, bookkeepers, specialists in plant and animal husbandry, and other sorts of experts. Moreover, in the train of the vast industrialization came a differentiation of urban occupations and callings almost as complicated and hierarchical as those to be found in the capitalistic societies of the West: engineers and managers of all kinds, plant foremen, and a classified personnel ranging from skilled machine operatives at the apex to untrained casual laborers at the bottom.

To plan, co-ordinate, direct, and govern the huge economic and political aggregations of the Russian Union, an immense bureaucracy was evolved. It was graded from the over-all executives at the top down through various territorial and specialized officials to the petty functionaries at the lowest rung of the ladder. Amid the exigencies of military preparations and war, an armed force of gigantic proportions was created and it also had its graded personnel ranging from the chief of staff down to non-commissioned officers and regimented men.

In the civil and foreign wars which immediately followed the Bolshevik Revolution of 1917, Soviet authorities had been compelled to rely upon improvisation—mainly upon the selection of military leaders from among the rank and file of soldiers and, indeed, from among civilians. The spectacular military performances of Trotsky as an amateur, in the period of the civil warfare, illustrates this point.

---

of animals, small implements, and gardens are now individually owned, but this branch of private enterprise is highly productive.

But, as time passed, more and more reliance was placed on men professionally trained for war, and provisions were made for their training. Thus a large body of professional military officers came into being, with a corresponding system of military education, selection, promotion, distinctions in rank, and *esprit de corps*. Unlike the officer class of Prussian Junkers, whose landed property gave them a certain degree of economic independence as against the state, the new Russian officer class was wholly dependent upon the state for its emoluments, prestige, and distinctions.

If, after years of such developments, the post-revolutionary Russian society was still nominally classless, in the sense that there were no longer classes based on the ownership of land and other productive property, it was in fact a highly differentiated society, with great divergencies in power, security, and income. If there were no propertied classes, there were income-classes, and classes with favored positions in respect of advancement and economic advantages. As the differentiation proceeded, a tendency to stratification appeared, first in fact and then more slowly in law. This process was quickened by an early abandonment of the communist formula: "from each according to his ability and to each according to his needs," and the substitution of "incentive pay" for industrial workers and graded salaries for members of the civil and military bureaucracy.

As a consequence of the larger incomes for members of the upper grades of workers in industries and for members of the higher civil and military bureaucracy, millions of Russians were able to accumulate money for personal expenditures or for deposit in savings banks or investment in government bonds. If nominally on the same footing as other Russian citizens, these recipients of higher incomes formed a substantial portion of the population differentiated from their less fortunate neighbors in the matter of claims to personal property and goods. The children of these people possessed privileges denied to the offspring of less favored families: privileges of leisure, comfort, convenience, and education, helpful in the gratification of tastes and ambitions. Such children could be better prepared for passing entrance examinations to the institutions of higher learning that trained youth for the civil and military professions and for occupations in the upper ranges of industry and the bureaucracy. After graduation they could call on powerful friends for help in securing lucrative positions in [the] economic hierarchy.

In this course of affairs, the family, treated by many of the early Bolsheviks as a moribund bourgeois institution, was gradually brought back into the history from which they had sought to expel it. Russian laws accelerated the restoration: for example, legislation relative to inheritance, marriage, maternal subsidies, divorce, and abortion. It is true that Russia was not reviving landed, industrial, and financial families of the old style. But Russia was reconstituting the family as an economic, cultural, and social institution, with all that this implied in terms of marked differentiations in society. By intermarriage among members of the upper-income families, family ties and family influences in economy, education, and the struggle for position were reinforced.[5]

These tendencies in Russian society did not signify, as some American innocents abroad liked to imagine, a return to historic capitalism or "free enterprise." They did indicate, however, that the communist ideal of free and equal individuals, having identical economic opportunities, having no special privileges of income and position, was not being realized. It also meant that, however "classless" Russian society might now be in theory, it had in truth highly differentiated and graded economic interests which

[5] From the standpoint of those old Bolsheviks who regarded the family as a form of bourgeois servitude to be abolished in favor of sex liberty, the most revolutionary piece of Soviet legislation in respect of the family is the Act of July 8, 1944, providing subsidies and special monthly pensions for mothers, graded in amount according to the number of their children. The Act also grants other special privileges to mothers, accords special protection to them and their children, creates medals and orders of maternity, imposes special taxes on childless and small families, and makes modifications in the former laws relative to matrimony, the family, and guardianship. A Spanish translation of this Act appears in *Boletín de Información* (Legation of the Soviet Union at Havana) for February 5, 1945. This number also contains valuable articles on the Russian family. One of the most interesting of these articles is entitled *La Familia Sovietica, Escuela de Patriotismo*, pp. 8–9. For criticism of the libertarian theories in respect of marriage during the early years of the Revolution, see pp. 10–11.

were recognized by government and law. Moreover, it meant that as such interests grew in vigor, they were bound to find expression in the thinking, the ideology, and, more or less, in the politics of the country.

Ten years after the Revolution of 1917 a stratification of the Russian communist society had already become marked. In 1927, when the Communist party claimed approximately 1,200,000 members, about 600,000 were officials and bureaucratic employees of the government, as against 150,000 workers on the land and 450,000 workers in factories. These officials and bureaucratic employees had accumulated considerable personal property. According to the figures for 1930, individual deposits in savings banks amounted to 476,000,000 rubles (apart from the deposits of co-operatives and collectives); and of this total, officials and bureaucratic employees held 205,000,000 rubles, while laborers held 90,000,000 rubles, and peasants held the balance.[6] In three years, between 1925 and 1928, the number of holders of internal-loan bonds in Soviet Russia increased from 100,000 to 10,000,000.[7] Exact figures for later dates are not available but it is estimated that in 1939 more than 50,000,000 people were holders of state bonds, and that at the end of 1944 internal bonds to the amount of 117,200,000,000 rubles were outstanding.[8] At the beginning of 1940 at least 37,000 savings banks were in operation and had on deposit a little more than 7,000,-000,000 rubles. The total number of depositors was then placed at 16,802,000 as compared with 15,547,000 in 1939.[9]

[6] A. Rosenberg, *Geschichte des Bolschewismus,* pp. 193, 229.

[7] A. Willehn (Alfred H. Vagts), *"Internationale Finanz und Internationale Politik,"* Europaische Gespräche, October, 1928, p. 514, note.

[8] From the total outstanding debt should be deducted gifts of bonds to the state by private citizens. These gifts have been large. In 1944 it was announced that gifts of state bonds to the amount of 4 billion rubles had been made to the Red Army Fund. But figures for the total amount of gifts do not seem to be available in the United States at the beginning of the year 1945.

[9] Among the sources for more recent figures on the Russian debt and savings bank deposits are: U. S. Department of Commerce, "Internal Debt Compiled from Announcements of

The statistical publications of Soviet Russia, at least those now available in the United States, provide little or no information about gradations in income-groups. They certainly do not permit the presentation of an exact picture showing: (1) all the various occupational groups and the exact number of persons in each group; (2) a classification of the Russian population according to incomes and the number of persons in each income-bracket (such as may be found in the official statistics of the United States); and (3) a classification of population according to holdings of property, such as household goods, government bonds, savings deposits, land and livestock allotments, authors' royalty rights, and so forth.

But Russian official documents do indicate that Russian society is divided into a number of classes, each consisting of individuals receiving incomes within a certain range, and all graded from low levels of income upward to annual salaries of 24,000 rubles and more per year. Though the Soviet government apparently does not make available the exact number of persons in each income category, the fact of the income categories is recognized and used in the tax legislation (Old Income Tax, 1940 rates; Housing and Cultural Tax, 1940 rates; and War Income Tax of December 29, 1941).

Special evidence bearing on the stratification of Russian society comes from reports on the tax and revenue system of the Soviet government. That system reflects and in some respects accentuates the gradations in Russian economy. It is not wholly grounded on the simple equalitarian principle that the tax laid on each person should be exactly adjusted to his income or ability to pay. In other words, the nature and rates of taxation in Soviet Russia are not such as to make the members of the various income groups carry tax burdens apportioned strictly and progressively according to their respective abilities in terms of wealth.

On this point we have recent information from Dr. Jerome Davis, a sympathetic and observant student of

Loans in Russian Newspapers" by E. C. Ropes; U. S. Department of Commerce, "Russian Economic Notes, March 15, 1940"; the *American Review of the Soviet Union*, June, 1941; *Soviet Information Bulletin*, September 29, 1944.

Russian institutions.[1] The largest single source of revenue for the Soviet state, he says, is "the turnover tax." Far less important as a revenue producer is the war income tax. Dr. Davis says that annual income up to 1,800 rubles is taxable to the amount of 120 rubles. The tax rate rises but apparently levels off at incomes of 24,000 rubles; it is 1,020 rubles on incomes between 9,600 and 10,800 rubles; and it is 2,700 rubles on incomes above 24,000 rubles. On farmers, it ranges from 150 to 500 rubles a year. There are, of course, various exemptions. Voluntary donations and lotteries afford substantial revenues. Another source is state loans. At the outset of the war in 1941 the state debt was about 50,000,000,000 rubles; three war loans of 1942, 1943, and 1944 brought in around 61,000,000,000 rubles.

Official reports and other publications issued under the auspices of the Soviet government or with its authorization permit, therefore, a classification of the Russian people on the basis of power, culture, and/or income, which often corresponds more or less closely to positions in the hierarchy. Exact figures are lacking, but the following general picture as of 1944 is based on a substantial documentation:

1. High officials in the Communist party. The party membership is about 5,000,000. High officials in the party are often high officials in the Soviet government on its political side and on its economic side.

2. High officials and intellectuals in Russian society, inside and outside the Communist party, often with relatively high incomes, especially those in posts of industrial management and those engaged in writing, editing, and propaganda.

3. Minor officials of the white-collar class, numbering millions: engineers, technicians, statisticians, economists, bookkeepers, chauffeurs, mechanics, teachers, police, and so forth.

4. Industrial workers of many types, crafts, and skills. Their number is variously estimated at from one-fifth of the population upward.

5. Workers on the land (peasants) comprising about

[1] *The New Republic,* January 1, 1945 (cabled from Moscow).

one-half of the population. The amount of time given by
the land worker to labor on state farms and the amount
given to the cultivation of his own allotment varies from
place to place and time to time.

6. Forced labor. Composed of prisoners of one kind
or another scattered about the country in labor camps.
Exact number unknown. Sometimes estimated in the
millions.

If long experiences in other ages and places are any
guide in making forecasts, certain things are likely to
happen in Russia during the coming years. As James Madison might put the case, these strong and often conflicting
interests will perdure and provide substance and force in
Russian politics in the future. Should Russia enter into a
long era of peace, the more powerful among these interests
could scarcely fail to seek representation and force in government, if not control over the state. Should the military
interest become supreme in the decades ahead, it would
subdue civilian interests to its will, perhaps for a long
period of time. For, as Daniel Webster's axiom runs, it is
only in the absence of the sword that economic interests
may rule (above, p. 38).

With military interests, foreign as well as domestic politics comes into consideration. No military body whose
directors are recruited largely from an officer, or military,
class can easily maintain itself in power, if at all, without
wars and rumors of war. Historically, Russia had been one
of the great warlike nations of Europe during more than a
century prior to the Bolshevik Revolution of 1917. For a
time, and partly owing to its internal weakness at first, Bolshevik Russia renounced imperialism and under compulsion
surrendered large areas of the country to her neighbors. To
some extent this repudiation of imperialism was due to the
hope of idealists that workers' revolutions would occur all
over Europe and lead to a federation of communist republics. But after 1939, and particularly after the sensational
victories over the Germans in the Second World War,
Russian leadership seemed to renew the territorial and
power ambitions of Tsarist Russia.

As everyone knows who has even an elementary acquaintance with Russian history since the age of Peter the

Great, Russian territorial and power ambitions have contemplated a wide sweep in Europe and Asia and have been accompanied by the rise and growth of Pan-Slavism. That Russian military planning and education will take these traditions into account, for strategic studies, preparations, and calculations of actions, is practically certain. Nor will the upper levels of the civilian bureaucracy be indifferent to the advantages that may be derived from economic and other forms of penetration into regions around the borders of the great Soviet Union. And here a peculiar factor may come into service. Unlike the interests behind the imperialist expansion of Western countries, Russian interests are vitalized by ideological ties with revolutionary parties in other areas, near and distant; they may profit by, if they do not foment, disturbances that will lead to intervention in a manner that resembles imperialistic action but may be defended on "moral" grounds.[2]

The upshot of all this seems to be that in a modern industrial society, the problem of property, so vital in politics, is not as simple as it was in old agricultural societies. It was one thing for peasants to destroy their landlords and go on tilling the soil as they had long been wont to do. It is another thing for workingmen to destroy capitalists as a class and assume all the complex and staggering burdens of management and exchange. It is also clear that, as efficient production depends to a great extent upon skill, skill itself is a form of property even if property in capital is abolished.

In short a great society, whether capitalist or communist, must possess different kinds and grades of skill and talent and carry on widely diversified industries. There must be miners, machinists, electricians, engineers, accountants, transport workers, draftsmen, managers, and a hundred other kinds of specialists. They may be temporarily welded together in a conflict with their capitalist employers, but they will be divided over the distribution of wealth among themselves after the capitalists have been disposed of. Conceivably a highly militarist government might destroy

[2] COMPILER'S NOTE: Here ends the passage on Russia shifted ahead from its original position in the 1945 edition of *The Economic Basis of Politics*.

their organizations and level them down, but the result would be the ruin of production and of the state itself. Even a communist could hardly defend his system on the theory that all must choose between military despotism and utter ruin.

The grand conclusion, therefore, seems to be exactly that advanced by our own James Madison in the tenth number of *The Federalist*. To express his thought in modern terms: a landed interest, a transport interest, a railway interest, a shipping interest, an engineering interest, a manufacturing interest, a public-official interest, with many lesser interests, grow up of necessity in all great societies and divide them into different classes actuated by different sentiments and views. The regulation of these various and interfering interests, whatever may be the formula for the ownership of property, constitutes the principal task of modern statesmen and involves the spirit of party in the necessary and ordinary operations of government. In other words, there is no rest for mankind, no final solution of eternal contradictions. Such is the design of the universe. The recognition of this fact is the beginning of wisdom—and of statesmanship.

C H A P T E R   V I I

POLITICAL AND MILITARY DOMINATION OVER "THE ECONOMIC MAN" IN OUR OWN AGE[1]

DURING the past quarter of a century radical changes have occurred in . . . the functions of government, particularly in those which call for wholesale intervention in economic operations. No doubt the nature and course of economy had been more or less shaped and directed by the state from early times. This was especially true under the mercantilist régimes of the seventeenth and eighteenth centuries. But in many Western countries during the nineteenth century economic interests enjoyed a high degree of freedom and independence as against the state. In these countries and amid such circumstances it was relatively easy for persons who held property to wield political power. In recent years, however, state intervention in economy has assumed systematic form almost everywhere and the number of persons employed by the state in giving effect to this intervention has greatly multiplied. As a result "the political man" has been gaining in independence from, and in

[1] COMPILER'S NOTE: This chapter is drawn from one in Beard's *The Economic Basis of Politics* labeled "Economics and Politics in Our Revolutionary Age." After the elimination of a few pages from the original version, to avoid duplication with material inserted in the present volume from other sources, some corresponding diminution in the scope of Beard's original title seemed advisable. The designation appearing here is the result.

power over, "the economic man" and is now often in a position to order him about rather than to take dictation from him. . . .

[For example, in the United States, by] [2] general agreement it had been early recognized that the great manufacturing and financial interests in the country were, in the main, on the Republican side of the political alignment. There were exceptions, of course, especially among manufacturers and financiers whose fortunes depended largely on export and import business and in the South where political attachments were nominally Democratic for special reasons. But on the whole the major manufacturing and financial interests were Republican, with all that signified in terms of protective tariffs, taxation, banking, government promotion of private enterprise, non-intervention in "the natural distribution of wealth," and *laissez faire* in many forms. And despite concessions to progressive and radical factions, the Republicans hewed rather close to the party line from 1921 to 1929, the period of so-called Republican prosperity.

At all events during that period (1921–1929), manufacturing and financial interests enjoyed a high degree of prosperity. There was some unemployment among industrial workers but the amount was not large enough to produce wholesale disaffection in their ranks. Only among farmers was there widespread economic distress. Although that distress made itself felt in politics, it was not strong enough to bring about a political overturn. Thus, Republican politics had a fairly secure economic basis during those years, while Democrats wandered in the political desert. Had their economic basis continued to be firm, Republicans might well have enjoyed an indefinite tenure of power. The election returns for 1928 certainly pointed in that direction.

In 1929, however, "prosperity" went to pieces. How far that crash was due to Republican policies, whether it could have been avoided by Democratic politicians had they been in power, and similar questions of "causation" are issues which simply cannot be resolved by any kind of analysis, economic, political, or historical. But according to the

[2] COMPILER'S NOTE: The bracketed start is mine.

scapegoat axiom of politics, the Republicans, who had claimed credit for the prosperity, were discredited by the depression, poverty, and unemployment which followed the crack of 1929, and in the election of 1932 they were swept out of office in an avalanche of votes.

This is not to argue that the voters in 1932 were convinced that the Democrats could or would restore "prosperity," or provide a degree of economic well-being sufficient to allay the political unrest which sprang from the depression. Nor is there warrant for claiming that in the campaign of 1932 the Democrats presented a clear outline of just what they intended to do in the way of "restoring," "recovering," or "creating" prosperity. In fact, apart from introducing various measures of regulation and social security long overdue, the Democrats, under President Franklin D. Roosevelt's leadership, failed to overcome the depression by the policies they put into effect in his first administration. In 1938 the number of unemployed workers was at least three times the number recorded during the peak months of "prosperity" under President Calvin Coolidge. It was not until the boom created by preparations for war and the still greater boom created by the war itself that Democratic politics achieved a temporary "prosperity" almost nation-wide in its range.

In the meantime, while the Democrats at the national capital were wrestling with the dislocations in economy and trying to get it into a higher speed of production, politics was gaining in power over economics. In part this gain represented a continuation of old tendencies, but in a larger part it was marked by so much novelty that it could be characterized, with some justification, as revolutionary in upshot if not in purpose. In any case, drastic shifts were effected in the methods of politics and in the economic basis of politics. Of these shifts only a few can be listed here, as illustrative.

At the head of the list belong the adoption and execution of the policy of *large-scale taxing, borrowing, and spending for many purposes under government, or political, auspices.*

Among the purposes were: to stimulate and promote private enterprise in industry and agriculture; to increase the amount of employment; to provide economic security for millions of dependent persons; to make preparations for war; and to wage war, after 1941.

It is true that for some of these operations there were precedents. When the panic broke in 1929 President Herbert Hoover urged the expansion of federal spending for public works and called upon the states to follow the federal example; and in other ways federal money and credit were used during the Hoover administration in aid of private enterprise and home loan institutions. But the degree of federal taxing, borrowing, and spending after 1933 reached such a height as to constitute an economic overturn, far-reaching in its consequences.

By numerous and complicated measures, sometimes connected with the policy of taxing and spending and sometimes standing alone, *manufacturing, commercial, financial, and agricultural interests, once treated as primarily private and as forming the chief economic basis of politics, were made dependent upon politics to an extent which in this respect signalized a breach with the past.*

To describe the new network of relationships would require a monumental treatise. Whole segments of industry, business, and agriculture now rely heavily upon government spending, for civilian and war purposes, as a main source of the popular buying power that keeps economy in motion and prosperity. Having lost their gold coins and bullion to the federal government and having filled their vaults with federal bonds and other paper, bankers have become in a large measure mere agents of the government in Washington. No longer do these powerful interests stand, so to speak, "outside the government" and in a position to control or dictate to it; all of them are closely linked in their fortunes to the fortunes of politics.

This must not be taken to imply, of course, that the powerful industrial and financial interests of the United States have been expropriated according to the formula of Marxian, as distinguished from American, communists or that they have become the mere servants of "political men." Far from it. The saying current in 1933 that the New Deal had saved frightened capitalists from a destructive revolution expressed a conviction then and still held by many Democrats high in the councils of the party. Furthermore, since 1933 numerous friends and patrons of the New Deal have complained that great capitalists have been all along entrenched in the strategic centers of the Roosevelt administrations. The controversy in 1945 over the selection of certain assistants as aides to the Secretary of State, Edward Stettinius, himself a former associate of the powerful Morgan interests, turned in part on this very point. So did the dispute about the ousting of Jesse Jones from the direction of federal lending agencies and the appointment of Henry Wallace as Secretary of Commerce.

With regard to the alleged power of big capitalists in the Roosevelt administrations two other facts have pertinence. The long list of capitalist contributors to the Republican campaign funds for the elections of 1936, 1940, and 1944 indicates that the amount of power exercised by capitalists in the federal government was not sufficient to meet their own conceptions of their interests in innumerable cases. Still more significant in this relation is the fact that capitalism, free enterprise, and "trust-busting" somewhat in the economic style of William Jennings Bryan in 1896 were supported by the very left wing of the New Dealers headed by Henry Wallace, endorsed by leaders in the Political Action Committee of the Congress of Industrial Organizations, and approved, temporarily at least, by American communists of the Stalin school. The expropriation of capitalists in favor of "political men" formed no part of the New Deal program as of 1945. Nevertheless in that year industrial and financial interests did not have any such independent power in politics as they had exercised in 1928 or 1916 or 1900.

During the evolution of the New Deal, another large interest, formerly regarded as essentially private, has assumed a semi-political and semi-official character. *Fourteen or fifteen million industrial and white-collar workers organized in trades and general unions have acquired a special position in law and have thus attached their fortunes to the fortunes of politics.* To consolidate and fortify this attachment one of the national federations of labor—the Congress of Industrial Organizations—established the Committee for Political Action in 1944 and, with no little reason, claimed to have assured the re-election of President Roosevelt in that year.

Nominally as yet, organized labor possesses a high degree of independence. But some of its privileges have been won by political instead of economic action; and it has entrusted the supervision of important elections and decisions in union affairs to federal agencies, thus regularly invoking the intervention and protection of the government directly in behalf of its interests. To this extent it has become entangled in the vicissitudes of politics and the state. Although organized labor had participated in campaigns and elections in limited ways for more than half a century, the degree and nature of its participation in 1944 indicated that it had reached a new stage in its relations to government and politics, and had made a deeper plunge into the opposition of interests that provides dynamics for politics, especially where freedom of opinion and elections is practiced.[3]

To carry out New Deal policies in general and particular, *an enormous body of public officials and employees, federal and state, has been added to the older and relatively small bureaucracy*. In other words, while the number of private citizens and concerns enjoying direct benefits from government expenditures increased, the apparatus of government, central and local, reached proportions never before attained in the United States. Now the political party in power has a huge army of officeholders dependent upon it for jobs, emoluments, promotion, and prestige, and hence by interest inclined to keep it indefinitely in all places of political authority.

Late in 1944 the United States Bureau of the Census reported that the federal government had 3,335,000 civil employees, and that state and local governments had 3,168,000, making a total of 6,503,000 public functionaries. Estimating the number of inhabitants at 138,100,875, the census bureau reckoned the number of place-holders at nearly one in twenty of the population. Since each place-holder usually has one or more family relatives, frequently dependents, it becomes evident that this class, whose for-

---

[3] COMPILER'S NOTE: The merger of the American Federation of Labor and the Congress of Industrial Organizations into one giant union, during 1956, would seem to clear the way for more powerful participation by organized labor, as an economic group, in American politics.

tunes are directly attached to those of government, is in a
position to wield immense power in politics and society. It
is true that in 1944 about two million of the civil employees
were in government places connected with the war and
that in time many of them may or will be returned to
private life. But even so, the number of place-holders will
remain large enough to exercise a decisive influence in
close elections under the rule of political equality—"one
person, one vote." Hence it must be recorded that a new
kind of class has appeared in America: a large and permanent bureaucracy composed of political men and women
whose economic support is derived mainly if not wholly
from politics.

Under the policies of taxing, spending, regulating, and
promoting, politicians have put a special sort of floor under
their operating machine. Millions of farmers, industrialists,
industrial workers, and government employees are made
directly dependent upon government actions, that is, politics, for part or all of their profits, wages, or other income.
Millions of aged and dependent persons are henceforward
to obtain all or a substantial portion of their economic
support from government, central or local or both in co-
operation. Until the war-boom demand for labor exceeded
the supply, millions of unemployed persons turned to the
federal government in search of employment or relief; but
the boom is admittedly temporary. An end to such prosperity is inevitable.

The political party phase of the economic shifts is patent.
In former times party organizations had been maintained
principally by contributions from private economic interests desirous of government favors. With funds derived
from such sources, party managers carried on campaigns
and employed many devices in influencing voters. But under the new régime Democratic politicians, while continuing old ways of collecting party funds, merely have to
remind a multitude of voters that they depend directly and
immediately upon politics for innumerable tangible benefits
received. Indeed it is likely that few of these voters need
to be reminded of anything so daily obvious to them. Once
Republican politicians had overtly called the attention of
manufacturers to the benefits derived from Republican
tariff policies; but the number of voters immediately rep-

resented by such interests was relatively small. Now the number of voters receiving economic returns from politics mounts upwards into the tens of millions. . . .

While "the political man" has been gaining in authority over "the economic man," American foreign policies and wars since 1898 have rendered necessary the enlargement of military interests in economy and politics. The significance of this development must be appreciated in any effort to understand the tendencies of our times; for it leads to the expectation that *"the military man" and "military force" will play an increasing role in the public affairs of the United States* as well as in the affairs of other countries.

This outcome of recent war experiences was not wholly unforeseen. For many years advocates of internationalism have insisted that "nationalism" and "isolationism," as well as "imperialism," require a huge military and naval establishment—"militarism," in short; and that only by a system of collective security on a world scale can this menace to civilian life and civilian government, including the burdensome cost, be avoided.

Arguments of this kind were prominent in the debate over the League of Nations at the close of the First World War and provisions were made in the Versailles Treaty for a reduction of armaments. Although the United States took part in the general conference on that subject, no agreement on reductions could be reached by the great Powers. Again, before and after the United States became involved in the Second World War, similar arguments respecting the dangers of militarism were advanced in favor of American participation in the war and in a permanent union of nations to prevent militarism.

However, early in 1945, after victory over Germany and Japan seemed assured and American membership in an organization of nations for collective security appeared almost certain, a demand arose in the United States for an extensive program of armaments, including universal military service, to be put into effect after the war as a permanent national system. In his message to Congress on January 6, 1945, President Roosevelt declared himself in favor of making universal training a regular feature of American military policy after peace was restored. It is true that he insisted on the creation of an international organization for collective security, but he evidently did not deem the achievement of that design a sufficient guarantee for the protection of the United States against foreign dangers.

If the new policy is adopted,[4] then the United States will have a gigantic military and naval establishment, modeled more or less on similar institutions long maintained by the great Powers of the world. That will be followed by an immense growth in the number of persons, especially officers, devoted entirely to the occupations of the armed services. This is not to contend that military men are more warlike than civilians; often they are in fact less warlike. But military men have, necessarily, a set of values which differ in many respects from civilian values; and the military interests, enlarged by universal conscription, will constitute a powerful influence in American affairs, with all that may involve amid the domestic and foreign contingencies of coming ages. . . .

[Moreover, outside the United States,][5] there has been a large-scale revival of belief in, quest for, and exercise of unlimited power in government as an end in itself or as a means to class, national, and imperialistic ends. Power has, of course, always been a characteristic of the state; but in the nineteenth century, with the growth of the middle class and the rise of democracy, it looked for a time as if autocratic authority was everywhere to be controlled by constitutional restraints in the interest of popular welfare and liberty of expression, person, and property. In nations which had made the most effective advances toward constitutional government, such as Great Britain and the United States, it was widely assumed that arbitrary power had been definitely subdued to "the will of the people." Although in other countries at the opening of the twentieth century, for example, Tsarist Russia, Imperial Japan, and Imperial Germany, popular supremacy had not been attained, even there movements in the direction of constitutional government were under way.

[4] COMPILER'S NOTE: Since this passage was written, the United States has placed the draft of men for the armed forces on a long-time basis.

[5] COMPILER'S NOTE: The bracketed words are mine.

When the absolutist order in Russia broke down during the First World War of our century, efforts were made to erect a constitutional system of government; but they failed, and power was seized by a communist faction under the leadership of a few determined men, notably V. I. Lenin and Leon Trotsky. To this type of power-action a new name was applied—Bolshevism. In sum and substance the philosophy of Bolshevism asserted the right of a small and resolute group to take power "in the name of the proletariat," to set up its own state, and to reduce the rest of the people to obedience.

For this arbitrary seizure and exercise of power the philosophers of Bolshevism, Lenin for instance, had at their command and proclaimed a moral or ideal justification. The dictatorship in the name of the proletariat was to be regarded as temporary, as the forerunner of equality and liberty to come after the state had "withered away." In the ideal order of the future the proletariat as well as every other class was to disappear and "the administration of things" by and for the good of the people was to supplant "the government of men."

In other parts of Europe, after the close of the First World War, the drive for democracy and constitutional government seemed to gain momentum for a period. Constitutions popular in form and containing bills of rights were adopted in Germany, Austria, Yugoslavia, and other European countries, and the suffrage was widened in Japan. But within a few years a reaction occurred, first in Italy. In several countries, governments established by the seizure of power and exercising unlimited power superseded governments checked by popular will and civil liberties.

To this new form of arbitrary power the name of Fascism was generally applied, even to the German type—Nazism. The Fascist state, notwithstanding variations, was the creation of a militant leader and his followers whose authority was sustained by terror and arms, even when some political stratagem was used. By philosphy and action, Fascism repudiated the ideal aims asserted by Bolshevism and likewise the institutions of democracy, constitutionalism, and civil liberty. It exalted and sought to fix permanently the right of a self-chosen élite to rule the rest of the people by the sword and the police. This fact was not and could not be disguised by any of the so-called "corporative constitutions" which Fascism proposed or produced in Italy or Spain.

Although Bolshevism and Fascism differed as to the proclaimed objectives, they agreed in their repudiation of constitutional government as understood in the West. Exponents of both ideologies treated democracy, elections, freedom of the press, and parliamentary politics as a kind of smoke-screen—"a mask for capitalism," to quote Benito Mussolini—devised by the bourgeoisie to conceal its "class dictatorship." In neither system of theory and practice was there any place for government by political majorities victorious at regular elections or for independent courts to uphold civil liberties against attacks by government officials. In short, both unqualifiedly rejected the democratic doctrine of political equality (above, Chapter V). While the Russian communists adopted in 1936 a constitution including a paper program of civil liberties, they were careful to keep sovereign power in the hands of the few—within the communist leadership and the party organization as directed by the supreme leader.

In ways utterly immeasurable and indescribable, two world wars have also altered the social, intellectual, and moral setting in which the theory of the economic basis of politics was discussed prior to 1914. From Aristotle's time down through the centuries the theory had been limited by the condition that economic forces operate freely only in the absence of military force (above, pp. 29, 31, 38 ff., 44, 64); but during the long period between the close of the Napoleonic wars in 1815 and the opening of the First World War in 1914, the conditional clause, which severely limited the theory, had been regarded as largely academic, particularly in the United States. Now a single generation has experienced the shattering impacts of military force around the globe on a scale beyond all precedents. Not an aspect of life—economic, political, intellectual or emotional—has escaped its actions and devastations. During the momentous years since 1914 "the military man" has again entered into full competition with "the economic man" and "the political man" for power over the state and its fortunes. . . .

Notwithstanding variations in the types of Fascism, particularly in "racist" theories and practices, the political and economic formulas and actions of Fascism were substantially identical wherever it appeared. The leader, supported by armed bands, was the head of the state—indeed the state itself; and the institutions associated with constitutional government and civil liberty were suppressed. All property was not taken over by the Fascist state, as it had been in Russia. Nor were the upper, middle, and farming classes liquidated. But the uses of property and the enjoyment of fruits and profits from property were so restricted as to destroy innumerable rights of persons in property as historically understood and defined.

It is true that the Weimar constitution designed for a republic in Germany after the First World War was not formally and entirely discarded by the Nazis. Yet for all practical purposes it was abolished. In Italy some efforts were made to give a voice in government to corporations, that is, to grant representation to specific organized classes —managerial, industrial, and commercial, for example— but these classes were denied all power of free choice in the selection of their agents. It was alleged in Italy that the goal of Fascism was the creation of "the corporative state," reproducing in a modern form something like the class hierarchy of estates in the middle ages. No such end was actually achieved, however. State power under Fascism in Italy as well as elsewhere remained absolutely independent of the people considered as political or economic individuals or as members of private associations. Economic interests of all kinds were in theory, and to a large extent in practice, subdued to the will of the state—namely, to the dictator, checked if at all only by the advice of his party council. Protests were smothered by the police.

Many attempts have been made to explain the rise and growth of the Fascist state in terms almost purely economic, as if the Fascist dictator and his colleagues were the mere automata of interests called "capitalistic." It has been claimed that Fascism was the logical and inevitable answer of sheer capitalist power to the menace of sheer communist power. Another explanation is to the effect that Fascism was simply the product of the unemployment, poverty, and social unrest which came in the wake of the

First World War—economic distresses with which democratic and parliamentary governments could not cope. A communist formula of explanation declares that Fascism is the last stage of exploitive capitalism and is to be succeeded by the final revolutionary triumph of the industrial proletariat under the banner of communism.

In the name of free enterprise or *laissez-faire* capitalism another economic explanation of Fascism has been offered; for instance, in F. A. Hayek's *The Road to Serfdom*. According to this thesis "the rise of Fascism and Nazism was not a reaction against the socialist trends of the preceding period but a necessary outcome of these tendencies." In other words, Fascism, in its German and Italian expression and in incipient expressions elsewhere, was due to the abandonment of the individualist tradition, the growth of capitalistic monopolies, the suppression of free competition, and the adoption of state intervention or planning in economy. Thus the Western democracies, as well as other countries, are on the road that leads to Fascist serfdom, for they have adopted protective tariffs, planning, and other types of state interference with the old "natural order of things" in which the competition of individuals prevailed. Here no distinction is made between state intervention by despotisms and state intervention by constitutional governments under popular mandates. Intervention in economy *per se* leads to Fascism.

Certainly economic interests figured in the rise and growth of Fascism. There were grave economic disturbances in Italy when Mussolini came to power in that country and undoubtedly the great depression in Germany made it easier for Hitler to seize the state in 1933. Unquestionably both Mussolini and Hitler appealed to industrial workers, peasants, and the lower middle classes as against the rich and the insurgent communists. Hitler practically promised "the people" everything they thought they wanted. Indisputably the two rising dictators received monetary aid from large financial and industrial interests. In both countries, perhaps more in Italy than in Germany, big industrialists were often granted special favors at the expense of the lower middle and laboring classes.

But purely economic interpretations of the rise, growth, and nature of Fascism are oversimplifications. They rest

upon a theory of the economic basis of politics unqualified
by the condition attached to it by the keenest thinkers who
made use of it—the condition that *only in the absence of
military force* does political power pass into the hands of
those who hold the property (above, p. 38 ff.). This is to
say that oversimplified economic interpretations treat economic interests as if they are always and everywhere independent "causes" of political actions and institutions; as if
they universally furnish the most powerful if not the sole
impetus to political action for the conquest of power in the
state, in times of war, civil and foreign, as well as in times
of peace.

Economic explanations pure and simple leave out of the
reckoning other aspects of human motivation; for instance,
the ambitions and force of unique personalities; the spirit
of resentment in Italy over the curt treatment received at
Versailles in 1919; and the passion for revenge in Germany after defeat in the First World War. They ignore
the role played in Fascism by those soldiers of that war
who were still filled with passion for destroying, killing,
and dominating. Nor must it be forgotten that the elements
of Fascist ideology had long been awaiting use by activists
in search of adventure and power in the war-torn world.
Among these elements were the racial doctrines of Count
Gobineau and H. S. Chamberlain; anti-semitic diatribes;
virulent abuse of "democracy" and "civilization"; exalta-
tions of irrationality and violence as masculine virtues;
and the systematic formulations of Sorel, Mosca, and
Pareto in criticism of the masses and popular government.
Economic forces undoubtedly entered into the rise of
Fascism but they do not wholly account for its appearance
and course. . . .

A RECONSIDERATION OF THE ECONOMIC THESIS

In reconsidering an idea as deeply entangled in powerful interests as the idea of the economic basis of politics,
no person can hope to be wholly "disinterested," wholly
detached and Olympian. He may strive to follow the example of Descartes and put preconceptions out of his
mind, but he is almost certain to find them returning,

perhaps by the "back door," as Descartes did. We are not under obligations to accept the associational psychology of John Locke as the whole truth; yet we are all, in some measure, victims of ideas derived from our experiences and associations.

There are few, if any, ideas relative to human affairs which all men and women of every class, clime, race, nation, and age can look upon coldly and agree upon as readily as they can upon the proposition that the circumference of a circle is equal to 3.1416 times its diameter, approximately. Certainly the proposition that "in the absence of military force, political power naturally and necessarily goes into the hands which hold the property" is not a statement likely to be viewed with chill detachment and universally accepted, defended, or criticized without emotion.

Even so, this does not imply that we may not with some success seek the utmost truth about particular aspects of human affairs in detail and in general. Indeed by an informed awareness of relevant preconceptions—sectarian, partisan, and factional, including our own—we may to some extent rise above them or shake off their tyranny. At all events, the theory of the economic basis of politics may be more effectively reconsidered if these admonitions are kept in mind.

Although this theory is ancient in origin, the modern statement of it was formulated in particular circumstances and on the basis of assumptions connected with those circumstances. It was in England and the United States that the thesis was earliest promulgated in comprehensive form and applied to practical politics. And in England civilian supremacy over the monarchy and army was attained by the end of the seventeenth century; in the United States civilian supremacy over all armed forces was guaranteed by the Constitution which went into effect in 1789.

The geographical position of these two countries, given the state of war technology, made unnecessary the maintenance of huge armies for purposes of offense or defense. While high standing was accorded to the military man in both nations, military virtues were subordinated to civilian virtues—in economic terms, industrial, commercial, and agricultural virtues. In England and the United States, from the latter part of the eighteenth century onward, constitutional government, with emphasis on civil liberties, generally prevailed; thus conditions favored the easy expression of economic interests in politics, and the exercise of power by such interests in affairs of state. Upon the assumption that these conditions would continue indefinitely, politics was extensively treated as if the theory of the economic basis of politics supplied the criteria for "explaining" politics always and everywhere.

It should also be remembered that Karl Marx, who reduced all history to class struggles and formulated the theory of materialist determinism near the middle of the nineteenth century, conducted his major economic studies in England and used English capitalism as the classic example. It is true that Marx and his collaborator, Friedrich Engels, gave some attention to war as a social phenomenon; but neither of them substantially qualified his "economic man" by reference to the role of the military man in universal history. In fact, Marx built his system largely on Manchester economics and then evolved his own theory of social dynamics, know as dialectical materialism. It may be truly said that in some ways he was a victim of capitalistic theories then in vogue and of Hegelian metaphysics.

The general conception of Manchesterism as applied to universal history was, up to a certain point, almost identical with that of Marxism. Capitalism was bound to spread throughout the world, reaching at length the most remote and backward places. Old military societies were to be transformed into industrial societies. "The economic man" would completely subdue "the military man," the state would shrink, and the administration of things for human welfare would take the place of government by force. Manchesterism saw this occurring as the area of capitalistic *laissez faire* was extended and as free trade among nations was progressively realized; and Marx introduced a proletarian revolution as a prelude to universal liberty and well-being. But both systems of historical interpretation looked forward to world peace, economic prosperity, and the decline, if not the disappearance, of "the military man" and the state. Even Marx himself thought that the socialist transformation might be effected in England and the United States by constitutional as distinguished from violent methods.

Nevertheless the prophecies of Manchesterism and Marxism have not been realized. The whole world has not been fully industrialized or turned to the peaceful pursuits of economic production. In recent years the area of the earth occupied by constitutional and democratic governments has diminished rather than increased. The multitude of people living under the sword of empires and under dictatorial states maintained by military force outnumbers by far the multitude living under systems of government which allow a high degree of economic and political liberty. "The political man" and "the military man" have gained at the expense of "the economic man." The state has not withered away, as the communists once confidently predicted, even under communism as enforced in Russia. Calculations respecting the future of both economic and political forces must still be balanced by calculations as to the possible weight of sheer power and the sword in the years ahead.

Yet amid recent changes one thing remains certain. Politics, including military aspects, must have an economic basis or perish. People must have food, clothing, and shelter before and while they engage in politics and fighting. Whatever the formulas for the ownership and use of property, the state—despotic or democratic—must secure for itself an economic underwriting sufficient to sustain it or it will in fact wither away, as many states and empires have in the past. "The man of war," with his insatiable demand for materials, is even more than ever dependent upon economic production and, if he strives for political sovereignty, he must make sure that an adequate economic underpinning is provided or he will be destroyed by his own works. It is in these circumstances and subject to such qualifications that the economic basis of politics needs re-examination; for it is a fundamental consideration in statecraft everywhere, all the time.

With economics left out of account, political science cannot rise much above the level of astrology. But when the forms and ownership of property, the productive methods, the economic institutions, and the economic groups and ideas of a given society have been described with the utmost accuracy and when long-term trends in the past have been plotted, pure analysis and representative thought have about reached the limits of their procedure. The findings and trends thus disclosed do not constitute an exact science which permits sure predictions as to the definite political consequences that will inexorably flow from the total economic situation or the trends.

Here then we confront the problem of great history, in which all economic, political, military, and other events take place. Inevitably, we also face the central problem of historiography and philosophy: the origin, nature, dynamics, and capacities of human beings in relation to one another and their environment.

But the human mind cannot actually lay hold of things alleged to be "original causes," or things called "causes" in the subsequent flow of personalities and events, and see them functioning independently in particular ways at particular times with inescapable effects discernible to the eye. We cannot picture realistically in the mind economic events or forces operating against "politics" and producing political "effects," as we can, for instance, picture a locomotive coming up behind a train of cars and pushing it ahead to a given destination. Such physical or mechanical images correspond to none of the realities associated with economic interests and activities in conjuncture with political interests and activities.

We may, of course, adopt some such formula as "economics comes first and determines politics." But this is an arbitrary act of will, and the formula is untenable in view of relevant historical knowledge. Human beings had to eat in order to live and they began eating before they established great societies and states; but human beings were more than mere eating-animals even in the most primitive times of which we have knowledge. At an early stage in social evolution, economics and government, such as they were, became inextricably entangled, and their influences upon each other were reciprocal. Not since the beginning of recorded history has this involved relationship been broken: economic changes have affected governments and changes in governments have affected economic institutions and interests. But the problem of which precedes which or what comes first has not been solved by any process of learning or thinking.

Unless we are to remain indefinitely in indecisive meditation upon an unanswerable question, the knot which cannot be unraveled by philosophy or historical inquiry and speculation must be cut by considering the economic basis of politics in terms of action. At bottom, the problem of comprehending, using, and testing the theory or fiction thus becomes one in active statecraft for all reflective persons concerned with living and operating in relation to public affairs. Immediately the theory, which is in itself mere idea, is attached to inner images and impulses and to visible circumstances. Having resolved to act, such persons will clarify their purposes as to economic or political ends, will make use of systematic knowledge and thought relative to economic and political interests, will strive to discern what is inescapable in the given conjuncture of events, and will at length come to a judgment on the general situation with reference to the time and form of proposed actions and their probable consequences.

Stated in another way, the political science of pure thought as an end in itself can ignore the economic basis of politics, but the political science of action cannot— unless forsooth it is wholly irrational and hence doomed to self-destruction. If rational, it will employ systematic knowledge of economic institutions, interests, and forces in all their forms, make conjectures or forecasts derived from this knowledge, reach informed judgments respecting the general situation and its details, make decisions so instructed, take appropriate actions, and submit the outcome to the test of human experience.

But here the absolutist who is sure that he *knows* precisely what will happen in every contingency, real or imagined, will file objections. He will declare that the above conclusion discloses no indefeasible or mathematical laws governing human affairs which will permit certainty in predictions and hence make perfectly plain the right thing to do or say at the right moment in order to accomplish a given end or ends. Besides, he will complain, it introduces the factor of human judgment, which is fallible and belongs to intuition, not knowledge and certainty; it is therefore "mystical" and "unscientific."

To such objections answers are possible. If human affairs are in fact determined under indefeasible or mathematical law, human beings are creatures of fate and have no choices, good or bad, as to the right thing to do or say at any time. They are mere automata in history. With reference to the factor of judgment or intuition, it also appears in the process of formulating theories of physical science, which may or may not be later subjected to the tests of action. At all events, human beings conduct their affairs as if they possess the power of insight, judgment, and choice.

In his volume *The Domain of Natural Science,* one of the most thoughtful and penetrating works on the subject, E. W. Hobson says (p. 460) that there are two kinds of scientific knowledge: the systematic scheme and the unsystematic synthesis (from which elements of the former may not be absent). "But besides these kinds of knowledge, there exists a kind of apprehension which is more immediate and direct, although it is often inextricably combined with knowledge of the other kinds. This knowledge is given by direct intuition, in which the object in the subject-object relation is apparently apprehended all at once, as a whole, and not by a conscious synthesis of all its parts and their relations. . . . An exceptional power of obtaining an intuitional grasp of a complex as a whole is an essential element in the mental outfit of a man of science of the highest order."

The exercise of "intuitional and imaginative apprehension" is prominent in the history of all the great statecraft that has steered nations through the storms of war and revolution and through years of advancing civilization in times of peace. An example of such statecraft on a large scale is to be found in the proceedings of the men who framed the Constitution of the United States in 1787. These men had at their command knowledge, both systematic and unsystematic; they were familiar with the history of government, tyranny, violence, and liberty; they were intimately acquainted with the political and economic interests involved directly and indirectly in their own undertaking. But, given the nature of their resolve to act, they also had to deal with imponderables, immeasurables, and unpredictables; to make calculations respecting the possibilities and probabilities of the occasion; to pass judgment on the general situation; and finally, without being certain as to the outcome, to make a decision on the forms of actions to be risked, in the hope of attaining the ends of union, government, and liberty, projected in the paper draft of the Constitution submitted to ratifying bodies and to validation by events.

By way of summary, the theory of the economic basis of politics may be restated in the following formulas:

Revolutions and wars on a world-shaking scale have been accompanied by accelerated alterations in the forms and functions of economies and governments.

If historical experience is any guide, drastic changes in economy will find expression in politics; and, on the other hand, changes in the functions of government will be followed by repercussions in economy.

In every civilized society, whatever the nature, ownership, and law of property, a diversity of economic interests appears and "the most common and durable source" of clashing interests in politics is the various and unequal distribution of property or income (above, pp. 35–6).

The practice of democracy as government by the will of majorities or pluralities, under the theory of free and equal heads, does not eliminate economic interests, prevent collisions among them, or guarantee a pacific conduct of government or an efficient solution of contradictions (above, Chapter VI).

In the absence of military force, economic interests will come to expression in political power.

If private economic interests, having achieved political power, cannot provide an efficient economic underpinning of society in the long run, they will lose their sovereignty to politics or military force.

If by force or stratagem politics achieves sovereignty over all private economic interests, it will have to maintain an efficient economic basis of its own or perish for want of life-giving support.

If military force triumphs over both economics and

politics, it must assure an economic basis of its own or collapse amid the ruins of sterile power.

If there are no individual or group economic interests possessing a high degree of independence as against the state, despotism will supplant constitutional government and then run its own historic course.

In the absence of military force, under constitutional government, that is, limited government, against which a high degree of freedom is provided by the supreme law, the statecraft loyal to such government is under obligation to recognize the nature and existence of economic interests, promote certain interests in particular times and circumstances, restrain specific interests in particular times and places, and in general facilitate voluntary and compulsory adjustments of conflicting interests within the framework of some common civil policy.

The principal alternative to such constitutional government and practice of statecraft is the pursuit of specific interests to the bitter end—to the test of sheer power to the uttermost. This will culminate in a resort to arms by one or more of the conflicting interests and may eventuate in the triumph of one among them (or a coalition); or, if long historical experience is conclusive, will result in the destruction of all factions in the ordeal of violence.

The realities to which the above formulas refer come within the sweep of total history in time. They are not self-contained and independent "tracts of matter and force." They are enmeshed in other human characteristics and events—biological, mental, moral, artistic, and religious—that also appear in total history. The origins of total history, like [those] of the physical universe, are shrouded in the darkness of pre-history, and the law or laws of total history, if there be any, have not been discovered. Given the fragmentary evidences available, these origins and law or laws cannot be discovered by the human mind. Hence the above formulas of economics and politics are not "laws of history" but are in the nature of conditioned and conditional axioms respecting probabilities of high degree, subject to modifications by the acquisition of new knowledge and by the experiences of a future that cannot be forecast with any mathematical or descriptive certainty worthy of the name.

TWO SPECIFIC EXAMPLES OF THE INTERPLAY OF ECONOMICS AND POLITICS IN EUROPEAN HISTORY

THE FUNCTION OF EUROPEAN CASE STUDIES
IN THIS VOLUME

COMPILER'S NOTE: There now occurs a significant change of pace in the presentation of Beard's writings within these covers. The effort to derive general principles regarding the discussion of human affairs, the writing of history, and the interplay of economics and politics during great reaches of time and space yields at this point to the simpler tasks of more ordinary research. The reader is now invited to look at a few selected studies of varied economic forces, operating over short periods, in small portions of the globe.

For those who may feel that they have acquired some broad background in Parts I and II with which to appraise case studies of the type now about to appear, the change in pace may afford opportunities to use Beard to analyze Beard, perhaps a unique experience. On the other hand, for those who remain unconvinced by Parts I and II that what Beard once termed "the historical uproar" can in fact be reduced to any general principles, the change in pace offers a chance for a fresh start. If the troubles of the general philosopher cannot be resolved, the question remains as to whether it is at least possible for a skilled researcher to cover the interplay of economics and politics on a small scale in such a way as to provide valuable and convincing unity, at least to some part of the human story.

The presentation of case studies begins with European examples. Rather than attempt to isolate Beard's contributions to composite works written in conjunction with others in the field of European history, notably Robinson and Breasted, reliance is had in Part III on passages bearing only Beard's signature.

Chapter VIII treats of the interplay of economics and

politics in Great Britain during the transition from feudalism to the modern factory system. It is a direct outgrowth of Beard's personal visits to British manufacturing areas and his studies in English history, around the turn of the century in 1900.

Chapter IX, "The Rise of the German Navy," appeared shortly before the Geneva Conference on disarmament met, in 1932). It offered a glimpse into what was behind a major arms development abroad, for the edification of American readers then deeply concerned over the mounting costs and hazards of naval construction in their own country.

CHAPTER VIII

THE BRITISH INDUSTRIAL REVOLUTION [1]

[COMPILER'S NOTE: In a volume published in 1906, Charles A. Beard made the statement that: "The general direction of the political movements and legislation in Great Britain during the last one hundred years has been determined by the interests and ideals of the three great economic classes: landlords, capitalists, and workingmen." [2] Concentrating on the influence of the landed aristocracy, then the capitalists, and lastly the working class, Beard, in the following passages, sketches some of the economic drives in British politics during the transition from feudalism to the modern factory system.]

[*The Landed Aristocracy in Mediæval England*]

Viewed from . . . an economic standpoint, agriculture was of supreme importance . . . on the eve of the Industrial Revolution. . . . In 1760, one-third of the workers of England were agricultural laborers, and a large number of those engaged in regular manufacturing industries continued to work in the fields during certain portions of the year. It is estimated that 3,600,000, out of a population of 8,500,000, lived in the country, and that their income was £66,000,000, out of a total national income of £119,-500,000. . . .

---

[1] From *The Industrial Revolution,* Swan Sonnenschein & Co., Ltd. (London, 1901).

[2] *An Introduction to the English Historians,* Macmillan (1906), p. 608.

On the eve of the Industrial Revolution . . . the government was in reality in the hands of a landed aristocracy more or less subject to royal dictates. . . . The various classes, from the king to the serf, took their places in society under arbitrary and hereditary contracts. The villein was bound to the soil; the lord of the soil to his overlord or directly to the king. However, at no time can we say that this order was absolute. Irresponsible kings, anarchy, foreign influence, the growth of towns and cities, and the rise of an artisan class, had been shaking the stability of the rigid fabric. Peasants' revolts, famines, and the rise of a free laboring class had the same tendency, and the commercial development, which began in the Tudor Age, also contributed to the destruction of the feudal organism. But by 1760 there had been no upheavals violent and far-reaching enough to affect the general character of the social hierarchy.

. . . The old view which regarded the whole system of social inequality as the divine order from the foundation of the world still held sway. . . . The mass of the people lived, performed their work, and died in the position to which they thought the Lord had called them, without questioning the causes which gave them their position. . . .

The whole social fabric was keyed together by the king, upon whose personality depended law, order, international relations, social and industrial changes. . . .

[King] George III had wielded a wonderful power for several reasons: (1) in the hands of the king rested the power to bestow all the honors, preferments, dignities, and positions which turn covetous politicians into sycophantic supporters of the hands which give; (2) the privileges and position of the peers were inseparable from those of the crown, and the greater part of their support and political influence was with the king; (3) but what was still more important, and added most to the placing of unlimited authority in the hands of the king, was the nonpopular character of the House of Commons. In the first place, the county representatives were nearly all under the dominion of the county aristocracy; (2) the boroughs which returned members were largely the property of peers or under their control; (3) election work done on behalf of the royal party was rewarded by positions and honor in the government service; (4) bribery was open and corrupt, and there were even "borough brokers," whose business it was to dispose of the right of representation at the highest prices.

At the close of the eighteenth century the House of Commons had 558 members, 354 of whom, according to legal form, were returned by "less than 15,000 electors, but actually on the nomination or recommendation of the Government, and 197 private patrons, including many peers." It is thus evident that the younger Pitt's declaration had its foundation in fact: "This House is not the representative of the people of Great Britain; it is the representative of nominal boroughs, of ruined and exterminated towns, of noble families, of wealthy individuals, of foreign potentates." As early as 1653, Oliver Cromwell attempted Parliamentary reform by increasing the county members, giving representation to Leeds, Halifax, and Manchester, and striking off small boroughs from the list. This laudable reform was, however, canceled when the Stuarts were restored to the throne. From the middle of the eighteenth century Parliamentary reform was again pressed forward, but without avail. The terrors of the French Revolution frightened the governing classes in England, and it was not until Napoleon was safe at Saint Helena that reform measures were seriously taken up.

[*The Emergence of Capitalism and "Rugged Individualism"*]

. . . The ancient doctrine of paternalism and state regulation was still recognized as expedient and desirable, and "though nominally free to move, both farmers and labourers were practically fettered to the manor by their ignorance and their poverty." The ancient theory of state made for a fixed order of society, and held it to be the duty of the government to care for the temporal, spiritual, and eternal welfare of the individual, especially in so far as these interests did not conflict with those of the privileged. Under the old economic doctrine, wages were regulated, and the quality and often quantity of wares determined by the powers that were. Especially as the regulation of wages and the guaranteeing of good quality of wares suited the temporal interests of the "upper classes," the system hung on from age to age, until it was finally broken by the sudden and vast movements of the Industrial Revolution. . . .

[At] the beginning of the Industrial Revolution every branch of trade, commerce, and industry was hampered and restricted by complicated regulations, while the majority of the people were held in political bondage, and national policies were determined in the light of mediæval doctrines. The wonderful expansion of trade and commerce which came with the great inventions broke the narrow bonds of the old mediæval order; the aristocratic and divine right foundations crumbled from beneath the institutions of state and the industrial structure; and society resolved into the chaos of unrestrained individualism in every activity. . . . The employment of land, capital, and labor in any way to make the largest returns for the "captains of industry" was recognized as legitimate, and upheld by the learned writers on political economy. Individual liberty was the battle-cry, and it is not to be wondered at when we understand the folly of the old restrictive doctrines which held on until the eve of the Revolution, and when we remember that the new principles of state control were not yet developed. The state was to be a passive policeman, according to the new theories of the sphere of legislative action, while workers and employers were to be allowed full freedom in selling and buying. Freedom from social and aristocratic dogmas, freedom from restriction, marked the coming of the new industrial order. . . .

Following in the main the doctrines of Adam Smith, but with vicious enlargements and interpretations, the economists were opposed to placing new restrictions on the rapidly developing industries. Having recognized the failures and fallacies of the mediæval trade regulations, they were naturally antagonistic to renewing, in any form, state interference. They strongly advocated the "enlightened self-interest" doctrine; they discovered natural law in the social world holding the free laborer to perpetual bondage, and the discovery was highly acceptable to the capitalists and mill owners. Malthus wrote about "the misery arising from a redundant population," and, suggesting a plan for the abolition of the poor laws, said: "We are bound in justice and honor to disclaim the right of the poor to support." The reverend gentleman added: "If parents desert their child, they ought to be made answerable for the crime. The infant is, comparatively speaking, of little value to society, as others will immediately supply its place." The conclusions of the old school were, in short, that man is a miserable, helpless creature here below, powerless to change anything, and that nature would have to take its course, starving, eliminating, and yielding up the hindmost to his Satanic Majesty.

. . . Capitalism, unrestrained by Acts of Parliament, and unhindered by public opinion, entered upon an era of full freedom of contract and unrestricted competition, and the results which followed upon the mad rush for wealth supply materials for the pessimist and cynic who make human nature a synonym for all that is mean and selfish. Labor became a commodity to be bought and sold on the market. Conditions of life became secondary to the production of wealth. . . .

As we have seen, the old domestic system of manufacturing had perished, and "contentment spinning at the cottage door" had become the dream of the poet. Instead came the factory system, with its organized armies of workers. Great factory buildings were rushed up by men ignorant of the elementary principles of sanitation. One who visits the Lancashire district today will see still standing many of the old factories with their low ceilings, small windows, and absence of sanitary arrangements. So wild was the rush for wealth that nothing was thought of save space enough to work the machines, and light enough to enable the operator to tend them. In these dingy buildings, choked with dust and worn with overwork, the English freeman enjoyed to the utmost the blessed privilege of freedom of contract. . . . Bodily and mental comfort, health, security from dangerous machines, and moral decency were hardly taken into consideration by the "captains of industry who were laying the foundations of England's greatness." . . . The horrors of the industrial conditions under unrestrained capitalism outrival those of black slavery in America. If the English worker died of starvation or was injured by accident in the mills, it mattered not to the employer, for he was not legally liable, and the worker's place could be supplied from among the thousands ready to work for even a bare subsistence. On the other hand, the body of the black slave was valuable to his master. Starvation or injury which diminished his power as a worker rendered him of less value to his owner, who was thus financially interested, at least in some degree, in the tolerable condition of his property. Contemporary reports, resolutions, personal accounts, and the Blue Books are so terrible that the reader today can scarcely believe that such ghastly stories of inhuman and infernal treatment can have a shadow of truth. For more than fifty years the reign of terror held sway in the peaceful walks of industry—a reign of terror that rivals that of the French Revolution, because it was so long, so coolly accepted, and even defended by political economists and servants of the Man of Galilee.

As early as 1795, Dr. Aikin noted that the invention of machinery [had] . . . called into the mills hands from all parts, and particularly children for the cotton factories. Millowners arranged with the overseers of the poor, and, after inspection of the paupers, selected the best, and had them shipped to the factories to wear their lives out as slaves to machinery. There were even regular traders in human flesh who acted as brokers in paupers for the mills. As soon as the children were in the hands of the mill proprietors, "they were simply at the mercy of their owners, nominally as apprentices, but in reality as mere slaves, who got no wages, and whom it was not worth while even to feed or clothe properly, because they were so cheap, and their places could be so easily supplied." These little slaves worked day and night in relays, so that the beds in which they slept never cooled, one batch following another in turn for its share of rest in the filthy rag piles. In the Parliamentary reports we read of children being knocked down and beaten as many as ten times a day; of boys working in heated glass factories, and being rewarded for negligence or failure to please the brutal overseer by severe beatings with irons. Children less than five years of age were found at work in coal mines, while in the pin factories, lads five years old were worked at full capacity for twelve hours a day. The story of adult labor is no less horrifying than that of child labor. Men and women were often worked just as long as the utmost limits of physical endurance would permit. . . . "We hear of children and young people in factories overworked and beaten as if they were slaves; of diseases and distortions only found in the manufacturing districts; of filthy, wretched homes where people huddle together like beasts; we hear of girls and women working underground in the dark recesses of the coal-mines, dragging loads of coal in cars in places where no horses could go, and harnessed and crawling along the subterranean pathways like beasts of burden. Everywhere we find cruelty and oppression. . . ."

[The Reaction—The Rank and File Gain Political Power]

. . . During these sad years in the history of English toil . . . the people were, fortunately, beginning to think a little for themselves. It soon became evident to the nation at large that unrestrained individualism in industry had failed to give health, happiness, or decent conditions of livelihood. The age of revolt was not far off.

. . . The conditions finally became so unbearable that the people, who had no voice in shaping the public policy, expressed their deep-seated resentment at the iniquities of the new order in occasional outbreaks. Rick burning and the destruction of machinery showed the determined spirit of the times. Discontent and unrest were rife throughout the North. The suspension of the Habeas Corpus Act and the Six Acts (1819) aimed at the suppression of sedition, revealed the fright of the government, and virtually declared England to be in a state of anarchy; while the so-called Peterloo Massacre added fuel to the flames of civil unrest. But it was not by riots and destruction of property that the people were to secure control over their conditions of life and labor. The work of individualism in striking down and clearing away the old economic, social, and political wreckage had been invaluable; but its failure to secure to the people the barest comforts of life soon became evident.

. . . When it became a physical impossibility to endure this terrible state of affairs any longer, the agitation for factory legislation began. However, the problem was approached with "bated breath and whispering humbleness," for fear of trenching upon the sacred rights of freedom of contract. Human life was nothing when measured against the holy obligation of precedent. Factory legislation in England has been brought about by curious forces. Philanthropists, scheming politicians, men with moral and social convictions, have joined with the workers in the struggle for better conditions. The first step in the direction of legislative control of the new industry was made in 1802. Terrible as were the conditions depicted in reports and pamphlets, they seem to have attracted little attention from the general public until the spread of disease created alarm outside the precincts of factories. Long hours, ill-ventilation, filthy homes, scanty food and clothing, and total lack of decent sanitary arrangements, led to the spread of epidemics in the factory districts, and action on the question could not be delayed longer without seriously involving public health. . . .

As a result of the agitation on the condition of factory operatives, two years after the opening of the new century a Statute was passed providing for the preservation of the health and morals of apprentices and others employed in the mills. This Act, which was passed largely through the continued effort of Sir Robert Peel, was intended chiefly to protect the little pauper apprentices. It *reduced* hours of labor for children to seventy-two per week, and regulated night work as well. . . . Each apprentice was to secure instruction in reading, writing, and arithmetic, and to be provided one suit of clothes a year. . . . However, Parliament could not undertake sweeping reforms owing to the selfishness of millowners and the dense ignorance of operatives, who had been taught to believe that a shortening of hours was inevitably accompanied by a fall in wages. . . . [A] select committee of the House of Commons reported in 1811 that "no interference of the Legislature with the freedom of trade, or with the perfect liberty of every individual to dispose of his time and his labour in the way and on the terms which he may judge most conducive to his interest, can take place without violating general principles of the first importance to the prosperity and happiness of the community . . ."

In 1815, Robert Owen, the great and revered friend of

the toilers of the world, lifted his voice in public protest against the iniquities of the industrial system. With him, interference was not a question of "economic theory," but one of human life. . . .

Owen framed three proposals which he wished to have embodied in a second Factory Act. . . . For four years Owen was at London attending the Parliamentary sessions, fighting for the passage of the Bill against ignorance, prejudice, selfishness, and personal abuse and slander. In 1819, after Owen's original draft had been mutilated beyond recognition, the Bill finally became a law. Owen tells us that he learned some things during the agitation. To use his own words: "My intimate acquaintance with these proceedings, for the four years during which this Bill was under the consideration of both Houses, opened my eyes to the conduct of public men, and to the ignorant, vulgar self-interest, regardless of means to accomplish their object, of trading and mercantile men, even of high standing in the commercial world." . . .

The new law forbade the employment of children under nine in the mills, and limited the hours of work to twelve a day, exclusive of mealtimes, for all between the ages of nine and sixteen. The first Act had only made the state a sort of a guardian for the pauper apprentices; but the Bill of 1819 was "legislative interference between the free labourer and his employer," which the opponents of the measure considered "a violent, highly dangerous, and unconstitutional innovation." It was certainly the first expression of the new doctrine that the state ought to protect the interests of the weaker citizens; and it opened the way for the later restrictive legislation. . . . In 1825, Saturday labor was shortened, and penalties provided for breach of factory regulation. These Factory Acts, however, did nothing toward assuring certainty of employment and living wages, and little toward improving the lot of the workers in any but the cotton industry. Misery, starvation, suffering, and degradation made up the common heritage of the laborers, in spite of the factory laws. The spirit of unrest, nevertheless, was abroad in the land. It became evident that the people themselves must assert their authority in the Halls of Parliament.

. . . [Notice] should be taken of William Cobbett, who

has been called the Father of English Radicalism. In 1816, his *Weekly Political Register* was reduced from 1s. ½ d. to 2 d., and by this means cheap political information, good and bad, was supplied to permeate the consciousness of the people with the new principles of reform. Orators, poets, writers, and pamphleteers were busy arousing the working classes, and Hampden clubs were founded all over the country for the purpose of pressing forward the demands for the suffrage. Under the leadership of Lord John Russell, such reform was again and again forced upon the House, until in 1832, after two defeats, and in spite of the bitter opposition of the House of Lords, the clergy, the universities, army and navy, and the Inns of Courts, the famous Reform Bill became law, and the tide set in toward democracy. The conflict was not waged in Parliament alone, however, for all over the country were groups of men determined not to abate their activities until the walls of political privilege were battered down. When the second bill was rejected by the House of Lords, rioting at once began in the large towns where the news had been anxiously awaited. The third bill was finally passed by the House of Lords, after threats from the prime minister, and warnings from the king.

The enfranchisement of the middle classes in 1832 opened the castle of the privileged to the assaults of the disinherited, and political history since that time centers about the struggles for enfranchisement of the masses. It is, however, well to bear in mind continually the significant words of Sidney Webb: "None of these enfranchised classes has ever sincerely desired to admit new voters to share the privileges, and submerge the power which it had won; but each political party in turn has been driven to 'shoot Niagara,' in order to compete with its opponents." By the Act of 1832, 143 seats were taken from "rotten" and small boroughs, and distributed among the new centers of population.

In 1867, radical agitation and rioting forced the Tory government to extend the electoral franchise in boroughs to householders and certain lodgers, and to reduce the county occupation franchise. In 1878, the tenement occupier was enfranchised. In 1885, the agricultural laborer became a "sovereign voter." The decentralizing local government acts of 1888–1894 have opened the way for local autonomy. Thus within the past one hundred years the world has witnessed a silent revolution in English politics, which has resulted in the vesting of power in the hands of the people.

. . . The first Parliament after the Reform of 1832 took up, among other things, the thread of factory legislation which had been dropped in the struggles over the franchise. In 1833–34, an important Act was passed which applied to all textile industries. The labor of children between the ages of nine and thirteen was limited to forty-eight hours, and that of young persons between thirteen and eighteen to sixty-nine hours per week. Night work for the young was forbidden, and ten hours a day made the limit for children in the silk mills. This Act met with a storm of opposition on the part of capitalists and millowners, but it did not prevent the conviction of one out of every eleven of the millowners for failure to observe its provisions. In 1842, the employment of women and children in underground work was forbidden. By the famous Ten Hours Act of 1847, and its supplement in 1850, the labor of women and children was restricted to ten hours a day. Since the labor of women and children could not be shortened without closing the mills where they were employed, the Ten Hours Bill practically applied to men also, and ten hours a day thus became the general rule for factories. . . .

After the breach was once made in the solid ranks of the individualists, and the desirability of collective action became apparent, act after act was passed curtailing the sphere of individual enterprise, and subjecting private gain to the welfare of society at large. . . . The battle has been long and hard, and even now only the first redoubts are in possession of the people. The power is theirs, however, but they will progress only so far as their intelligence and character will permit. . . .

. . . When the Industrial Revolution made capital and machinery relatively more important than labor, there was developed a large class of workers doomed by necessity to remain employees all their lives. The mediæval guild regulations were without avail, and in the chaos of the beginning of the new order there were no generally recognized principles of organization. The workers were not only compelled to accept the bondage, with its shocking conditions as to hours and wages, but they were also forbidden to combine for mutual assistance and for the defense of a standard of life. In addition to the Law of Settlement which, though intended for paupers, actually prevented laborers from going from one parish to another in search of work, in 1799 and 1800 acts were passed definitely forbidding workmen to combine for the purpose of securing better conditions. Agitation carried on by Francis Place, assisted by Joseph Hume and J. R. Mulloch, succeeded in forcing a repeal of the restrictive laws in 1824; but the strikes and disorders which followed frightened the government, and Parliament passed an Act rendering illegal any action arising from the deliberations of the unions. . . . It was not, however, until 1871–76 that unions were placed on a legal basis.

CHAPTER IX

THE RISE OF THE GERMAN NAVY [1]

IN DUE COURSE the representatives of the Great Powers will assemble to consider armaments. Economy suggests a reduction; fear of revolution to follow another war haunts the boldest of the "natural-born fighters." At this grand conclave will appear high-hatted diplomats looking wise, bespangled naval officers wearing airs of omniscience and assurance, hopeful pacifists dreaming dreams, advocates of peace with their appropriate "formulas," agents of the heavy industries safeguarding profits, and many journalists, always worldly wise in small things and usually devoid of historic sense. And around the edges will hover Bolshevik observers convinced that capitalists cannot develop protective intelligence and hence are doomed in advance, twist and turn as they will. Success means defeat to the chief participants and failure means disaster still more magnificent in the next great day.

Unfortunately for the functioning of the conference, the intellectual background has not been prepared. In spite of the millions spent by peace societies for research and propaganda, there does not exist in any language a realistic description and analysis of all the forces now at work and all the fundamental problems at stake in armament rivalries. What is national interest? Who has the right to define it? What is adequate defense? Adequate to what and to whom? Why do armies and navies grow bigger and better?

[1] Originally appearing as "Making a Bigger and Better Navy" in *The New Republic,* Oct. 14, 1931, pp. 223–6; reprinted by permission of the *New Republic.*

What is to be gained by war? Who gains it, when, as, and if? Do navalism and imperialism pay? Pay whom? The questions are not even asked officially and the materials for answering them are not yet assembled.

Happily, however, there is now available one excellent treatise on a phase of the subject, which those who wish understanding instead of illusion may consult. At the close of the World War the secret archives of Germany were extensively opened, and it is now possible for one nation on earth to know what went on behind its governmental façade during momentous years, to discover how navalism operates—its methods, hopes, and mentality. Taking full advantage of this situation, Dr. Eckart Kehr has given us a deep insight into the political, social, and ideological presuppositions of German imperialism in his *Schlacht-flottenbau und Parteipolitik 1894–1902* (Berlin, 1930)—a work which is thoroughly documented and has wrought havoc among the apologists of von Tirpitz and company. Dr. Kehr's book opens with an introduction on the evolution of opinion respecting naval imperialism from 1867 to 1894. Then comes a minute survey of the rise and development of the battle over big navalism, sketched in meticulous detail, with data on profit-makers, prices of steel and shipyard stocks, intrigues, newspapers, journalists, officials, millionaires, propagandists and politicians, all set down with frosty precision. This is followed by a calm analysis of the "opinions" of parties, classes and orders of state on imperialism and sea power. At the end is a section showing that the naval-armament struggle is a phase of the domestic social and economic conflict, mirrored in patriotic ideology. Not often since Eve handed Adam the apple have those who wish to distinguish truth from moonshine had a better opportunity to eat of the fruit of the tree of knowledge.

This close study of German naval policy furnishes hard lessons for those Marxians who think that ideas automatically arise from given economic conditions, inexorable in spirit and form, and also to the theorists who imagine that the world can be ruled by ideas without reference to realities. In the German chronicle we do not at the outset see capitalists and merchants drawing together on their own motion, evolving an inevitable ideology and swinging the government into line as their agency or tool. On the contrary, the clarification and elaboration of the big-navy policy for Germany was largely the work of Captain Alfred von Tirpitz and a small group of men whom he assembled around him.

That von Tirpitz knew precisely what he was doing, that he had picked England as "the enemy" at the outset, that he had a grand dream of German security, is nowhere apparent in the record. Personally ambitious, restless and eager for power, placed by fortune in the navy, he simply made the most of his opportunity. Assuming a kind of technical omniscience, he flatly decided that battleships were better than cruisers, and that squadron formation and line tactics were better than English empiricism. Having come to these conclusions with the dogmatism that usually characterizes the engineer, whose social knowledge is as a rule sadly deficient, von Tirpitz then cast about for the best way to sell his idea to the powers that ruled Germany, not overlooking the man in the street. After a brief search he hit upon the slogan that "the navy pays," that sea armaments make economic returns to industry, and that upon this hard foundation of economic cupidity must the ideological structure of navy propaganda be built.[2]

Von Tirpitz' idea was not his own invention. Great Britain had long before found out by experience that the sea power was an efficient agency with which to build empire, protect trade, exploit backward places and peoples and smash rivals. The British, to be sure, had not theorized much about it; they had been content to "rule the waves" in fact, to write the law of the sea and to dictate terms in all conflicts on the water. It had been left to an American, Captain Alfred T. Mahan, to formulate systematically the gospel of *Welt- und Machtpolitik* in his writings on the sea power in history—works written not without an eye to doing for the American navy what von Tirpitz wanted to do for his, and not without powerful effects on politicians devoted to the strenuous life, such as Theodore Roosevelt and Henry Cabot Lodge, and equally powerful effects on our captains of steel for whom Marcus A. Hanna was soon

[2] Consider "The United States Navy as an Industrial Asset," Office of Naval Intelligence (Washington, 1924).

to speak so effectively in the Senate of the United States. As the noted naval critic, Sir John Laughton, said in commenting on Mahan's *The Influence of Sea Power upon the French Revolution and Empire,* "the book is throughout a splendid apotheosis of English courage and English endurance, of English skill and English power, the more splendid, the more glorious as these are put forward not as a matter of boasting or of laudation, but philosophically, scientifically, as illustrating propositions in naval strategy or in commercial war."

Mahan's first "masterpiece" came out in 1890 and his second in 1892. Of the latter Sir John Laughton remarked, "important as it is to naval officers, [it] is still more so to the statesman, the administrator, the shipowner, the merchant and the tradesman." Both of these works went to the head of the Kaiser and von Tirpitz like heavy wine. . . .

Von Tirpitz had *The Influence of Sea Power upon History* translated and made it a kind of marine bible for his officers and propagandists, especially as it not only expounded the gospel of might but also indicated the parties who could be interested in the outcome, namely, statesmen, *shipowners, merchants and tradesmen*—from whom the possessors of shipyards and the manufacturers of armor plate were not sharply divorced. Old Germany, dozing on the land and still infected by Kantian idealism, was to be rudely awakened and set to "glorious" tasks, and the acquisitive instincts of every group likely to profit from the operation were now to be stirred by propaganda. At last, in Mahan's works, von Tirpitz had the scientific, systematic, economic and moral justification for the enterprise in hand.

Within less than ten years von Tirpitz had converted enough hesitant and uncertain Germans to his program to assure victory for his battle fleet. When his operations are examined in detail, they are found to fall into the following pattern: the preparation of "literature," the alignment of interested classes, the enlistment of facile journalists and publicists, the adjustment of party conflicts and the conquest of the intellectuals.

The literature of propaganda took all appropriate forms. A special division in the Navy Office assumed general charge of it. . . . To make sure that lay periodicals were kept current, the Allgemeine Marine- und Handelscorrespondenz was established and regularly supplied the public with specific "information" about the Navy, especially the close relation between economic and the sea power.

All this, however, was merely a beginning. Money by the billions could not be wrung from the nation unless its governors, particularly businessmen and agrarians, could be convinced. Although the fleet would "pay," according to the new philosophy, taxes had to be raised to meet the cost of construction. It was not difficult, of course, to enroll powder manufacturers, coal owners, armor-plate makers and shipbuilders. For them patriotism was clearly a paying proposition. If any of them had any doubts on the point, they were quickly reassured when they saw the stocks of pertinent industries shoot upward in a bull market as soon as the first great grant of money to the Navy had been voted. And after the building had begun and plants had been extended to meet additional requirements, gentlemen of this order thought the navy should be still bigger. Otherwise their enlarged establishments would be partly idle and, as they pitifully urged, their workingmen would be unemployed. Among them all, apparently, there was not a single steel magnate to weep with Carnegie and Schwab over the thought of death and destruction to come. Indeed, taking advantage of the opportunity, the coal men of the Ruhr organized a syndicate, raised prices on the Navy, and in spite of its protests forced it to pay more per ton than the rate on the world market. If some patriots were shocked at what seemed to be greed on the part of coal owners, they were not shocked enough to produce any effect on "the technical evolution of the situation."

While it was easy to prove to munition makers and shipbuilders the "necessity" for a big navy, that was not enough. Other capitalists, who were to be "paid" indirectly, if at all, could not see their earnings so easily. They had to be taught. So, the navy propagandists began to round up chambers of commerce by enlisting the great industrialists, apparently on the theory that the small yes-men in the rear would come when called. . . . [The] majority were brought into the fold, singly and in groups, until at last capitalism was well mobilized behind the program and duly informed

as to the best methods for swinging recalcitrant members
of Parliament into line when navy budgets were voted. . . .

The agrarian side of the conflict over sea power presented many aspects. Out of the agricultural situation
flowed no simple answer to this problem in statecraft. Yet
obviously agriculture was tied into the question of armaments. Naturally the landed classes of Germany, led by
the Prussian gentry, wished to preserve their ascendancy
and to keep the Prussian monarchy and the Empire on
the old foundation of the land and the army, commanded
by officers of their social order. That much was clear.

Now if Germany went out upon the high seas, increased
her industries and enlarged the industrial population, many
things would happen to the economic system. The balance
of power would pass to industrial and finance capitalism,
and the landed aristocracy would be beaten by the bourgeoisie. If German manufacturers were to sell their commodities abroad on a large scale, they would import in
exchange huge quantities of agricultural produce, as a
necessity of trade and to feed the growing multitudes of
the cities; that meant fierce competition for the agrarians.
A great battle fleet also offered perplexities. While the
industrialists saw in it an instrument for keeping the seas
open in time of war, the agrarians looked on that as a
dubious blessing, because a blockade, instead of injuring
them, would bring an immense upswing in the prices of
their farm produce.

In the issue they also saw national defense imperiled
. . . the agrarians resented a diversion of money from the
army to the navy—a diversion that ultimately weakened
the main lines of defense. . . .

Hemmed in on all sides by a narrowing destiny, the
agrarians chose what seemed to be the only way out—a
compromise with capitalism, not because they were converted to *Welt- und Machtpolitik* but because they had to
make adjustments to live at all. So in the end they voted
for the fleet demanded in the name of industry; in return,
the capitalists granted to agriculture the tariffs on grain
demanded for its protection; and the two groups united on
a program designed to prevent the conquest of the state by

social democracy. Perhaps never in history was a more fateful decision made by directing statesmen.

The foreign-policy correlate of this compromise had grave implications. On the one hand, it involved a surrender of the industrialists to the anti-Russia sentiment of the agrarians who had felt the competition of that agricultural giant and had preferred to retain English friendship. On the other hand, the agrarians were forced to give the industrialists a free rein to compete with England in commerce and sea power. Another result was to accelerate the transfer of Russia to French capitalists for development and exploitation. At the same time the coalition of the bourgeois and the landed gentry put a check on the liberal tendencies in domestic politics, which the former would have otherwise favored within limits, hardened class lines and placed an embargo on thinking. But when the combination was duly effected, both parties were chained to it, and government by reasoned policy—enlightened, supple, ingenious statecraft—became impossible. No Greek tragedy was ever more exact. Foreign and domestic policies were caught in an iron framework.

In lining up other political factions behind his big-navy program, von Tirpitz had difficulties. The socialists, of course, were intransigent in their opposition, those "fatherlandless fellows"; they were firmly convinced at the turn of the century that his policy would lead to a competitive struggle among imperialist nations which in turn would end in a crash for all Western civilization—a crash which, as one of them said, would make the Thirty Years' War look like a summer idyl. It happened that the socialists were nearer the truth than any of the official prophets, but in the eyes of the great and wise the former were merely contemptible traitors, out of whose mouths could come nothing good.

Between the industrial-agrarian coalition on the one side and the proletariat on the other stood the Center Party, Catholic in religion and astute in politics. Uniting under its banner some big industrialists, a part of the proletariat and many peasants, it cut across class lines. For a long time it hesitated, while negotiations went on among its leaders behind the scenes, but at last, in exchange for power and the spoils of office, the Center went over to von Tirpitz. . . .

In the spread of "enlightenment," journalists and publicists were easily enlisted. A large number of these birds of passage, circling around in search of fleshpots and lighting places, were easily collected about the Navy Office, nominally independent but actually receiving their rewards from that source. . . . So, suddenly the German press broke out with the rash in the late nineties, with the fever of a bigger and better navy. . . . Two newspapers were engineered directly by the armament interests: Stumm's *Post* and Krupps' *Neueste Nachrichten,* and they served as feeders for outlying editors whose knowledge of the sea power and its profits was likely to be deficient.

Finally, there were the teachers and the professors. The former, as cogs in the bureaucratic machine, were quickly subdued to the formula that every patriot must believe in a big Navy. That was easy, for conscientious objectors could be ousted and ruined. But professors claimed to be scientific and impartial. How could they sail in the winds of propaganda? The Navy Office found a way by suggesting appropriate subjects for academic research and by supplying statistics for computation and analysis—all calculated to stir up interest in the sea power. . . . In due time the intellectuals were brought into line.

With the stage all set and the money voted, the navy grew and grew. At last "the" enemy was needed. If one had not been manufactured by the course of events, it would have been necessary to designate one for the purpose of keeping up the furor. Soldiers and sailors become restless when their good weapons rust. So the enemy was discovered on the horizon; it was no mirage; it was England. In the end the gentlemen who worked so hard and so long to build the fleet blew up with their own works, and since that dénouement a number of German people have begun to suspect the omniscience of naval "intelligence."

PART IV

SOME ECONOMIC ASPECTS
OF AMERICAN
POLITICAL HISTORY

SHIFTING THE SPOTLIGHT TO THE
AMERICAN SCENE

COMPILER'S NOTE: Attention now turns from the European theater (Part III) to the shores of the New World in Part IV. Here material drawn from Beard's numerous investigations of the economic aspects of American political history is presented approximately in chronological order.

Writing of colonial times, Beard pointed out that "When the representative system was transplanted to these shores the old English practice of associating representation with property came with it. To be sure, there were no estates in Colonial America—clergy, barons, and burgesses—in the legal sense, but there were men with different degrees and kinds of property, to use James Madison's accurate phrase. These people alone could vote and sit in colonial assemblies in the great year of grace, 1776." [1] As has previously been reported (pp. 53–4), the same linkage of property with representation is to be found in the first American state constitutions.

Such was the political atmosphere in which the Constitution of the United States was drafted. While property qualifications for voting and public office did not find their way into that great document, as Beard shows in Chapter X, this certainly does not signify that economic considerations were ignored by those who formulated it. Chapter XI goes on to deal with some of the economic forces that affected the vote on its ratification. [2]

[1] "Whom Does Congress Represent?" *Harper's Magazine*, Jan., 1930, pp. 144–52, quoted with the magazine's permission.

[2] Beard greatly amplified the story here presented in his *An Economic Interpretation of the Constitution of the United States,* Macmillan (1913). However, as the volume is still (1956) in print, extracts from it have been purposely left out of this compendium.

Beard's emphasis on economic factors influencing the writing and adoption of the Constitution evoked a torrent of criticism. In self-defense, he pointed out that those who avoided such elements did not, in his opinion, go deep enough. When discussing Theodore Clarke Smith's interpretation that the formation and adoption of the Constitution was "a contest between sections ending in the victory of straight-thinking national-minded men over narrower and more local opponents," Beard declared: "An economic interpretation does not inquire whether men were straight-thinking or crooked-thinking. It inquires not into their powers of mind or virtues, but into the nature and effects of their substantial possessions. Nor is it necessarily in conflict with Mr. Smith's conclusions. It pushes the inquiry one step further than he does. It asks how it happened that some men were national-minded and others were local-minded, and perhaps throws some light upon the subject." [3]

Chapters XIII through XX collectively pick up the thread of American politics shortly after the national administration was established under the new Constitution. They start with the strong differences of opinion that developed over the policies of the young government—differences which soon found expression in the first great and enduring national party alignments. They then proceed to carry the account down to the year 1928, with major emphasis on the economic aspects of American domestic politics. (For comments on domestic affairs in the period subsequent to 1928, the reader is referred back to pp. 84 ff.)

Finally, Chapter XXI brings the text to a close with an economic commentary on American foreign policy as it stood shortly after World War I. This concluding material appeared originally as a part of a series of lectures delivered by Beard at Dartmouth College on the Guernsey Center Moore Foundation in June 1922.

[3] "That Noble Dream," *The American Historical Review,* Oct. 1935, pp. 85–6, quoted by permission.

CHAPTER X

FRAMING THE CONSTITUTION [1]

As BLACKSTONE[2] shows by happy illustration the reason and spirit of a law are to be understood only by an inquiry into the circumstances of its enactment. The underlying purposes of the Constitution [of the United States], therefore, are to be revealed only by a study of the conditions and events which led to its formation and adoption.

At the outset it must be remembered that there were two great parties at the time of the adoption of the Constitution—one laying emphasis on strength and efficiency in government and the other on its popular aspects. Quite naturally the men who led in stirring up the revolt against Great Britain and in keeping the fighting temper of the Revolutionists at the proper heat were the boldest and most radical thinkers—men like Samuel Adams, Thomas Paine, Patrick Henry, and Thomas Jefferson. They were not, generally speaking, men of large property interests or of much practical business experience. In a time of disorder, they could consistently lay more stress upon personal liberty than upon social control; and they pushed to the extreme limits those doctrines of individual rights which had been evolved in England during the struggles of the small landed proprietors and commercial classes against royal prerogative, and which corresponded to the economic conditions prevailing in America at the close of the eight-

[1] From *The Supreme Court and the Constitution*, Macmillan (1912).

[2] COMPILER'S NOTE: Blackstone, Sir William (1723–1780). Distinguished commentator on the laws of England, judge, and teacher.

eenth century. They associated strong government with monarchy, and came to believe that the best political system was one which governed least. A majority of the radicals viewed all government, especially if highly centralized, as a species of evil, tolerable only because necessary and always to be kept down to an irreducible minimum by a jealous vigilance.

Jefferson put the doctrine in concrete form when he declared that he preferred newspapers without government to government without newspapers. The Declaration of Independence, the first state Constitutions, and the Articles of Confederation bore the impress of this philosophy. In their anxiety to defend the individual against all federal interference and to preserve to the states a large sphere of local autonomy, these Revolutionists had set up a system too weak to accomplish the accepted objects of government; namely, national defense, the protection of property, and the advancement of commerce. They were not unaware of the character of their handiwork, but they believed with Jefferson that "man was a rational animal endowed by nature with rights and with an innate sense of justice and that he could be restrained from wrong and protected in right by moderate powers confided to persons of his own choice." Occasional riots and disorders, they held, were preferable to too much government.

The new American political system based on these doctrines had scarcely gone into effect before it began to incur opposition from many sources. The close of the Revolutionary struggle removed the prime cause for radical agitation and brought a new group of thinkers into prominence. When independence had been gained, the practical work to be done was the maintenance of social order, the payment of the public debt, the provision of a sound financial system, and the establishment of conditions favorable to the development of the economic resources of the new country. The men who were principally concerned in this work of peaceful enterprise were not the philosophers, but men of business and property and the holders of public securities. For the most part they had had no quarrel with the system of class rule and the strong centralization of government which existed in England. It was on the question of policy, not of governmental structure, that they had broken with the British authorities. By no means all of them, in fact, had even resisted the policy of the mother country, for within the ranks of the conservatives were large numbers of Loyalists who had remained in America, and, as was to have been expected, cherished a bitter feeling against the Revolutionists, especially the radical section which had been boldest in denouncing the English system root and branch. In other words, after the heat and excitement of the War of Independence were over and the new government, state and national, was tested by the ordinary experiences of traders, financiers, and manufacturers, it was found inadequate, and these groups accordingly grew more and more determined to reconstruct the political system in such a fashion as to make it subserve their permanent interests.

Under the state constitutions and the Articles of Confederation established during the Revolution, every powerful economic class in the nation suffered either immediate losses or from impediments placed in the way of the development of their enterprises. The holders of the securities of the Confederate government did not receive the interest on their loans. Those who owned Western lands or looked with longing eyes upon the rich opportunities for speculation there chaffed at the weakness of the government and its delays in establishing order on the frontiers. Traders and commercial men found their plans for commerce on a national scale impeded by local interference with interstate commerce. The currency of the states and the nation was hopelessly muddled. Creditors everywhere were angry about the depreciated paper money which the agrarians had made and were attempting to force upon those from whom they had borrowed specie. In short, it was a war between business and populism. Under the Articles of Confederation populism had a free hand, for majorities in the state legislatures were omnipotent. Anyone who reads the economic history of the time will see why the solid conservative interests of the country were weary of talk about the "rights of the people" and bent upon establishing firm guarantees for the rights of property.

The Congress of the Confederation was not long in discovering the true character of the futile authority which the Articles had conferred upon it. The necessity for new sources of revenue became apparent even while the struggle for independence was yet undecided, and, in 1781, Congress carried a resolution to the effect that it should be authorized to lay a duty of five per cent on certain goods. This moderate proposition was defeated because Rhode Island rejected it on the grounds that "she regarded it the most precious jewel of sovereignty that no state shall be called upon to open its purse but by the authority of the state and by her own officers." Two years later Congress prepared another amendment to the Articles providing for certain import duties, the receipts from which, collected by state officers, were to be applied to the payment of the public debt; but three years after the introduction of the measure, four states, including New York, still held out against its ratification, and the project was allowed to drop. At last, in 1786, Congress in a resolution declared that the requisitions for the last eight years had been so irregular in their operation, so uncertain in their collection, and so evidently unproductive, that a reliance on them in the future would be no less dishonorable to the understandings of those who entertained it than it would be dangerous to the welfare and peace of the Union. Congress, thereupon, solemnly added that it had become its duty "to declare most explicitly that the crisis had arrived when the people of the United States, by whose will and for whose benefit the federal government was instituted, must decide whether they will support their rank as a nation by maintaining the public faith at home and abroad, or whether for the want of a timely exertion in establishing a general revenue and thereby giving strength to the Confederacy, they will hazard not only the existence of the Union but those great and invaluable privileges for which they have so arduously and so honorably contended."

In fact, the Articles of Confederation had hardly gone into effect before the leading citizens also began to feel that the powers of Congress were wholly inadequate. In 1780, even before their adoption, Alexander Hamilton proposed a general convention to frame a new constitution, and from that time forward he labored with remarkable zeal and wisdom to extend and popularize the idea of a strong national government. Two years later, the Assembly of the

State of New York recommended a convention to revise the Articles and increase the power of Congress. In 1783, Washington, in a circular letter to the governors, urged that it was indispensable to the happiness of the individual states that there should be lodged somewhere a supreme power to regulate and govern the general concerns of the confederation. Shortly afterward (1785), Governor Bowdoin, of Massachusetts, suggested to his state legislature the advisability of calling a national assembly to settle upon and define the powers of Congress; and the legislature resolved that the government under the Articles of Confederation was inadequate and should be reformed; but the resolution was never laid before Congress.

In January, 1786, Virginia invited all the other states to send delegates to a convention at Annapolis to consider the question of duties on imports and commerce in general. When this convention assembled in 1786, delegates from only five states were present, and they were disheartened at the limitations on their powers and the lack of interest the other states had shown in the project. With characteristic foresight, however, Alexander Hamilton seized the occasion to secure the adoption of a recommendation advising the states to choose representatives for another convention to meet in Philadelphia the following year "to consider the Articles of Confederation and to propose such changes therein as might render them adequate to the exigencies of the union." This recommendation was cautiously worded, for Hamilton did not want to raise any unnecessary alarm. He doubtless believed that a complete revolution in the old system was desirable, but he knew that, in the existing state of popular temper, it was not expedient to announce his complete program. Accordingly no general reconstruction of the political system was suggested; the Articles of Confederation were merely to be "revised"; and the amendments were to be approved by the state legislatures as provided by that instrument.

The proposal of the Annapolis convention was transmitted to the state legislatures and laid before Congress. Congress thereupon resolved in February, 1787, that a convention should be held for the sole and express purpose of revising the Articles of Confederation and reporting to itself and the legislatures of the several states such alterations and provisions as would when agreed to by Congress and confirmed by the states render the federal constitution adequate to the exigencies of government and the preservation of the union.

In pursuance of this call, delegates to the new convention were chosen by the legislatures of the states or by the governors in conformity to authority conferred by the legislative assemblies.[3] The delegates were given instructions of a general nature by their respective states, none of which, apparently, contemplated any very far-reaching changes. In fact, almost all of them expressly limited their representatives to a mere revision of the Articles of Confederation. For example, Connecticut authorized her delegates to represent and confer for the purpose mentioned in the resolution of Congress and to discuss such measures "agreeably to the general principles of Republican government" as they should think proper to render the Union adequate. Delaware, however, went so far as to provide that none of the proposed alterations should extend to the fifth part of the Articles of Confederation guaranteeing that each state should be entitled to one vote.

It was a truly remarkable assembly of men that gathered in Philadelphia on May 14, 1787, to undertake the work of reconstructing the American system of government. It is not merely patriotic pride that compels one to assert that never in the history of assemblies has there been a convention of men richer in political experience and in practical knowledge, or endowed with a profounder insight into the springs of human action and the intimate essence of government. It is indeed an astounding fact that at one time so many men skilled in statecraft could be found on the very frontiers of civilization among a population numbering about four million whites. It is no less a cause for admiration that their instrument of government should have survived the trials and crises of a century that saw the wreck of more than a score of paper constitutions.

All the members had had a practical training in politics. Washington, as commander-in-chief of the Revolutionary

[3] Rhode Island alone was unrepresented. In all, sixty-two delegates were appointed by the states; fifty-five of these attended sometime during the sessions; but only thirty-nine signed the finished document.

forces, had learned well the lessons and problems of war, and mastered successfully the no less difficult problems of administration. The two Morrises had distinguished themselves in grappling with financial questions as trying and perplexing as any which statesmen had ever been compelled to face. Seven of the delegates had gained political wisdom as governors of their native states; and no less than twenty-eight had served in Congress either during the Revolution or under the Articles of Confederation. These were men trained in the law, versed in finance, skilled in administration, and learned in the political philosophy of their own and all earlier times. Moreover, they were men destined to continue public service under the government which they had met to construct—Presidents, Vice-Presidents, heads of departments, Justices of the Supreme Court were in that imposing body. . . .

As Woodrow Wilson has concisely put it, the framers of the Constitution represented "a strong and intelligent class possessed of unity and informed by a conscious solidarity of interests." [4] . . .

The makers of the federal Constitution represented the solid, conservative, commercial and financial interests of the country—not the interests which denounced and proscribed judges in Rhode Island, New Jersey, and North Carolina, and stoned their houses in New York. The conservative interests, made desperate by the imbecilities of the Confederation and harried by state legislatures, roused themselves from their lethargy, drew together in a mighty effort to establish a government that would be strong enough to pay the national debt, regulate interstate and foreign commerce, provide for national defense, prevent fluctuations in the currency created by paper emissions, and control the propensities of legislative majorities to attack private rights. . . . The radicals, however, like Patrick Henry, Jefferson, and Samuel Adams, were conspicuous by their absence from the convention.[5] . . .

[The makers of the Constitution were convened] to frame a government which would meet the practical issues that

[4] *Division and Reunion*, p. 12.

[5] COMPILER'S NOTE: The contents of this paragraph have been taken from positions on pp. 75–6 and 88 of the original text and placed here to emphasize the economic theme.

had arisen under the Articles of Confederation. The objections they entertained to direct popular government, and they were undoubtedly many, were based upon their experience with popular assemblies during the immediately preceding years. With many of the plain lessons of history before them, they naturally feared that the rights and privileges of the minority would be insecure if the principle of majority rule was definitely adopted and provisions made for its exercise. Furthermore, it will be remembered that up to that time the right of all men, as men, to share in the government had never been recognized in practice. Everywhere in Europe the government was in the hands of a ruling monarch or at best a ruling class; everywhere the mass of the people had been regarded principally as an arms-bearing and tax-paying multitude, uneducated, and with little hope or capacity for advancement. Two years were to elapse after the meeting of the grave assembly at Philadelphia before the transformation of the Estates General into the National Convention in France opened the floodgates of revolutionary ideas on human rights before whose rising tide old landmarks of government are still being submerged. It is small wonder, therefore, that, under the circumstances, many of the members of that august body held popular government in slight esteem and took the people into consideration only as far as it was imperative "to inspire them with the necessary confidence," as Mr. Gerry frankly put it.[6]

Indeed, every page of the laconic record of the proceedings of the convention preserved to posterity by Mr. Madison shows conclusively that the members of that assembly were not seeking to realize any fine notions about democracy and equality, but were striving with all the resources of political wisdom at their command to set up a system of government that would be stable and efficient, safeguarded on one hand against the possibilities of despotism and on the other against the onslaught of majorities. In the mind of Mr. Gerry, the evils they had experienced flowed "from the excess of democracy," and he confessed that while he was still republican, he "had been taught by experience the danger of the levelling spirit." [7] Mr. Ran-

[6] Elliot's *Debates*, vol. v, p. 160.
[7] *Ibid.*, vol. v, p. 136.

dolph in offering to the consideration of the convention his plan of government, observed "that the general object was to provide a cure for the evils under which the United States labored; that, in tracing these evils to their origin, every man had found it in the turbulence and follies of democracy; that some check therefore was to be sought for against this tendency of our governments; and that a good Senate seemed most likely to answer the purpose." [8] Mr. Hamilton, in advocating a life term for Senators, urged that "all communities divide themselves into the few and the many. The first are rich and well born and the other the mass of the people who seldom judge or determine right."

Gouverneur Morris wanted to check the "precipitancy, changeableness, and excess" of the representatives of the people by the ability and virtue of men "of great and established property—aristocracy; men who from pride will support consistency and permanency. . . . Such an aristocratic body will keep down the turbulence of democracy." While these extreme doctrines were somewhat counterbalanced by the democratic principles of Mr. Wilson who urged that "the government ought to possess, not only first, the force, but second the mind or sense of the people at large," Madison doubtless summed up in a brief sentence the general opinion of the convention when he said that to secure private rights against majority factions, and at the same time to preserve the spirit and form of popular government, was the great object to which their inquiries had been directed.[9]

They were anxious above everything else to safeguard the rights of private property against any leveling tendencies on the part of the propertyless masses. Gouverneur Morris, in speaking on the problem of apportioning representatives, correctly stated the sound historical fact when he declared: "Life and liberty were generally said to be of more value than property. An accurate view of the matter would, nevertheless, prove that property was the main object of society. . . . If property, then, was the main object of government, certainly it ought to be one measure of the influence due to those who were to be affected by

[8] *Ibid.*, vol. v, p. 138.
[9] *The Federalist,* No. 10.

the government." [1] Mr. King also agreed that "property was the primary object of society";[2] and Mr. Madison warned the convention that in framing a system which they wished to last for ages they must not lose sight of the changes which the ages would produce in the forms and distribution of property. In advocating a long term in order to give independence and firmness to the Senate, he described these impending changes: "An increase of population will of necessity increase the proportion of those who will labor under all the hardships of life and secretly sigh for a more equal distribution of its blessings. These may in time outnumber those who are placed above the feelings of indigence. According to the equal laws of suffrage, the power will slide into the hands of the former. No agrarian attempts have yet been made in this country, but symptoms of a levelling spirit, as we have understood have sufficiently appeared, in a certain quarter, to give notice of the future danger." [3] And again, in support of the argument for a property qualification on voters, Madison urged: "In future times, a great majority of the people will not only be without landed, but any other sort of property. These will either combine, under the influence of their common situation,—in which case the rights of property and the public liberty will not be secure in their hands, —or, what is more probable, they will become the tools of opulence and ambition; in which case there will be equal danger on another side." [4] Various projects for setting up class rule by the establishment of property qualifications for voters and officers were advanced in the convention, but they were defeated. . . .

The absence of such property qualifications is certainly not due to any belief in Jefferson's free-and-equal doctrine. It is due rather to the fact that the members of the convention could not agree on the nature and amount of the qualifications. Naturally a landed qualification was suggested, but for obvious reasons it was rejected. Although it was satisfactory to the landed gentry of the South, it

[1] Elliot's *Debates,* vol. v, p. 279.

[2] *Ibid.,* vol. v, p. 280.

[3] *Ibid.,* vol. v, p. 243.

[4] Elliot's *Debates,* vol. v, p. 387.

did not suit the financial, commercial, and manufacturing gentry of the North. If it was high, the latter would be excluded; if it was low it would let in the populistic farmers who had already made so much trouble in the state legislatures with paper-money schemes and other devices for "relieving agriculture." One of the chief reasons for calling the convention and framing the Constitution was to promote commerce and industry and to protect personal property against the "depredations" of Jefferson's noble freeholders. On the other hand a personal-property qualification, high enough to please merchant princes like Robert Morris and Nathaniel Gorham would shut out the Southern planters. Again, an alternative of land or personal property, high enough to afford safeguards to large interests, would doubtless bring about the rejection of the whole Constitution by the trouble-making farmers who had to pass upon the question of ratification.[5] . . .

Nevertheless, by the system of checks and balances placed in the government, the convention safeguarded the interests of property against attacks by majorities. The House of Representatives, Mr. Hamilton pointed out, "was so formed as to render it particularly the guardian of the poorer orders of citizens," [6] while the Senate was to preserve the rights of property and the interests of the minority against the demands of the majority.[7] In the tenth number of *The Federalist*, Mr. Madison argued in a philosophic vein in support of the proposition that it was necessary to base the political system on the actual conditions of "natural inequality." Uniformity of interests throughout the state, he contended, was impossible on account of the diversity in the faculties of men, from which the rights of property originated; the protection of these faculties was the first object of government; from the protection of different and unequal faculties of acquiring property the possession of different degrees and kinds of

[5] COMPILER'S NOTE: This single paragraph from "Whom Does Congress Represent?" *Harper's Magazine*, Jan., 1930, pp. 144–152, has been inserted here because of its value in amplifying the passages from *The Supreme Court and the Constitution*. Reprinting from this article by Beard has been done with the permission of *Harper's Magazine*.

[6] Elliot's *Debates*, vol. v, p. 244.

[7] *Ibid.*, vol. v, p. 203.

property immediately resulted; from the influence of these on the sentiments and views of the respective proprietors ensued a division of society into different interests and parties; the unequal distribution of wealth inevitably led to a clash of interests in which the majority was liable to carry out its policies at the expense of the minority; hence, he added, in concluding this splendid piece of logic, "the majority, having such coexistent passion or interest, must be rendered by their number and local situation unable to concert and carry into effect schemes of oppression"; and in his opinion it was the great merit of the newly framed Constitution that it secured the rights of the minority against "the superior force of an interested and overbearing majority."

This very system of checks and balances, which is undeniably the essential element of the Constitution, is built upon the doctrine that the popular branch of the government cannot be allowed full sway, and least of all in the enactment of laws touching the rights of property. The exclusion of the direct popular vote in the election of the President; the creation, again by indirect election, of a Senate which the framers hoped would represent the wealth and conservative interests of the country;[8] and the establishment of an independent judiciary appointed by the President with the concurrence of the Senate—all these devices bear witness to the fact that the underlying purpose of the Constitution was not the establishment of popular government by means of parliamentary majorities.

Page after page of *The Federalist* is directed to that portion of the electorate which was disgusted with the "mutability of the public councils." Writing on the Presidential veto Hamilton says: "The propensity of the legislative department to intrude upon the rights, and absorb the powers, of the other departments has already been suggested and repeated . . . It may perhaps be said that the power of preventing bad laws included the power of preventing good ones; and may be used to the one purpose as well as the other. But this objection will have little

[8] COMPILER'S NOTE: Popular election of Senators was achieved in 1913 through the XVIIth Amendment to the Constitution.

weight with those who can properly estimate the mischiefs of that inconstancy and mutability in the laws which form the greatest blemish in the character and genius of our governments. They will consider every institution calculated to restrain the excess of law-making and to keep things in the same state in which they happen to be at any given period, as more likely to do good than harm; because it is favorable to greater stability in the system of legislation. The injury which may be possibly done by defeating a few good laws will be amply compensated by the advantage of preventing a number of bad ones."

When the framers of the Constitution had completed the remarkable instrument which was to establish a national government capable of discharging effectively certain great functions and checking the propensities of popular legislatures to attack the rights of private property, a formidable task remained before them—the task of securing the adoption of the new frame of government by states torn with popular dissensions. They knew very well that the state legislatures which had been so negligent in paying their quotas [of money] under the Articles [of Confederation] and which had been so jealous of their rights, would probably stick at ratifying such a national instrument of government. Accordingly they cast aside that clause in the Articles requiring amendments to be ratified by the legislatures of all the states; and advised that the new Constitution should be ratified by conventions in the several states composed of delegates chosen by the voters.[9] They furthermore declared—and this is a fundamental matter—that when the conventions of nine states had ratified the Constitution the new government should go into effect so far as those states were concerned. The chief reason for resorting to ratifications by conventions is laid down by Hamilton in the twenty-second number of *The Federalist:* "It has not a little contributed to the infirmities of the existing federal system that it never had a ratification by the people. Resting on no better foundation than the con-

[9] COMPILER'S NOTE: The original text, p. 75, comments: "It was largely because the framers of the Constitution knew the temper and class bias of the state legislatures that they arranged that the new Constitution should be ratified by conventions."

sent of the several legislatures, it has been exposed to frequent and intricate questions concerning the validity of its powers; and has in some instances given birth to the enormous doctrine of a right of legislative repeal. Owing its ratification to the law of a state, it has been contended that the same authority might repeal the law by which it was ratified. However gross a heresy it may be to maintain that a party to a compact has a right to revoke that compact, the doctrine itself has respectable advocates. The possibility of a question of this nature proves the necessity of laying the foundations of our national government deeper than in the mere sanction of delegated authority. The fabric of American empire ought to rest on the solid basis of the consent of the people. The streams of national power ought to flow immediately from that pure original fountain of all legitimate authority."

Of course, the convention did not resort to the revolutionary policy of transmitting the Constitution directly to the conventions of the several states. It merely laid the finished instrument before the Confederate Congress with the suggestion that it should be submitted to "a convention of delegates chosen in each state by the people thereof, under the recommendation of its legislature, for their assent and ratification; and each convention assenting thereto and ratifying the same should give notice thereof to the United States in Congress assembled." The convention went on to suggest that when nine states had ratified the Constitution, the Confederate Congress should extinguish itself by making provision for the elections necessary to put the new government into effect. . . .

After the new Constitution was published and transmitted to the states, there began a long and bitter fight over ratification. A veritable flood of pamphlet literature descended upon the country, and a collection of these pamphlets by Hamilton, Madison, and Jay, brought together under the title of *The Federalist*—though clearly a piece of campaign literature—has remained a permanent part of the contemporary sources on the Constitution and has been regarded by many lawyers as a commentary second in value only to the decisions of the Supreme Court. Within a year the champions of the new government found themselves victorious, for on June 21, 1788, the ninth state, New Hampshire, ratified the Constitution, and accordingly the new government might go into effect as between the agreeing states. Within a few weeks, the nationalist party in Virginia and New York succeeded in winning these two states, and in spite of the fact that North Carolina and Rhode Island had not yet ratified the Constitution, Congress determined to put the instrument into effect in accordance with the recommendations of the convention. Elections for the new government were held; the date March 4, 1789, was fixed for the formal establishment of the new system; Congress secured a quorum on April 6; and on April 30 Washington was inaugurated at the Federal Hall in Wall Street, New York.

CHAPTER XI

THE ADOPTION OF THE CONSTITUTION [1]

THE NEW CONSTITUTION was ratified by conventions of delegates chosen at the polls; but it should be remembered that, under the property qualifications then imposed upon the suffrage, a large portion of the adult males were debarred from participating in the elections. Generally speaking, the propertyless, who were disgruntled with the handiwork of the Philadelphia conference, could do nothing but gnash their teeth.

Among those who led in the ratification of the new Constitution everywhere were men of substantial property interests who had suffered most from the enterprises of the state legislatures. The supporters of the new instrument in the states included in their ranks the leaders in every economic activity: merchants, traders, shippers, land dealers, lawyers, capitalists, financiers, and professional men. This fact is conclusively demonstrated by Dr. Libby's study[2] of the ratification of the Constitution and it is illustrated by the following letters and papers written by keen observers during the period of the struggle over the adoption of the new system of government.

[1] From *The Supreme Court and the Constitution*, Macmillan (1912).

[2] *Geographical Distribution of the Vote of the Thirteen States on the Federal Constitution*, Wisconsin University Publications (1897).

WILLIAM GRAYSON TO JAMES MONROE.
New York, May 29, 1787.

The delegates [to the Philadelphia convention] from the Eastward are for a very strong government, and wish to prostrate all the state legislatures, and form a general system out of the whole; but I don't learn that the people are with them, on the contrary in Massachusetts they think that government too strong and are about rebelling again, for the purpose of making it more democratical: In Connecticut they have rejected the requisition for the present year decidedly, and no man there would be elected to the office of a constable if he was to declare that he meant to pay a copper towards the domestic debt:—Rhode Island has refused to send members—the cry there is for a good government after they have paid their debts in depreciated paper:—first demolish the Philistines, *i.e.* their creditors, and then for *propriety*.

New Hampshire has not paid a shilling, since peace, and does not ever mean to pay one to all eternity:—if it was attempted to tax the people for the domestic debt 500 Shays would arise in a fortnight.—In New York they pay well because they do it by plundering New Jersey and Connecticut.—Jersey will go great lengths from motives of revenge and Interest: Pennsylvania will join provided you let the sessions of the Executive of America be fixed in Philadelphia and give her other advantages in trade to compensate for the loss of state power. I shall make no observations on the southern states, but I think they will be, perhaps from different motives, as little disposed to part with efficient power as any in the Union.[3]

D. HUMPHREYS TO GEORGE WASHINGTON.
New Haven, Sept. 28, 1787.

All the different classes in the liberal professions will be in favour of the proposed Constitution. The clergy, lawyers, physicians and merchants will have considerable influence on society. Nor will the officers of the late army be backward in expressing their approbation. Indeed the well affected have not been wanting in efforts to prepare the minds of the citizens for the favorable reception of what-

[3] *Documentary History of the Constitution,* vol. i. pp. 170–1.

ever might be the result of your proceedings. I have had no inconsiderable agency in the superintendence of two presses, from which more newspapers are circulated, I imagine, than from any others in New England. Judicious and well-timed publications have great efficacy in ripening the judgment of men in this quarter of the continent.[4]

CONJECTURES ABOUT THE NEW CONSTITUTION
BY HAMILTON, AUTUMN, 1787.

The new Constitution has in favor of its success these circumstances—a very great weight of influence of the persons who framed it, particularly in the universal popularity of General Washington—the good will of the commercial interest throughout the states which will give all its efforts to the establishment of a government capable of regulating, protecting and extending the commerce of the Union—the good will of most men of property in the several states who wish a government of the union able to protect them against domestic violence and the depredations which the democratic spirit is apt to make on property;—and who are besides anxious for the respectability of the nation—a strong belief in the people at large of the insufficiency of the present confederation to preserve the existence of the union and of the necessity of the union to their safety and prosperity; of course a strong desire of a change and a predisposition to receive well the propositions of the convention.

Against the success is to be put the influence of many *inconsiderable* men in possession of considerable offices under the state governments who will fear a diminution of their consequence, power and emolument by the establishment of the general government and who can hope for nothing there—the influence of some *considerable* men in office possessed of talents and popularity who partly from the same motives and partly from a desire of *playing a part* in a convulsion for their own aggrandisement will oppose the quiet adoption of the new government—(some considerable men out of office, from motives of ambition may be disposed to act the same part)—add to these causes the democratical jealousy of the people which may be alarmed at the appearance of institutions that may seem

[4] *Documentary History of the Constitution*, vol. i, p. 302.

calculated to place the power of the community in few hands and to raise a few individuals to stations of great preëminence—and the influence of some foreign powers who from different motives will not wish to see an energetic government established throughout the states.[5]

JAMES MADISON TO THOMAS JEFFERSON. DEC. 9, 1787.

It is worthy of remark that whilst in Virginia and some of the other states in the middle and southern districts of the Union, the men of intelligence, patriotism, property, and independent circumstances, are thus divided; all of this description, with a few exceptions, in the eastern states, and most of the middle states, are zealously attached to the proposed Constitution. In New England, the men of letters, the principal officers of Govt., the judges and lawyers, the clergy, and men of property, furnish only here and there an adversary. It is not less worthy of remark that in Virginia where the mass of the people have been so much accustomed to be guided by their rulers on all new and intricate questions, they should on the present which certainly surpasses the judgment of the greater part of them, not only go before, but contrary to, their most popular leaders. And the phenomenon is the more wonderful, as a popular ground is taken by all the adversaries to the new Constitution. Perhaps the solution in both these cases, would not be very difficult; but it would lead to observations too diffusive; and to you unnecessary. I will barely observe that the case in Virga. seems to prove that the body of sober and steady people, even of the lower order, are tired of the vicissitudes, injustice and follies which have so much characterized public measures, and are impatient for some change which promises stability and repose.[6]

H. KNOX TO GEN. WASHINGTON. NEW YORK, JAN. 14, 1788.

Colonel Wadsworth writes me that the present Governor and Lieutenant Governor, the late Governor, the judges of the Supreme Court and the Council were of the convention and all for the constitution excepting Jas. Wadsworth.

[5] *Documentary History of the Constitution*, vol. i, pp. 288–9.
[6] *Documentary History of the Constitution*, vol. i, p. 398.

The Massachusetts convention were to meet on the 9th. The decision of Connecticut will influence in a degree their determination and I have no doubt that the Constitution will be adopted in Massachusetts.—But it is at this moment questionable whether it will be by a large majority.

There are three parties existing in that state at present, differing in their numbers and greatly differing in their wealth and talents.

The 1st is the commercial part, of the state to which are added, all the men of considerable property, the clergy, the lawyers—including all the judges of all the courts, and all the officers of the late army, and also the neighbourhood of all the great towns—its numbers may include 3/7ths of the state. This party are for the most vigorous government, perhaps many of them would have been still more pleased with the new Constitution had it been more analogous to the British Constitution.

The 2d party, are the eastern part of the state lying beyond New Hampshire formerly the Province of Main— This party are chiefly looking towards the erection of a new state, and the majority of them will adopt or reject the new Constitution as it may facilitate or retard their designs, without regarding the merits of the great question— this party 2/7ths.

The 3d party are the Insurgents, or their favorers, the great majority of whom are for an annihilation of debts, public and private, and therefore they will not approve the new Constitution—this party 2/7ths.

If the 1st and 2d party agree as will be most probable, and also some of the party stated as in the insurgent interest, the Constitution will be adopted by a great majority notwithstanding all the exertions to the contrary.[7]

IN LETTERS WRITTEN BY RUFUS KING TO MADISON DATED IN JANUARY, 1788, HE SAID:

Our convention [in Massachusetts] proceeds slowly; and apprehension that the liberties of the people are in danger, and a distrust of men of property or education have a more powerful effect upon the minds of our opponents than any specific objections against the Constitution. . . . The friends of the Constitution, who in addition to their own

[7] *Documentary History of the Constitution*, vol. i, p. 442.

weight are respectable as they represent a very large proportion of the good sense and property of this state, have
the task not only of answering, but also of stating and
bringing forward the objections of their opponents. The opposition complains that the lawyers, judges, clergymen,
merchants and men of education are all in favor of the
Constitution—and that for that reason they appear to be
able to make the worse appear the better cause. But say
they, if we had men of this description on our side, we
should alarm the people with the imperfections of the Constitution and be able to refute the defence set up in its
favor. Notwithstanding the superiority of talent in favor of
the Constitution, yet the same infatuation which prevailed
not many months since in several counties of this state, and
which emboldened them to take arms against the government, seems to have an uncontrollable authority over a
numerous part of the convention. These objections are not
directed against any part of the Constitution, but their opposition seems to arise from an opinion that is immovable,
that some injury is plotted against them—that the system
is the production of the rich and ambitious, that they discover its operations and that the consequence will be the
establishment of two orders in the Society, one comprehending the opulent and great, the other the poor and il-
literate. The extraordinary Union in favor of the Constitution in this state of the wealthy and sensible part of it, is in
confirmation of these opinions and every exertion hitherto
made to eradicate it, has been in vain.[8]

JABEZ BOWEN TO GEORGE WASHINGTON.

Providence, Dec. 15, 1789.

The towns of Newport, Providence, Bristol, etc., with
the whole mercantile interest in the other towns in the
state are federal, while the farmers in general are against
it. Their opposition arises principally from their being much
in debt, from the insinuations of wicked and designing men,
that they will lose their liberty by adopting it; that the
salaries of the national officers are so verry high that it will
take the whole of the money collected by the impost to
pay them, that the intrest and principal of the general debt
must be raised by dry taxation on real estates, etc. We have

[8] Rufus King, *Life and Letters,* vol. i, pp. 314, 316.

exerted our utmost abilities to convince them of the errors that they have imbibed by hearing to the *old Tories* and *desperate debtors,* but all in vain, what further, sir, is to be done? if we knew what our duty was, we are willing to do it, tho' I have no idea that the Antis will or can be induced to come in without the arm of power is exerted and that they shall be taught that the principles that they hould and Disseminate among the citizens of the neighboring states as well as this is inconsistent, and not proper to be professed by any person or persons that live on the territories of the United States: their wish is to overturn the whole Federal Government rather than this state should submit to it. If we fail in getting a convention at the next meeting of the general assembly, will Congress *protect* us if we separate from the State Government and appoint us officers to col-lect the revenue; if this should be thought well of and should be put in practice but in part I have no doubt but it will bring the country part of the community to their senses soon—and that one town and another will be a dropping off so that the opposition will be done away. Be pleased, sir, to give me an answer to this proposition as soon as convenient.[9]

*   *   *

On reading these papers by representative and thoughtful men of the period, it is difficult to escape the conclusion that the Constitution was looked upon as a bulwark against populism of every form. Surely men of the type here quoted as in support of the new instrument of government must have rejoiced in the knowledge (spread abroad by *The Federalist*) that an independent judiciary was to guard the personal and property rights of minorities against all legislatures, state and national.

Indeed, it would seem to be a work of supererogation to argue such a proposition, were it not for the misleading notions about the American political system which are all too current. Every serious student of the history of our public law and policy has known that the defense of the rights of minorities against majorities is one of the funda-mental purposes of our system of government. "I have

[9] *Documentary History of the Constitution,* vol. ii, p. 226.

thought," said Mr. Choate in his moving argument in the Income Tax Cases before the Supreme Court, "that one of the fundamental objects of all civilized government was the preservation of the rights of private property. I have thought that it was the very keystone of the arch upon which all civilized government rests, and that this once abandoned, everything was at stake and danger. . . . If it be true, as my friend said in closing, that the passions of the people are aroused on this subject, if it be true that a mighty army of sixty millions is likely to be incensed by this decision, it is the more vital to the future welfare of this country that this court again resolutely and courageously declare, as Marshall did, that it has the power to set aside an act of Congress violative of the Constitution, and that it will not hesitate in executing that power, no matter what the threatened consequences of popular or populistic wrath may be."

CHAPTER XII

NATURE OF POLITICAL PARTIES [1]

[COMPILER'S NOTE: Shortly after the new government created in conformity with the Constitution began to function, there arose differences of opinion as to what it should do. Those having strong convictions on the subject helped to form national political parties. It is to this partisan period of American history that attention is now devoted.]

ORIGIN OF PARTIES

Why do political parties arise? The question is hard to answer. Certainly the solutions of the problem offered by writers on the subject are vague and contradictory.

According to one view, politics is merely a great game or sport, an endless contest between the ins and outs, full of sound and fury, springing from no substantial interests, affecting in no vital way the state of the people. Citizens divide into political parties for reasons no more important than those which separate them into partisans of Gene Tunney or Jack Dempsey. Politics is all a question of finding slogans that will capture the crowd or discovering candidates that will awaken enthusiasm. "If the Republicans can find the proper candidate," remarked Dr. George B. Cutten, President of Colgate University, in the Sunday *Times* of May 13, 1928, "almost any kind of a slogan will do; if the Democrats can find the proper slogan almost any kind of a candidate will do."

[1] From Chapter I of *The American Party Battle,* Macmillan (1928).

Another explanation of party origins is to be found in the writings of the English historian, Lord Macaulay. According to his interpretation men (and presumably women) divide *naturally* into two groups—one devoted to order, conservative in disposition, and the other devoted to progress, adventurous in character. In short, the problem is one in psychology.

A similar answer to the riddle was made a few years ago by a distinguished professor of literature, Brander Matthews. Americans, he declared, divide *instinctively* into Hamiltonians and Jeffersonians. "The Hamiltonian," he said, "believes in government by the best, by the selected leaders, competent to guide the less competent mass; and this is true aristocracy in the best sense of that abused word. The Jeffersonian believes that the average man, however unenlightened, actually knows his own business, or at least knows what he wants, better than any superior person can know it for him; and this is true democracy in the best sense of that abused term. These two attitudes are inevitably antagonistic; they are instinctive, intuitive, innate." [2]

Of course this is like saying: "God made Democrats and Republicans, and that is all there is to it." When anyone states that human actions spring from innate, inherent, intuitive sources, he denies the force of environment and with a final air disposes of such little questions as: "Why are they innate? How do you know that they are innate? Where is the proof?"

Furthermore, a detailed study of political parties, always disconcerting to the makers of simple hypotheses, reveals some data not easily disposed of by the literary theory of politics. Parties in Europe do not divide into two sections: conservative and progressive, Hamiltonian and Jeffersonian. There we find labor parties, agrarian parties, clerical parties, industrialist parties, Hungarian, German, Polish, and what-not parties. A study of the early distribution of party membership in the United States shows that the major portion of the Hamiltonian party had its center of influence in the cities and towns where financial, industrial, and commercial interests were predominant. Hamilton was a New York lawyer. Leadership in the Jeffersonian party came

[2] *New York Times Magazine,* September 24, 1916.

from the slave-owning planters of the South. Jefferson was a Southern planter.

How did it happen that most of the businessmen of the country were instinctive Hamiltonians, intuitive "aristocrats," and most of the aristocratic planters of the South became instinctive Jeffersonians, intuitive "democrats"? The matter is not as simple as Brander Matthews imagined.

On about the same footing may be placed the explanation of party divisions offered by James Bryce in his great work, *The American Commonwealth*. According to his view, the history of American parties began about 1787 when two opposing tendencies were "revealed"—one in favor of strengthening the central government and the other in favor of upholding the "sovereign" rights of the states. Broadly speaking, one party has advocated an extensive use of federal powers and the other has opposed that operation. Perhaps this may be called the orthodox theory of American party differences.

To this interpretation two objections can be made. The first is that neither party has been consistent in upholding its creed—particularly whenever its vital interests have been affected. For example, the Jeffersonians used federal powers to the limit in purchasing Louisiana, in putting an embargo on commerce, and in enacting the fugitive slave law of 1850 for the return of runaway property. On the other hand, the Hamiltonians, who stretched federal powers in establishing a bank and making protective tariffs, became advocates of states' rights when they opposed the purchase of Louisiana and resisted the enforcement of the embargo.[3]

The second objection to the Bryce theory is that it explains nothing. Why did some of the American people think that the federal government should be strong and others give their affection to the states—that is, when upon occasion it suited their pleasure to do so? Did this division have a direct relation to the occupations and interests of the people? Was it not geared up to pre-existing differences in work and economy? As the theory stands, it merely offers another illustrative "innate" clue to the origin of parties.

More realistic and therefore more illuminating is the key

[3] For further comment see below, p. 234.

to party differences given in the tenth number of *The Federalist* by James Madison, the "Father of the federal Constitution" and twice President of the United States. "The most common and durable source of factions [that is, in eighteenth century language, parties]," Madison said, "has been the various and unequal distribution of property. Those who hold and those who are without property have ever formed distinct interests in society. Those who are creditors and those who are debtors fall under a like distinction. A landed interest, a manufacturing interest, a mercantile interest, with many lesser interests grow up of necessity in civilized nations and divide them into different classes actuated by different sentiments and views. The regulation of these various and interfering interests forms the principal task of modern legislation and involves the spirit of party and faction in the necessary and ordinary operations of government."

In other words, the division of voters into parties according to their political sentiments and views springs from the possession of different kinds and amounts of property. Illustrations of this theory may be readily recalled by those familiar with the role of the farmer vote, the labor vote, and the business vote in American politics.

Though realistic, this theory must not be taken too narrowly. We are in great danger of being misled by such words as capitalists, farmers, and laborers. Capitalists, that is, people engaged in using money to make money, are certainly not all occupied in identical processes. Some are manufacturers of commodities which come into sharp competition with European products and favor high protective tariffs on their particular goods. Others are engaged in producing commodities not subject to competition and may be stanch free traders.

Again, capitalists interested in railways may be utterly indifferent to protective tariffs because it matters little to them whether they haul domestic or foreign freight.

A third group of capitalists are merchants who import many of the commodities they offer for sale and may look with pleasure upon low tariffs promising cheaper prices and larger turnovers.

Finally, there are the financiers, the bankers, who lend money to industries and governments, foreign and domestic, apparently without patriotic preference, considering the terms and security of their loans more important than national advantages. They may be indifferent as to the schedules in tariff bills; or they may approve low rates on imports which facilitate the payment of interest and charges on loans floated abroad. Indeed there is apparent now a rift between the bankers and manufacturers of the United States with respect to tariff policies.

Hence we may conclude that bankers, railway investors, and importing merchants, all capitalists, might readily line up with Democratic cotton growers of the South in support of a low-tariff campaign, assuming that the latter did not propose other radical measures calculated to alarm their allies.

Nor is the case much different with regard to the "agricultural interest." It too is divided into special interests. The cotton growers of the South produce a staple which is sold largely in foreign markets and they are subjected to little competition as yet from cotton raisers in other countries. Consequently they need no protection on their commodity and naturally favor a low tariff on the manufactured goods which they consume. On the other hand, the raisers of wheat, corn, livestock, and fruits have many formidable competitors and are generally found in the protective-tariff lobbies when their particular commodities are under consideration. All this is made so clear by A. N. Holcombe in his book on *The Political Parties of To-day* that comment is superfluous. One of the difficult tasks of political managers is to work out the proper combination that will unite the major portion of the farmers under one political roof.

Not a whit more solid is the much vaunted "solidarity of labor." Busily concerned with the question of wages, trade unionists cannot be entirely oblivious to the conditions which determine wages. Those who labor in mills heavily protected against foreign competition may easily allow their practical interests (supposed, at least) to outweigh their opposition to capitalists and vote with their employers. Again, one industry may be very prosperous while others are in a state of depression. Miners may be starving while railway conductors and engineers are living well and making large deposits in their union banks.

It is also necessary to emphasize the "various and unequal distribution of property" mentioned by Madison. There are big and little capitalists, big and little farmers. Some are prosperous for one reason or another. Others are struggling along near the margin of subsistence or are heavily in debt. Hence the capitalistic and agricultural interests are crisscrossed by intricate lines due to "the various and unequal distribution of property." It takes a great deal of research and discernment to find the roots of "different sentiments and views" in any particular political situation, especially as it is hard to get all the pertinent data in the case.

Additional difficulties in applying Madison's theory arise from the fact that two persons in the same economic situation and cherishing the same "sentiments" may differ as to the best plan of action to advance their interests. Their motive may be purely economic and their prejudices identical, but their reasoning divergent. For example, two capitalists confronted by a menacing labor agitation may utterly disagree as to the best method for dealing with it. One may favor calling in the police and the other urge the expediency of conciliatory tactics.

Presumably most of the directing classes know what their interests are, at least in detail; but they often make wrong guesses as to policies calculated to bring advantages to them in the long run. Moreover, as society becomes more complicated, the difficulties of figuring up the exact results likely to flow from particular types of action increase. It is at this point that intelligence and information enter into policy-determining operations. If two people of the same economic class, seeking the same economic advantage, disagree on methods, evidently in this case the theory of economic interpretation breaks down; that is, it does not explain the divergence in political view. Even the dictatorship of the proletariat in Russia is marked by bitter dissensions over policy. Still, though it does not by any means exhaust the science of the subject, economics is a fundamental branch of politics and offers the most satisfactory clue to the origin and development of political parties.

Economics also runs into political situations which wear racial aspects. It is a matter of common observation, for example, that Irish-Americans are generally Democrats. A great deal of light can be thrown on this fact by economic history. In the beginning, the Irish who migrated to America were extremely poor in this world's goods and settled in the cities as laborers. For a generation or two most of them were hewers of wood and drawers of water—until other races from southern and southeastern Europe came to take their places and enabled them to move up in the industrial scale. As laborers, the Irish were generally drawn into the party of the masses and lined up against the classes. On the other hand, when German migration set in heavily the federal government was giving away land in the West and thousands of Germans owed their farms to the bounty of the Republicans. This debt they did not forget.

To some degree religious sentiments are connected with economic situations. Catholic writers are fond of saying that the Protestant revolt against the Roman Church sprang from a lust of the rising middle class for the property of the clergy. Undoubtedly this was a factor in a momentous religious change. Its importance is now demonstrated in many scientific works. To use another illustration, the prevalence of Democratic party views among Catholics may be, to a considerable extent, attributed to the fact that a large proportion of the Catholics are of immigrant stock and are to be found in or close to the laboring ranks of American industrial society.

It is almost safe to say that, where diverse economic interests divide groups, common religious sentiments will not completely weld them. In other words, religious ties are not often strong enough to bind opposing economic interests into the same party. Protestant churches were divided in America over slavery, the Southern branches sustaining their "peculiar institution." Methodists and Baptists split over tariff schedules, the regulation of railway rates, farm relief, and other economic questions.

Confusion with respect to the roots of party differences is darkened by the very nature of party organization. It often happens that an institution, established for a clear and definite object, continues after its end has been attained. Herbert Spencer tells an amusing story of a society founded in England for the purpose of carrying on an

agitation for a particular reform. It had its president, sec-
retaries, agents, paid workers, and petty officers. After a
long season of agitation, Parliament finally adopted the
reform. Shortly after the triumph, Spencer called at the
organization headquarters, expecting to find great rejoicing.
Instead he found universal sorrow. The achievement of the
purposes of the society had abolished all the lucrative jobs
which it maintained. So in politics.

A political party has offices and positions yielding gains
and profits. When in possession of the government it dis-
tributes honors, privileges, favors, and emoluments of one
kind or another. The spoils of office alone are sufficient to
sustain a large party. Once in power and enjoying its advantages, professional politicians are loath to lose what they
have gained. Out of power, they hesitate to espouse any
ideas that will defeat their efforts to capture the government. Hence on both sides regular party workers often
prefer to avoid rather than to define issues, especially when
there is risk in definition. . . .

THE ROOTS AND SOURCES OF PARTY STRENGTH

Why is it that party organization has become so minute
in its ramifications and so powerful in the United States?
To answer that question adequately, one would have to ex-
plore the structure of American society; but some of the
more obvious reasons are agreed upon and may be enumerated here.

In the first place, the large number of elective offices
makes it impossible for the mass of the people to take an
active part in nominating candidates and running the political machinery. Wherever elective officers are provided for,
machinery for making nominations inevitably follows. . . .
Party business of necessity falls into the hands of professional workers experienced in the art of managing
primaries and elections.

Even the very structure of our federal system makes
party government and strong party organization indispensable if the will of the voters is to be realized. The legislative powers are divided between Congress and the states, so
that if a party has a policy which requires federal and state

action it must be in power in both governments. . . . If a party, therefore, has a systematic and national policy covering the important questions of our day relative to railways, insurance, conservation . . . it should be strong enough to control state and national legislatures.

The legal separation of executive and legislative powers serves to strengthen the political party; for democracy or majority rule, as now understood, requires the co-ordination of those two branches of government, and the political party is employed to bring them into harmony with each other. . . .

Passing outward from the structure of government, which in itself makes for strong party organization, we encounter the "spoils system" as a contributing factor. To some extent, of course, civil service reform has reduced the relative number of offices to be filled by party adherents, but there still remains an enormous number of federal and state positions to be divided among the victors. The political appointments subject to the President's orders have an annual value of millions. The multiplication of the functions of state administration has enlarged the appointing power of the governor and the state senate. Every state legislature has within its gift legislative offices and positions available for partisan purposes, usually free from civil service control. For example, there are sergeants-at-arms and assistant sergeants-at-arms, principal doorkeepers, first and second assistant doorkeepers, journal clerks, executive clerks, index clerks, revision clerks, librarians, messengers, postmasters, janitors, stenographers, and mesengers to the various committees and assistants first and second, too numerous to mention. Then there are city offices, high and low, steadily multiplying in number, and, in spite of the civil service restrictions, within the gift of the political party that wins at the polls. Finally there are the election officers, a veritable army of inspectors, ballot clerks, and poll clerks for the primary and regular elections, who derive anywhere from ten dollars to fifty dollars a year for their services. Every large city annually pays thousands of dollars to the officials who preside at primaries and elections.

Party machines are strengthened by huge levies on the candidates. Generally speaking, no one can hope to be elected to office today without being nominated by one of the political parties. The party organization wages the campaign which carries the candidate into office. What is more natural and just than the demand that the candidate shall help to pay the legitimate expenses of the campaign? It is a regular practice, therefore, for party organizations, state and local, to collect tribute from candidates for nomination as well as nominees to office—as a rule in proportion to the value of the office they seek. There are, in addition, levies on officeholders after election, sometimes in spite of the laws forbidding them. Officeholders do not always wait to be pressed by party managers in this matter. It is not expedient.

The construction of parks, school buildings, highways, and other public works yields revenues to the party organization which controls the letting of contracts. High bids may be accepted on the condition that the surplus shall go to the party war chest or to the party leaders. The capitol building and grounds at Albany cost New York nearly $25,000,000, and the plunder of the public treasury in the construction of the capitol at Harrisburg is a notorious chapter in Pennsylvania history.

Even more important, as an economic factor, than the spoils of office are the large funds secured by party organizations from private interests and distributed by their officers and workers.[4] Perhaps the most fruitful source of revenue for party treasuries during recent years has been contributions from business corporations—even though prohibited by law in many states. They must all apply to the government—national, state, or municipal—for the right to come into existence in the first place, and for the right to extend their operations in the second place. They are subject to constant regulation by municipal councils, state legislatures, or Congress (possibly by all three agencies); they are compelled to do things which cost them large sums of money or abstain from doing things which are highly profitable. In these circumstances, corporations often find it cheap to pay party "bosses" for favors and immunities. With a kindred concern for practical ends, industrial concerns which thrive under protective tariffs often "insure themselves against free trade" by contributing gen-

[4] J. K. Pollock, *Party Campaign Funds.*

erously to party war chests. Far more elusive is the collection of party revenues in return for the protection of gambling, liquor selling, and vice in various forms. The extent to which this source of funds is exploited at any time by any party is, of course, impossible to ascertain; but authentic documents show that in the not distant past huge sums for party war chests have come from the government protection of those who violate its laws.

Sometimes the private interests affected by governmental action give money to parties to secure favors or prevent regulations really designed in the public interest. Sometimes they are forced to contribute, "blackmailed," by party leaders under threats of punitive legislation if they do not. On many occasions, they have given money to both the leading parties with a view to getting a "friend at court" without fail. . . .

Like a church or any other society, the political party may be used as a social club through which a young man or woman may make valuable acquaintances and secure business, clients, or patients as the case may be. The social power of the party organization enables it to intrench itself by drawing into its ranks the best energies and talents of young people who, though by no means devoid of idealistic motives, cannot be blind to the stern necessities of the struggle for existence. In some cities, it is well for the young lawyer practicing in certain courts to be known as a prominent worker in the party to which the presiding judges belong. A Democratic doctor in a strongly Republican district of a Northern city would doubtless find his rise in the world somewhat handicapped if he were over-zealous in the support of his party, and a belligerent Republican lawyer in a Southern city might very well find his business limited to practice in the federal courts. The subtle influences of party control are doubtless more powerful than the gross influences which appear upon the surface. . . .

[Also] contributing to party strength is the assistance given to the voters by the [party] machine. Party leaders and workers favor the poor voters by a thousand charitable acts. They give outings, picnics, clambakes, and celebrations for them; they help the unemployed to get work with private corporations or in governmental departments; they pay the rent of sick and unfortunate persons about to be dispossessed; they appear in court for those in trouble, and often a word to the magistrate saves the voter from the workhouse or even worse; they remember the children at Christmas; and, in short, they are the ever watchful charity agents for their respective neighborhoods. A kind word and a little money in time of pressing need often will go further than an eloquent sermon on civic virtue. Thus politics as it operates through party organization is a serious and desperately determined business activity; it works night and day; it is patient; it gets what it can; it never relaxes.

CHAPTER XIII

FEDERALIST-REPUBLICAN
ALIGNMENT [1]

IT IS CUSTOMARY to separate American political history into three periods, using changes in party names as the basis of the division. According to this scheme, there have been three great party alignments since the formation of the Constitution: Federalists against Republicans (1789–1816); Whigs against Democrats (1830–1856); and Republicans against Democrats (1856 to the present time). Although the dates are merely approximate, they furnish useful chronological clues.

But this division is arbitrary and only for convenience. In fact, there has been no sharp break in the sources of party strength, in policy, or in opinion. On the contrary, these three alignments have been merely phases of one unbroken conflict originating in the age of George Washington and continuing without interruption to our own time. . . .

The first of these alignments—Federalists against Republicans—was connected more or less directly with the contest over the framing and adoption of the federal Constitution.[2]

[1] From Chapter II of *The American Party Battle*, Macmillan (1928) with the exception of one passage from *The American Historical Review*, duly noted below.

[2] The roots of party antagonism lie deep in colonial times. In Virginia, there were contests between the upland farmers and the gentlemen planters of the seaboard before the seventeenth century closed. During the stirring prelude to the Revolution against Great Britain, the division between the Patriots and

Authorities are generally agreed that the main support for the Constitution came from merchants, manufacturers, government bondholders, and other people of substantial property interests "along the line of the seaboard towns and populous regions." They are likewise agreed that the opposition came mainly from the inland farmers, from debtors, and from those in less prosperous sections of the country.[3]

[THE FUNDING AND ASSUMPTION OF THE REVOLUTIONARY DEBT]

The feelings aroused by the contest over the Constitution had not disappeared when the first administration was organized in 1789 with Washington as President and friends of the new system installed in all branches of the government—executive, legislative, and judicial. With Alexander Hamilton, first Secretary of the Treasury, in the lead, the advocates of the new order, soon to be known as Federalists, carried through a series of economic measures which in time divided the country into two powerful parties. In summary form, [the first two of] these measures were as follows:

1. *The funding of the national debt.* All the old bonds, certificates, and other evidences of indebtedness issued by the Continental Congress during the Revolution were called in and new bonds for face value given to the holders.

2. *The assumption of the revolutionary debts of the states.* The federal government also called in the revolutionary debts of the states and issued new federal

the Tories was supplemented by sharp divisions among the former. More than once the mechanics of the towns frightened the merchants by radical demands and serious rioting. All through the War of Independence, the revolutionists were split into radical and conservative factions—mechanics and poor farmers against the merchants and possessors of large property. *See* Beard, *Rise of American Civilization,* Vol. I, pp. 266–8.

[3] Beard, *An Economic Interpretation of the Constitution of the United States,* pp. 292–9, and *Economic Origins of Jeffersonian Democracy,* pp. 1–9.

bonds instead; that is, the federal government assumed the obligations of the states and added them to the general debt of the nation.

These two operations, funding and assumption, deeply affected the purses of classes and masses. Before Hamilton began his work, the old bonds and notes issued during the Revolution had been selling at from ten to twenty cents on the dollar, because the national government and several states had failed to meet their obligations. During the dark days of uncertainty, a large part of this paper had been bought by speculators from the original holders at low prices with a view to profit-taking. In the end, funding and assumption increased the value of the depreciated securities to the amount of approximately forty million dollars—a huge sum for those days. To raise the money to pay the interest on the debt, the federal government had to lay heavy taxes on the people, most of whom were farmers, not bond-holders.

[COMPILER'S NOTE: A short passage from an article by Beard [4] has been inserted here for the valuable evidence it offers as to the alignment of economic forces during the vote in Congress on federal refunding and assumption plans. The addition, beginning immediately after this NOTE, runs to the next cross-head—entitled OTHER FEDERALIST MEASURES.]

[Under] the funding system set up by the new government, nearly all holders of old paper brought their securities to the Treasury or to the loan offices of their respective states to be transformed into new certificates of indebtedness. If the Treasury records at Washington were complete (unfortunately they are not) it would be possible to discover the names of all those who funded public securities under the law of August 4, 1790, except perhaps those represented by attorneys.

The incompleteness of the records makes it impossible,

[4] "Some Economic Origins of Jeffersonian Democracy," *The American Historical Review,* Jan. 1914, pp. 282–98, quoted by permission. Beard later broadened the study, offering the results as *Economic Origins of Jeffersonian Democracy,* Macmillan (1915), still in print in 1956.

however, to discover positively what members of Congress did *not* have securities; but the mass of materials which remains enables us to find a large number who did hold public paper at the time of the funding of the debt . . . unless we are to assume that the members of Congress who appear on the ledgers were attorneys for other parties. . . .

The proposition to assume the state debts was taken up in the House of Representatives in February, 1790 . . . and on April 12 the assumption plan was defeated in the House by a vote of thirty-one to twenty-nine. . . . The way in which the "innocent" Jefferson was . . . used to bring about [the ultimate movement of the capital to Washington, D.C., in] exchange . . . for the assumption of state debts, on July 7, has often been told. . . . Jefferson informs us that "two of the Potomac members (White and Lee, but White with a revulsion of stomach almost convulsive) agreed to change their votes and Hamilton undertook to carry the other point." Daniel Carroll, a large property holder in the region where the new capital was to be located, also considerately changed his vote.[5] Thus the bargain whereby the capital was located on the Potomac and the debts of the states were assumed by the federal government was brought to a conclusion at a private dinner given by Jefferson. The funding bill with the assumption amendment was carried in the Senate on July 21. . . . Three days later the motion of Jackson, of Georgia [in the House], to disagree with the Senate amendment, was defeated by a vote of thirty-two to twenty-nine. . . .

Of the fourteen senators who voted in favor of the funding bill, with the assumption amendment, on July 21, 1790, at least ten . . . appear on the Treasury records as holders of public securities at the time of the funding process. To this list Pierce Butler doubtless should be added.

Of the twelve who voted against the funding bill on

[5] COMPILER'S NOTE: Eventually, Beard reports in the same article, Carroll "had the satisfaction of helping to engineer the laying out of the City of Washington in such a manner as to give an immense appreciation to the value of his farm lands in the vicinity."

July 21, 1790, at least five . . . were holders of public debt. . . .

A study of the Treasury records shows that the senators who held securities and voted for the funding bill were, with one or two exceptions, among the large holders of public papers, and that the senators of the same class who voted against the bill (with the possible exception of Johnston of North Carolina) were among the minor holders. . . . Seven of the twelve votes in opposition came from Southern states. Virginia, North Carolina, and Georgia were solid against it. These were the states (particularly Georgia and North Carolina) in which the debt had been so largely bought up by speculators. . . .

The temptation to draw too many conclusions . . . should be resisted. The one conclusion which is indisputable, however, is that almost one-half of the members of the first Congress were security holders. . . . This certainly justifies Jefferson's assertion that had those actually interested in the outcome of the funding process withdrawn from voting on Hamilton's proposals not a single one of them would have been carried. . . .

Finally, . . . an examination of the vote with reference to geographical distribution of the public securities would seem to show beyond question that nearly all of the members, security holders and non-security holders alike, represented the dominant economic interests of their respective constituencies rather than their personal interests. In many instances there was, it is evident, a singular coincidence between public service, as the members conceived it, and private advantage; but the charge of mere corruption must fall to the ground. It was a clear case of a collision of economic interests: fluid capital versus agrarianism. The representation of one interest was as legitimate as the other, and there is no more ground for denouncing the members of Congress who held securities and voted to sustain the public credit than there is for denouncing the slave-owners who voted against the Quaker memorials against slavery on March 23, 1790.[6]

[6] COMPILER'S NOTE: Here ends the passage from *The American Historical Review*.

[OTHER FEDERALIST MEASURES]

3. *Protective Tariff.* The third measure on the Federalist program was the protection of American industries by the imposition of customs duties on imports coming into competition with American products. Hamilton openly favored an elaborate system of protection. Although his plans were not adopted in full, the first revenue bill passed in 1789 was mildly protective and, in time, other protective features were added.

4. *The United States Bank.* Under Hamilton's leadership, Congress chartered a banking corporation, authorized it to raise a large capital composed, three-fourths, of new federal bonds, and empowered it to issue currency and do a general banking business.

5. *A sound national currency.* Under the new Constitution, the states had to stop issuing paper money. The gold and silver coin of the United States now provided by law became the money of the country, with the notes of the United States Bank circulating on a parity.

6. *Discrimination in favor of American shipping.* To encourage the construction of an American merchant marine, Congress provided that the tonnage duties on foreign-built and foreign-owned ships should be five times as high as the duties on American ships. In line with this, other concessions were made to native shipping, especially that engaged in the China trade.

7. *National defense.* In creating a navy and a standing army, Congress had more in mind than the mere defense of the country against foreign foes. The navy was useful in protecting commerce on the high seas and the army in suppressing uprisings such as had occurred in Massachusetts in 1786. In other words, economic factors as well as patriotism were involved in the process.

8. *Foreign affairs.* When the wars of the French Revolution broke out in Europe, the Washington administration, largely inspired by Hamilton, frankly sympathized with England as against France and looked on the contest in the Old World as a conflict between prop-

erty and order on the one side and democracy and anarchy on the other—akin in fact to the political dispute at home.

THE RISE OF OPPOSITION

Now these measures were not excursions in theory. They were acts of power involving the pocketbooks of groups, affecting the distribution of wealth and the weight of classes in politics. Certainly the first six of them bore directly upon the economic interests of the citizens.

Under these laws, large sums of money were paid to the holders of government bonds who had been receiving little or nothing; people who were moderately well off one day found themselves rich the next. Under these laws, stockholders in the United States Bank earned handsome profits on their investment, protected manufacturers entered upon a period of prosperity, and merchants and moneylenders were enabled, by the sound currency system and adequate judicial assistance, to carry on their operations safely in all parts of the country. Under these laws, heavy taxes were collected to pay the interest on the bonds and to maintain the new government.

Were these things done for beneficiaries at the expense of other classes, notably the farmers, or did the increased production caused by the operations more than cover the cost? On this point economists disagree and the historian cannot answer the question mathematically.

At all events, however, a considerable portion of the American people came to the conclusion that the Federalist measures and policies above enumerated in fact transferred money to investors, merchants, manufacturers, and the capitalistic interests in general, at the expense of the masses—a majority of whom were farmers and planters. "This plan of a National Bank is calculated to benefit a small part of the United States, the mercantile interest only; the farmers, the yeomanry, will derive no advantage from it," complained a member of Congress from Georgia. The protective tariff on steel will operate "as an oppressive, though indirect, tax upon agriculture," lamented a Congressman from Virginia. "The funding system was intended to effect what the Bank was contrived to accelerate: 1. Accumulation of great wealth in a few hands. 2. A political moneyed engine," protested another Virginia statesman.

In time, the citizens who took this view of the Hamiltonian program were marshaled, first as Anti-Federalists and later as Republicans, under the leadership of Thomas Jefferson, who was by occupation and opinion well fitted for his mission. A planter, Jefferson was acquainted with the interests of agriculture. Moreover, he believed and said openly that "cultivators of the earth are the most valuable citizens. They are the most vigorous, the most independent, the most virtuous, and they are tied to their country and wedded to its liberty and interests by the most lasting bonds." In logical relation, he had a low opinion of commerce and industry, which created urban masses. "The mobs of great cities," he asserted, "add just so much to the support of pure government as sores do to the strength of the human body."

Holding such opinions, Jefferson set out to enlist a large following in his struggle against the capitalistic measures of Hamilton. He made his strongest appeal directly to the agriculturalists of the country. And when his party was fully organized he took pride in saying that "the whole landed interest is republican," that is, lined up on his side of the contest.

Speaking of the Federalists arrayed against him on the other side, Jefferson said that they included all the federal officeholders, "all who want to be officers, all timid men who prefer the calm of despotism to the boisterous sea of liberty, British merchants and Americans trading on British capitals, speculators and holders in the banks and public funds, a contrivance invented for the purposes of corruption."

Appealing to the farmers and the masses in general against the larger capitalistic interests, Jefferson's party inevitably took a popular, that is, a democratic turn. This was in keeping with his theories, for he thought that kings, clergy, nobles, and other ruling classes of Europe had filled their countries with poverty and misery and kept the world in turmoil with useless wars. The common people, he reasoned, if given liberty and let alone, would be happier under their own government than under any ruling class.

To their economic arguments, the Jeffersonians added a constitutional theory. They declared that the Constitution did not give Congress the power to charter a bank, provide protection for manufacturers, and pass certain other measures sponsored by the Federalists. This was a "strict construction" of the Constitution; that is, the powers of Congress were to be interpreted narrowly and the rights of the states liberally. Although the Federalists included in their ranks most of the leading men who had made the Constitution, they were thus accused of violating the very fundamental law which they had conceived and adopted. In this way arose the wordy battle over the "true meaning" of the Constitution and the "rights of states," which occupies such a large place in the history of American political loquacity.

To the disputes over domestic questions were added differences of opinion about foreign policies. In the very spring in which Washington was inaugurated with such acclaim, the Estates General met at Versailles and opened the first scene in the great drama of the French Revolution; in 1791 a new constitution was put into effect and the power of the king was practically destroyed; the next year the first French republic was established; in 1793 Louis XVI was executed, and war was declared on England. These events were watched with deep interest by American citizens.

The more radical elements of the population, fresh from their own triumph over George III, remembered with satisfaction the execution of Charles I by their ancestors, and took advantage of the occasion to rejoice in the death of another ruler—the French monarch. A climax came in 1793, when France called on the United States to fulfill the terms of the treaty of 1778, in return for the assistance which had been given to the Americans in their struggle with England. The radicals wanted to aid France, either openly or secretly, in her war on England, but Washington and his conservative supporters refused to be drawn into the European controversy. So the Americans were divided into contending groups over foreign policy, and the division ran in the main along the line already cut by the Federalist-Republican contest over domestic questions.

THE FEDERALIST-REPUBLICAN BATTLE

As the critics of the administration, known at first as Anti-Federalists, slowly changed from a mere opposition group into a regular party and took on the name Republican, the friends of the administration, with Hamilton, John Jay, and John Adams in the lead, began to organize for political warfare under the banner of Federalism. In the third presidential election, the party alignment was complete. Jefferson, the leader of the Republicans, was roundly denounced as an atheist and leveler; while Adams, the Federalist candidate, was condemned by his opponents as "the monarchist." So sharply drawn was the contest that Adams was chosen by the narrow margin of three electoral votes.

During Adams's administration, the Federalist party was thoroughly discredited. The Republican newspapers heaped indiscriminate abuse upon the head of the President and the Federalists generally. As a result Congress pushed through the Alien and Sedition Acts—the first authorizing the President to expel certain aliens deemed dangerous to the safety and peace of the country, and the second making the publication of attacks on any branch of the federal government a crime.

Under the Sedition Act, many Republicans were severely punished for trivial criticisms of the administration. For example, Callender, a friend of Jefferson, was convicted for saying, among other things: "Mr. Adams has only completed the scene of ignominy which Mr. Washington began." In letter and spirit the Act seemed contrary to the amendment to the federal Constitution guaranteeing freedom of press and speech against federal interference. At all events, the two laws called forth the famous Kentucky and Virginia Resolutions, and convinced even those moderately inclined toward democracy that Federalism meant the establishment of political tyranny. The death knell of the Federalist party was rung. Jefferson was elected in 1800 by a substantial majority over the Federalist candidate.

It has been the fashion to ascribe to the Federalists a

political philosophy born of innate ill-will for the people. "Your people, sir," Hamilton is supposed to have said, "is a great beast"—as if in a burst of petulance.

Now this imputation is not entirely just. No doubt some of the emotions to which Federalists gave free vent were the feelings common to persons of large property—feelings of superiority and virtue. But there were practical grounds for distrusting "the people." Throughout the Revolution "the lower orders" had given trouble to the right wing of patriotism, threatening to upset the new ship of state before it was launched. Indeed, some blood had been shed in conflicts among the Patriots themselves before independence was won.

To the Tories who remained in America and rallied to the Federalist cause, the masses were, of course, contemptible in opinion and conduct. In the eyes of the Patriots of the right, the new democracy was responsible for the failure to pay the interest on the national and state debts between 1783 and 1789, for the refusal to grant aid and protection to American industry, for the uprising against the "rich and well-born" in Massachusetts in 1786, and for sundry other disturbances in the body politic. When, therefore, Federalists cursed the people—as they did in gross and in detail—they were not merely expressing a conservative temper. Rather were they reasoning, so they thought, from experience, bitter, realistic experience at that.

CHAPTER XIV

TWENTY-EIGHT YEARS OF THE JEFFERSONIAN PARTY [1]

FOR TWENTY-EIGHT YEARS, from 1801 to 1829, Presidents calling themselves Republican occupied the White House—Jefferson, Madison, Monroe, and John Quincy Adams—and except for a short time at the beginning they were well supported in Congress by party members of their own persuasion. During this period, the Federalist party, as a national organization, died a lingering death. It continued to put up candidates until 1816, but after that failure it disappeared from the national theater. Deprived of a shelter all their own, active Federalists then went into the Republican organization and did what they could to bend it in their direction, while the intransigents of the old generation often sulked in their tents, lamenting the evil days upon which they had fallen.

Although they possessed the power of government, the Republicans, it must be said, did not have a perfectly free hand in carrying their policies into effect. For more than half of this period, the nations of Europe were engaged in the devastating Napoleonic wars which interfered with the shipment of American agricultural produce to Europe, and for a brief time the United States was at war with Great Britain. Owing to foreign events beyond their control, the Republicans were compelled to adopt many devices not to their liking, or at least contrary to their professions.

[1] From Chapter III of *The American Party Battle,* Macmillan (1928).

REPUBLICAN ECONOMIC MEASURES

Nothing had caused more discussion among the Republicans than the national debt. Members of the extreme left had argued that it should be repudiated, that inasmuch as soldiers had given their lives to the Revolutionary cause property owners should sacrifice their financial contributions. Not many, of course, held this extreme opinion, but some did, and the Federalists had attributed such views to the Republicans in general. A middle faction of Republicans opposed repudiation but thought that some reduction should be made in the generous terms adopted by Hamilton. All Republicans agreed that, in any case, the debt was a burden on the taxpayers, most of whom were farmers, that it was a source of speculation and corruption in Congress, and that it should be discharged in full as soon as possible.

Hence the Republicans paid off the national debt as fast as they could, and they were in a fair way to extinguish it when they got into a war with Great Britain in 1812 and were simply forced to increase it.

Hamilton's second great political institution, the United States Bank, likewise came in for its full share of Republican attack. On this point there was no compromise. In 1811, at the end of the twenty-year term, the charter of the Bank expired, and the Republicans refused to renew the life of the great "money power." The banking business passed into the hands of banks chartered by the states and the paper notes of these concerns flooded the country, some of them good, many of them bad.

If it had not been for a crisis, the Republicans probably would have stood firmly against any revival of the United States Bank. But during the war with Great Britain, which they undertook against the wishes of the business and commercial sections, they were driven into a corner in their efforts to pay their bills. In the end, they had to choose between surrendering to the private banks, which had sprung up in the business centers such as Boston, New York, and Philadelphia, and establishing a semi-political government bank under their own control. In the dilemma, they naturally chose the latter plan; in 1816 a Republican Congress chartered the second United States Bank and a Republican President approved it. Members on the left wing opposed this action and in growing numbers waged war on the new "money power." As we shall see, they split the party and destroyed the Bank. Even members of the middle and right factions accepted the Bank as a measure of necessity merely to save the government in their hands from a worse fate.

Into the tax program of the Republicans, the War of 1812 broke with incredible force. They had bitterly opposed the Federalists' direct taxes, which fell heavily upon land, and their internal taxes, especially the tax on whisky which reached into the pockets of thousands of farmers who had little stills of their own. Once installed in office, the Republicans reduced and abolished until they cut the direct and internal revenue taxes and duties down almost to the vanishing point. These burdens so odious to agriculture had nearly disappeared when several of them had to be revived after war was declared on Great Britain. Wars cost money and somebody must pay for them! Yet it could be truly said that, until necessity compelled them to choose another course, the Republican statesmen had done their best to ease the taxes distasteful to their agricultural constituents.

Tariff schedules likewise became involved in war necessities. Those established under Federalist auspices were mildly protectionist in character. Hamilton's thoroughgoing program had been rejected by Congress. As the rates which the Republicans found in force on coming into office were light and yielded large revenues to pay off the hated debt, no radical changes were made in a downward direction.

On the contrary, the opposite happened. The wars in Europe, the War of 1812, the blockades, and the depredations played havoc with American farmers and planters. Unable to ship their produce abroad freely, they found it spoiling on their hands or sinking in price for the want of a market. Why not have a home market, therefore, beyond the reach of wars? Manufacturers approved the idea and offered to furnish the market for the produce of farms and plantations if they could get sufficient protection against foreign competition.

Despite loud protests on the left wing, the Republicans adopted in 1816 a protective tariff bill which would have delighted Hamilton had he been alive to see it. In a long oration, John C. Calhoun, a South Carolina planter, defended the bill in Congress on the ground that it would furnish a market for the produce of the soil. And the stoutest opposition came from New England whose shipping interests, engaged in a lucrative carrying trade, did not want foreign imports reduced by high tariffs. The business was economic but tables were reversed. As we shall see, when conditions changed, planters and farmers could alter their tariff policies. At no time did they forget to cherish the land.

Land—the source of Jefferson's party interest—also figured in two other strokes of policy made by the Republicans during this period. In 1803 they purchased the Louisiana Territory from Napoleon and thus added enough land to satisfy, it seemed, farmers and planters for a century or more. True to their class, the financial and commercial Federalists on the seaboard opposed the purchase on the ground that it would soon enable the agricultural interests of the South and West to dominate the country. That dominance was exactly what the Republicans wanted and, as they had a majority in Congress, the treaty of purchase was ratified.

The question of land similarly entered the War of 1812. According to the usual schoolbook traditions, this war was fought in defense of American rights against British depredations on the sea, but Professor Julius W. Pratt, in his *Expansionists of 1812*, has demolished that theory. Commercial interests were generally opposed to the war. Planters and farmers voted for it. The grand outcome was to be the annexation of the two Floridas for the planters and the annexation of Canada for the farmers. In the process, the Indian allies of Great Britain on the frontier were to be reduced to order so that pioneers could take up their abode in peace on the edges of American civilization. Owing to inadequate military preparations the plans failed.

The truth is that the Republicans did not believe in a

powerful navy and a powerful standing army. In Jefferson's eyes, a navy was a costly Federalist device for which farmers and planters had to pay in taxes simply to protect the property of American shippers on the high seas.

Loyal to farmer traditions, Jefferson feared a strong regular army. It was expensive, he thought, and unnecessary because the popular militia could be relied upon to keep order and defend the country. Although Jefferson used the navy with vigor and telling effect on the Barbary pirates, he and his party reduced rather than strengthened the regular armed forces of the country. The failure to achieve their ends in the War of 1812 may be laid at their door. Farmers did not realize that banking and fighting were professions that could not be learned overnight.

On the whole, it could be said that the Republicans were loyal to the landed interest which they frankly championed in politics. Most of their apparent veerings in the Federalist direction were due to that loyalty rather than to any conversion of heart. . . .

CHAPTER XV

NATIONAL REPUBLICAN
(WHIG)-DEMOCRATIC
ALIGNMENT [1]

THE CHANGING ECONOMIC ORDER

DURING the long years of Republican supremacy, certain fundamental economic changes occurred which strengthened the left wing of that party. These great changes were connected with the settlement of the Northwest Territory, the extension of cotton culture into the Southwest, and the revolution wrought in Eastern industry by machinery.

In the process, the balance of power was shifted from the seaboard states to the West. Kentucky was admitted to the Union in 1792, Tennessee in 1796, Ohio in 1803, Louisiana in 1812, Indiana in 1816, Illinois in 1818, Mississippi in 1817, Alabama in 1819, and Missouri in 1821.

In these Western states there arose a type of economic society such as had never before appeared in the history of the world, at least on a large scale. A vast region was settled by hardy and restless pioneers who crossed the mountains, cut down the forests, built houses, and founded homes. In the possession of this world's goods they were, for the most part, substantially equal; it was easy to acquire land; any thrifty and industrious farmer with his family could readily secure the comforts of a rude but healthful and independent life. Practically every white man could

[1] From Chapter IV of *The American Party Battle,* Macmillan (1928).

vote. In the log cabins were developed political ideas fundamentally different from those entertained by the rich merchants of the East or the aristocratic landholders in the manors along the Hudson.

In the West, the leveling theories of Jefferson were fairly realized. Owing to the simple life which farmers lived, government was to them a simple thing; anyone could hold the office of sheriff, county clerk, road supervisor, state auditor, or governor. Since the duties of the offices were easily understood and the emoluments connected with them attractive, especially to men who earned their bread with the ax and the plow, the Western settlers seized with eagerness upon the doctrine of short terms and rotation in office.

Needing capital to develop their resources and provide means of transportation, these Western people were always borrowers in the money market. Of necessity, they had to depend largely upon Eastern financiers for credits and, being far from the center of business, they had to pay high rates of interest on their loans. In the best of times they were hard driven and during depressions they were plunged into distress. Naturally they sought a remedy for their difficulties and came to the conclusion that it consisted in currency inflation—perhaps through the agency of state banks empowered to issue bills of credit. By such a device they hoped to pay their debts more easily and to command a higher price for their produce—economic operations which threw them into opposition to creditors and buyers.

No less significant for politics than the development of the West was an economic revolution in the agricultural system of the South created by invention of textile machinery and the cotton gin. With the extraordinary demand for cotton came a demand for more land to cultivate and more slaves for labor. The slave population now rapidly increased and the lust for money seized the dominant planting class as it had seized the millowners of New England. Under the old plantation system, masters and slaves dwelt side by side from generation to generation, mitigating the bondage of slavery by a somewhat patriarchal relation, but under the new system slaves were worked in gangs with less regard for humane considerations, and the profit-making motive swept everything before it. Once condemned or merely condoned, slavery was now defended as "a positive good," and inevitably drew to its support the best intellectual strength of the South.

During these crowded years, the East, as well as the West and South, was being transformed. The industries of New England and the Middle States, founded in colonial times and fostered by a protective tariff especially after the war of 1812, began their spectacular career. Mechanics from England came to America in large numbers, bringing with them the designs of machines which had recently wrought a revolution in English industry. In 1807, Fulton inaugurated steam navigation on the Hudson; and far and wide hamlets were expanded into manufacturing centers through the magic of steam. The tide of immigration from Europe steadily increased, and most immigrants found their homes in the growing cities of the East. In the twenty years from 1800 to 1820, the population of Boston almost doubled, while that of New York rose from 60,000 to 123,700. Owing to the property qualifications placed on the suffrage by the constitutions of the Eastern states, most of the immigrants and native workers in the factories were excluded in the beginning from the right to vote; but before the first quarter of the nineteenth century had elapsed, the restrictions on the suffrage had been broken down by popular agitation.

JACKSON'S LEFT-WING MOVEMENT

Here were the changed social conditions which made the United States of 1825 as different from the United States of Washington's day as the England of Cobden and Bright was different from the England of Bolingbroke and Walpole. The financial and industrial interests of New England and the Middle States had now aligned against them the laboring classes, the farmers of the West, and the slave owners who raised cotton principally for the British market.

In 1828, there was found a standard-bearer who, curiously enough, seemed to represent these three diverse elements. That was Andrew Jackson, a resident of Tennessee, a bold frontiersman, immensely popular on account of his victory over the English at New Orleans and his unqualified championship of what he called "the rights of the people." Triumphantly elected, and feeling behind him the irresistible pressure of popular support, he began an executive policy which seemed for a time to transfer the seat of government from the capitol to the White House. He adopted the most novel notions about the rights of the President under the Constitution; he ousted old officeholding "aristocrats" without regard to appearances and circumstances, and gave their places to his friends and supporters; he destroyed the United States Bank, the stronghold of powerful financial interests, in spite of the opposition raised up against him in Congress; and when nullification appeared in South Carolina, he issued a ringing proclamation which showed that he was a stanch defender of nationalism as against states' rights. During his two administrations, the Republicans gradually dropped their old name and proudly assumed the title of Democrats—a word that savored of anarchy a generation before and was then abhorred by most respectable people.

In short, Jackson, a representative of the agrarian South and West, ardently supported by the working classes in the East, took his place firmly in the left wing of the party started by Jefferson. His position with respect to the main Federalist institutions and articles of political faith makes this evident beyond argument.

The Federalists, besides funding the national debt, looked upon it as an excellent permanent device for drawing moneyed men to the support of the government. Jeffersonian Republicans, on the other hand, had done their best to get rid of the debt by paying it off, but the necessities of the War of 1812 had piled it up again. In his first annual message, Jackson favored the extinction of the entire debt by payment, rejoiced that the moment for extinction was at hand, and reached this goal before he went out of office.

Second on the Federalist list was the United States Bank. On the expiration of its charter in 1811, the Republicans destroyed it, but during the financial distress created by the War of 1812 they had been forced to re-establish it. For that reversal their radical followers never forgave them, and early in his administration Jackson opened a battle on this engine of "the money power." He practically demolished it by a drastic use of executive authority and finished the work by preventing a renewal of its charter in Congress.

From the beginning, Federalist businessmen and statesmen had insisted on a sound national currency, including notes of the Bank circulating on a parity with gold and silver. Republican philosophers on the right opposed the issue of paper money on the ground that it added nothing to the wealth of the country. As they thought, the bankers, with government sanction, merely used the printing press liberally to manufacture notes which were lent to the public at six per cent interest or more—a very profitable transaction for the bankers. But Republican philosophers on the left, while bitterly opposing the United States Bank currency, favored a more generous issue of notes by state banks, on the theory that they could pay their debts easier and sell their produce at higher prices if a great deal of money was afloat. Jackson likewise favored banks under state supervision. Judges appointed by him interpreted the Constitution in such a fashion as to permit states to charter banks, hold the stock, and issue money—a very ingenious way of avoiding the constitutional provision to the effect that states could not make anything but gold and silver legal tender in the payment of debts. In their paper-money practices, the Jacksonian Democrats went beyond the Constitution back to the time of Daniel Shays.

With respect to the protective tariff, Jackson was true to Republican theory when he said that "it is principally as manufactures and commerce tend to increase the value of agricultural productions . . . that they deserve the fostering care of government." But he vaguely added that they deserved such fostering care because they catered to the "wants and comforts of society." This uncertainty the Democrats later cured by reducing the tariff drastically in the direction of a revenue basis. None of them wanted to abolish the tariff entirely, for that would have brought about direct taxation on land, an alternative not pleasant to farmers and planters.

Federalists boasted of having "the rich and well-born" in their ranks. Jackson, in waging war on the Bank, made himself the open champion of "the humbler members of society—the farmers, mechanics, and laborers" against "the rich and powerful."

Faithful to the Jeffersonian tradition, Jackson looked upon the federal judiciary with a critical eye. He refused to accept as binding upon himself the decision of the Supreme Court upholding the constitutionality of the United States Bank. "Mere precedent," he said, "is a dangerous source of authority, and should not be regarded as deciding questions of constitutional power, except where the acquiescence of the people and the states can be considered well settled."

More than once he defied the Court by refusing to execute its mandates and in one case he is reported to have said: "John Marshall has made his decision:—now let him enforce it."

NATIONAL REPUBLICAN-WHIG COMBINATION

Holding strongly to such opinions and commanding wide popular support among farmers and mechanics, Jackson seemed to be sovereign in Washington; but nevertheless the factions opposed to his policies steadily gained in unity and power. The banking and financial interests of the East had every reason to fear that a calamity would follow the destruction of the United States Bank and the flooding of the country with paper money through the state banks; many members of his party in the South, who sympathized with the nullification policy of South Carolina, violently attacked Jackson for his determined stand against the action of that state. Furthermore, there was a well-organized group of Eastern manufacturers who wanted to extend the system of protective tariffs beyond the point to which Jackson was willing to go. In addition to this host of enemies, Jackson raised up against himself many disappointed officeseekers, as well as the old officeholders whom he had turned out. There was also in the West a growing number of persons who wanted to secure larger federal grants for internal improvements—roads, harbors, canals, and river facilities—than he was willing to concede.

These elements of opposition to Jackson were finally brought together in a new organization. Making use of a clever vote-catching device, they called themselves National Republicans, and nominated for the presidency in

1831 Jackson's powerful foe, Henry Clay, of Kentucky. In its platform of that year, the party declared in favor of "an adequate protection to American industry," "a uniform system of internal improvements sustained and supported by the general government," "the preservation of the authority and jurisdiction" of the Supreme Court, and the maintenance of the Senate as "preëminently a conservative branch of the federal government." Defeated on this straightforward Federalist program, the National Republicans widened their base and about 1834 merged into a more miscellaneous collection calling themselves "Whigs" —a title taken from English politics, signifying antagonism to high executive prerogative. Marshaled under this banner, they appealed to everybody who was discontented with Jackson.

Nominally the Whig party lasted until the close of the presidential campaign of 1856. It enjoyed two brief periods of triumph. In 1840, without having made any declaration of principles at all, it elected William Henry Harrison, a military hero. After a second defeat four years later, with Clay as the candidate, the party once more resorted to the old device and in 1848 carried the day with another popular hero, General Taylor. Even this design failed the Whigs the next time, for their third military hero, General Scott, was utterly routed.

Operating in a country predominantly agricultural, the Whigs had to be circumspect in their conduct. Their choice of military heroes as candidates lent confusion to the period, but there was no doubt about the measures which the Whig leaders cherished in their hearts. In their program, the Federalist creed was repeated in full, or rather, it would be more correct to say, continued unbroken. Indeed, many a Federalist of the old school who had held his nose during the years of Republican supremacy under the Jeffersonians and during Democratic uproar under Jackson lived to rejoice in the election of Harrison in 1840. Nor should it be forgotten that Daniel Webster, the hope and pride of the Whigs, "the merchants' pet," as he was dubbed by Democrats, began his career as a Federalist. His father was a Federalist and "it is said, being taken sick in a Democratic town had himself removed lest he should die in such pollution." The great Daniel himself, loyal to his early discipline, fired his first political gun in 1804 by writing a pamphlet showing the virtues of Federalism and the vices of Democracy.

Upholding the Hamilton tradition, the Whigs placed the protection of American industry high among the objects to be attained by political action. Words they followed by deeds. Although the tariff compromise of 1883, which temporarily "scotched" secession in South Carolina, was a sort of gentlemen's agreement to regulate rates downward according to a sliding scale, the Whigs, with the aid of Democrats from special sections, broke the understanding and raised the rates in 1842. A cry of rage went up from the planters, but the Whigs were determined and in a hurry.

In attempting to restore the second Federalist institution —the United States Bank—the Whigs were not so fortunate. But their defeat on this issue was due to the death of President Harrison a short time after his inauguration— not to any lack of will on their part. They were prepared to re-establish the Bank and were simply outwitted by Harrison's successor, John Tyler, a Virginia politician nominated for the Vice-Presidency to catch Democratic votes in the South. With their defeat on this issue, their designs for a sound currency system also fell to the ground. . . .

That other interest dear to the Federalists—commerce— was also steadily supported in every direction by the Whigs. It was under Whig auspices that the movement for subsidizing mail steamers on the high seas was inaugurated, culminating in the Subsidy Act of March 3, 1845. It was mainly with Whig support that this Act was maintained and extended. It was under a Democratic President, James Buchanan, that notice of "complete abrogation of contracts" for such subsidies was served on American shipping interests in 1859.

Less hampered by Democratic opposition in the field of executive action, the Whigs, whenever in possession of the Presidency, used the navy and the State Department to advance the sale of manufactured goods in the Far East and other places in the Pacific where agencies of power could be plied with effect. It was under Whig direction that formal relations were established with China in 1844, that

Japan was broken open by Commodore Perry ten years later, and that the governments of the Old World were warned against trespassing on American preserves in Hawaii—all foreshadowing the days of William McKinley. In other words, the Whigs believed that the flag went before and after trade and understood the nature of commercial empires.

THE FRUITS OF DEMOCRATIC TRIUMPH

Between 1828 and 1860 the Democrats won every presidential election except two, and during most of that period they controlled Congress. Not long after the death of Marshall, they got complete possession of the Supreme Court. The numerical supremacy of farmers and planters seemed to promise an indefinite lease of power. If conservative planters had little liking for the leveling doctrines of Jacksonian Democracy, they were practical men and finally became convinced that they could only hope to hold their own in politics against advancing industrialism by an alliance with farmers.

On fundamentals of economic action the two wings of agriculture were long able to agree. In fact, while the Whigs were trying to get possession of the government by nominating military heroes and avoiding a clear statement of principles, the Democrats were making their doctrines more and more precise.

In their platform of 1840, they wrote their agrarian creed in language so plain that any farmer or mechanic could understand it. They opposed protective tariffs, the establishment of another United States Bank, internal improvements, the creation of public debts, and all interference with slavery—the labor supply of the planters. At every presidential election until 1860, the Democrats repeated this profession of economic faith, and in every presidential campaign their orators refined it.

In practice, the Democrats carried out most of their promises. They defeated every attempt to restore the Bank which Jackson had destroyed. They struck a smashing blow at the protective tariff in their revenue law of 1846 and again in 1857, indicating their determination to destroy the Hamiltonian system root and branch. In 1859, the last of the subsidies for transatlantic steamships was ordered discontinued by Congress, and shippers were given to understand that they were to receive no such favors from the federal government. In the meantime, as the Federalist members of the Supreme Court, with Justice Marshall at their head, passed away, Democrats were appointed to take their places; and Hamilton's theories about the Constitution were generally abandoned in favor of the rights of states. In particular, the clause of the Constitution forbidding states to issue paper money—bills of credit—was reinterpreted in such a way as to permit states to set up banks which flooded the country with paper currency; and the clause respecting the obligation of contracts was practically destroyed by new judicial reasoning.

Loyal to the anti-commercial sentiments of Jefferson, the Democrats were indifferent to various proposals made in the middle period for using the navy to occupy strategic trading posts in the Pacific and the Far East; but they were not partisans of a "little America." On the contrary, as the party of planters and farmers, they were advocates of that kind of expansion which yielded more land for slave owners and freeholders. They brought Texas into the Union in 1845, and waged a war on Mexico which ended in magnificent additions of land in 1848, in spite of opposition from the Whig side. If it had not been for resistance in that quarter, the Democrats would have probably annexed Cuba and huge slices of Latin America on the mainland and in the Caribbean, thus strengthening the landed interest founded on slave labor. To the influence of Whig opposition must be added that of many free farmers enrolled under the Democratic banner, who feared and sometimes disliked the dominance of the slave-holding planters in their partnership.

CHAPTER XVI

DEMOCRATIC-REPUBLICAN
ALIGNMENT [1]

WHILE THE DEMOCRATS were refusing to support industrial enterprise, vital economic forces were preparing the way for an intensification of the battle between agriculture and capitalism. . . .

SHIFTS IN THE ECONOMIC SETTING

In the Northeast, manufacturing and railways were rapidly expanding, employing more labor and increasing the number and wealth of businessmen. By 1850, the value of the property employed in mills, mines, railways, and urban undertakings generally exceeded the value of all the farms and plantations between the Atlantic and the Pacific. A fact immense and ominous, as Carlyle would say.

In the South, cotton planting, stimulated by the development of the cotton gin and textile machinery, became the dominant interest, as against tobacco, rice, and sugar; by 1860 nearly two-thirds of the slaves were engaged in cultivating that crop. Cotton raising rapidly exhausted the soil and led the planters to push steadily westward, occupying new land.

In the Northwest, farmers were pressing across the Mississippi, demanding the opening of more territories to the plow and the granting of free homesteads to all who cared to ask for them. There was also a rapid growth in

[1] From Chapter V of *The American Party Battle,* Macmillan (1928).

industrial cities like Cincinnati and Chicago and in the
construction of railways uniting the Mississippi Valley with
the Atlantic ports of Philadelphia, New York, and Boston.
Once the stronghold of Jacksonian Democracy, the Northwest was now being assimilated to the economic system of
the Northeast—severed from its affiliation with the Southern planters.

THE SLAVERY ISSUE

Into the issues inherited from Hamilton's day—the tariff,
[banking], internal improvements, sound currency, and subsidies for business enterprise—was now injected a new
issue, slavery. . . . Had the abolition question stood alone
and had the slave owners been content with maintaining
slavery in the states where it was lawful, the controversy
over the subject might never have taken a serious turn.

It so happened, however, that slavery could not be
isolated. It was a labor system, the basis of planting, the
foundation of the Southern aristocracy. And that aristocracy, being agricultural in interest, generally opposed high
protective tariffs, ship subsidies, internal improvements,
and other measures deemed advantageous to business enterprise.

Moreover, that aristocracy, eager to protect itself against
adverse legislation at Washington, was constantly afraid of
being outvoted in Congress. Especially did it object to the
exclusion of slavery from the territories because that policy
meant the erection of new free states to "overbalance"
the Southern states.

Declaring that the Western territories had all been won
by common sacrifices, Southern planters never ceased to
regard it an act of justice to open the West to slavery.
Although they accepted the Missouri Compromise of 1820,
excluding slavery from the northern portion of the Louisiana territory, and the compromise of 1850, their most
ardent leaders refused to abide by the settlement as final.

At last, in 1854, they came out boldly with their demand.
Under the leadership of Stephen A. Douglas, supported
by an almost solid delegation from the South, Congress, in
that year, passed the Kansas-Nebraska Act which expressly

repealed the Missouri Compromise and provided that two Western territories then erected, Kansas and Nebraska, could come into the Union as states with or without slavery, as their constitutions might stipulate.

RISE OF THE THIRD REPUBLICAN PARTY

On the very morning after the House of Representatives took up the Kansas-Nebraska bill, several members of that body held a conference and agreed that the "slave power" could only be checked by the formation of a party directly opposed to its plans for expansion. About the same time a mass meeting was held at Ripon, Wisconsin, and a resolution adopted to the effect that a new organization, to be called Republican, should be formed on the question of slavery extension, if the bill passed.

Indeed, all through the North and East, there were signs of dissolution among the Democrats and Whigs, and a general realignment; in the spring and summer of 1854, meetings were held in Illinois, Maine, Vermont, Michigan, Iowa, Indiana, Massachusetts, and New York, at which the Kansas-Nebraska bill was roundly denounced. On July 6, 1854, a state convention was held at Jackson, Michigan, at which a full state ticket of Republican candidates was nominated.

Thus launched, a third Republican party—bearing the vote-getting title which Jefferson had given to his hosts in 1800 and Clay's party had taken in 1831—held its first national convention at Philadelphia in June, 1856, on a call issued by a preliminary meeting assembled at Pittsburgh, in the preceding February. At this convention, John Charles Frémont was nominated as the candidate on a platform which declared that it was the right and duty of Congress to prohibit slavery in the territories. In the campaign which ensued, Frémont won 1,341,264 votes against 2,712,703 votes cast in favor of the Democratic and the Whig candidates.

During the four years which followed, the Republican party gained in strength. It gathered recruits among Northern farmers and mechanics, who believed that the federal lands should be given away in homesteads to poor men. It added to its farmer and mechanic regiments, manufacturers of the East who objected strenuously to the reduction of the protective tariff by the Democrats in 1857, and demanded an increase in the rates.

Responding to the requirements of these powerful groups, the Republicans, at their convention in Chicago in 1860, favored a homestead law and a protective tariff, as well as the exclusion of slavery from the territories. Thus they appealed to many farmers and mechanics who had formerly voted the Democratic ticket and at the same time made a bid for support among the Whig manufacturers who clung to the doctrines of Alexander Hamilton. By selecting as their candidate Abraham Lincoln, of Illinois, they made a shrewd and fateful stroke.

Fortunately for the Republicans, the Democrats now split into two factions, one headed by Stephen A. Douglas, who hoped to solve the slavery question by allowing the people of each territory, on admission to the Union as a state, to decide it for themselves; the other by John C. Breckinridge, who held to the extreme Southern view that Congress had no power to prevent slavery in the territories. By another faction, composed of conservative Whigs and Democrats, known as Constitutional Unionists, John Bell was nominated on a platform that begged the slavery issue. Owing to the division among their opponents, the Republicans were able to win the Presidency, although their popular vote was only 1,866,452 as against 2,815,617 cast for their opponents.

A FEDERALIST PROGRAM UNDER REPUBLICAN AUSPICES

During the Civil War and Reconstruction, the Republicans repudiated the policies which the Democrats had laboriously supported between 1830 and 1860, and substituted other policies more in accord with the historic principles of the Federalists and the Whigs, thus illustrating again the essential continuity of the American political battle. . . .

1. *National debt.* The Federalists had funded and defended a great national debt, drawing the creditors to the support of the federal government. In 1865, the Republicans had a war debt more than twenty times the size of

Hamilton's accumulation, and all holders of federal bonds looked to the Republican party for the strict payment of interest and principal. The old Jefferson-Jackson idea of a debtless government seemed far removed again.

2. *Protective tariff.* After many years of debate and agitation, the Democrats, by 1857, had pushed the tariff far down the scale in the direction of free trade. During their tenure of power from 1861 to 1865, the Republicans more than realized the Hamiltonian ideal by raising the duties again and again, to the highest peak of protection yet reached in the history of the country.

3. *Banking system.* With respect to no issue had the Democrats been more consistent than in dealing with the United States Bank. Jeffersonian Republicans had been against it and had only yielded to a demand for its restoration in 1816 under the necessities of war finance. In Jackson's administration, the Bank was completely demolished and the most heroic efforts of the Whigs could not revive it. But in 1863—once more in time of war distress—the third Republican party managed to create another national banking system, drawing to the support of the government a powerful economic interest.

4. *Currency.* When the Civil War broke out, the country was flooded with paper money issued by local banks chartered by the states. There were hundreds of varieties of all denominations, some sound, but much of it depreciated and fluctuating.

This was . . . disturbing to business and pleased only debtors and farmers. Returning to Hamiltonian principles in 1865, the Republicans abolished this state currency by taxing it out of existence. Unfortunately, however, for the cause of sound money, they had to issue huge quantities of paper themselves to finance the war; but a few years later they put it all on a specie basis.

5. *The commercial empire.* The extension of trading operations, particularly in the Pacific and the Far East, which the Federalists had favored with special legislation and the Whigs had promoted by vigorous executive action through the Navy and State Departments, was not overlooked even during the dark days of the Civil War.[2]

William H. Seward, whom Lincoln selected as head of

[2] See above, pp. 191–2.

the State Department, was the most outspoken imperialist in the country. During the campaign of 1860 he had proclaimed the future of the American empire. Canada was to be annexed, our southern borders were to be pushed down to include Latin-American republics, the Pacific was announced as the theater of the coming centuries, and a conflict between the United States and Russia on the plains of China was prophesied as a fruit of destiny. Such was the creed of the master in charge of foreign affairs from 1861 until 1869.

Fantastic as most of Seward's doctrines may have appeared in 1860, they were not all mere rhetoric. Some of them took practical form within a few years. When the Pacific railway was authorized in the very midst of the civil conflict, its value to merchants engaged in Far Eastern trade, as well as its importance to the Union, was recognized by the initiated. In 1867, Seward purchased Alaska from Russia, carrying the frontier of the United States near to the Asiatic shore. About the same time, through the good offices of the Navy Department, Seward arranged for the acquisition of a naval base in Santo Domingo, for the purchase of the Virgin Islands, and for American control over the Isthmus of Panama. In these three undertakings he was defeated by opposition in Congress where such designs were not yet fully understood.

But his schemes were not forgotten. In 1869, President Grant arranged for the annexation of Santo Domingo, only to be baffled by Congress; to the end of his administration Grant favored the project on the ground, as he said himself, that "the soil would soon have fallen into the hands of United States capitalists." In 1872, an American naval officer secured a coaling station from a local prince in Samoa, far away in the South Seas. In 1875, a treaty with the ruler of Hawaii bound him not to alienate any of his territory except to the United States and a few years later a supplementary treaty gave the United States exclusive use of Pearl Harbor. Thus it could be said that the managers in the party of Hamilton, Webster, and Seward were consistent in their solicitude for commercial and naval empire and prepared the way for the administration of William McKinley, which finally let mankind know, what was already a fact, that America was a world power.

6. *Judicial supremacy*. From its Jeffersonian forerunner, the Democratic party, with its theory of majority rule, had inherited a tradition of criticism with respect to the federal judiciary. In the middle period, however, after all the old Federalist judges had died or resigned and good Democrats had been appointed to the bench, the tradition faded. When the Supreme Court, in the Dred Scott case (1857) upheld slavery in the territories, Democrats demanded unqualified loyalty and obedience to the decisions of that great tribunal. It was the new Republican party, whose anti-slavery plank had been splintered by the decision, that now criticized the Court and talked about "reconstructing" it. But once more time and politics worked a reorganization of the Court and Republicans conveniently forgot their former resolutions of protest against its actions.

They even effected a revision of the Constitution which gave the federal judiciary a power over the states far greater than it had ever enjoyed. . . . In due time hundreds of state laws interfering with capitalistic undertakings were declared null and void by the judiciary acting under the terms of the Fourteenth Amendment.[3]

7. *Free land for farmers and mechanics*. While the Republicans were effecting these important economic reforms, they fulfilled a promise made to farmers and mechanics in their platform of 1860. By the Homestead Act of 1862, they offered a farm of 160 acres from the national domain, free of all charges except petty fees, to citizens and aliens who had declared their intention of becoming citizens. Applicants merely had to comply with certain conditions in order to secure full ownership. Thus hundreds of thousands of farmers in the West were indebted to the Republican party for the very soil they tilled, and nothing short of a crisis could make them forget their obligation.

This union of businessmen and free farmers could function rather smoothly now that the Democratic planters were ruined by the Civil War. Defeated on the field of battle, deprived of their slaves by abolition, and for a long time governed under military authority from Washington, the planters could not recover their former position of

[3] For a fuller account of this development, see below, pp. 209–11.

power in the Democratic party. Even after the wounds of the War were healed, this important agricultural group, once the bulwark of the landed interest, did not regain its old place of continuous dominance in politics. Giant industry, marching in seven-league boots, outstripped it in the race.

YEARS OF REPUBLICAN SUPREMACY

From the period of Civil War and Reconstruction the Republicans emerged as a powerful, consolidated party fortified by an intense patriotism, by the support of the manufacturing interests which had flourished under the war tariffs, by the patronage of capitalists eager to swing forward with the development of railways and new enterprises, and by farmers grateful for many favors, including homesteads. In possession of all the important offices, controlling the federal legislature, executive, and judiciary, with the Democratic party prostrate and branded with treason, the Republicans had a dominion over the destinies of the country greater than the Democrats had ever wielded.

Wherever there is such tremendous power, vigilant self-seekers of every kind are sure to congregate. During the years which followed the war, the ranks of the Republican party were permeated with mercenaries of every type—spoilsmen hunting offices, railway promoters seeking land grants and financial aid from the government, manufacturers demanding more discrimination in the tariff legislation, and the great army of hangers-on who attached themselves to these leaders. The integrity of the party was further injured by the "carpet-baggers" in the South, who, in the name of the federal government and the Republican party, plundered the Southern states and heaped upon them an enormous burden of debt.

In these circumstances, the Democratic party began to revive. It had had a long and triumphant history previous to the Civil War; it had great traditions, and numbered on its roll some of the most distinguished men in American history. The population of the country was still principally agricultural and the cotton planters were soon producing as

many bales a year as in the "flush times" before the Civil
War.

It is not surprising, therefore, that the Democratic party
sought to close up its shattered ranks in opposition to Republican rule. In the South, the whites recovered their
predominance; in the North and West, farmers protested
against the high protective tariffs; here and there throughout the Union discontent with the railway and corporation
policy of the Republican party began to appear; and the
spoils system which had flourished since Jackson's day
stirred to action a small but vigorous minority of "civil
service reformers."

As a result, the Democratic party, in 1884, was able to
bring together an effective opposition and to elect Grover
Cleveland President, with the support of the "mugwumps"
who bolted the Republicans after the nomination of James
G. Blaine at their Chicago convention. This Democratic
triumph was short-lived, however, for four years later,
when Cleveland raised the tariff issue by his celebrated
message of 1887, the Republicans were able to elect Benja-
min Harrison by a slight majority. Taking advantage of
their victory, they forced through the McKinley tariff
bill, though it was regarded by many members of the
party as entirely too drastic. In the succeeding election of
1892, Cleveland was again able to lead his party to success, but it could scarcely be said that any vital issues now
divided the two contending parties.

CHAPTER XVII

SOME POLITICAL ASPECTS
OF THE AMERICAN
INDUSTRIAL REVOLUTION [1]

LONG BEFORE the Civil War, steam and machinery had begun to invade American industries. . . . The census of 1860 reported nearly a million and a half wage earners in the United States, and more than a billion dollars invested in manufacturing. By that year over thirty thousand miles of railway had been constructed, including such important lines as the New York Central, the Erie, the Baltimore and Ohio, and the Pennsylvania. . . .

But the spectacular conflict over slavery prevented the political results of the economic transformation from coming to the surface. Those who had occasion to watch the proceedings of Congress during the two decades just before the [Civil] War discovered the manipulations of railway corporations seeking land grants and privileges from the federal government and the operations of the "protected" interests in behalf of increased tariffs. Those were also harvest days for corporations and companies in the state legislatures where special charters and privileges were being bartered away by the wholesale. There was emerging in a number of the larger industrial centers a small, though by no means negligible, labor movement. But the slavery issue overshadowed everything. The annexation of Texas, slavery in the territories, the Compromise of 1850, the Nebraska bill, and Bleeding Kansas

[1] A composite of Chapters II and III of *Contemporary American History*, 1877–1913, The Macmillan Co. (1914).

kept the mind of the North from the consideration of the more fundamental economic problems connected with the new order. The politicians, to be sure, did not live by the slavery agitation alone, but it afforded the leading topics for public discussion and prevented the critical from inquiring too narrowly into the real staples of politics.

The Civil War sharply shifted the old scenery of politics. It gave a tremendous impetus to industry and railway construction. The tariff measures during the war gave to manufacturers an unwonted protection against foreign competition; the demand for war supplies, iron, and steel, railway materials, textiles, and food supplies, quickened every enterprise in the North; the great fortunes made out of speculations in finances, contracts for government supplies, and land grants placed an enormous capital in private hands to carry forward business after the war was over.

Within little more than a quarter of a century the advance of industry and commerce had made the United States of Lincoln's day seem small and petty. The census of 1905 showed over twelve billion dollars invested in factories and nearly five and one-half million wage earners employed. In that year, the total value of manufactured products was over fourteen billion dollars—fifteen times the amount turned out in 1860. . . .

The building of railways more than kept pace with the growth of the population and the increase in manufacturing. There were 30,000 miles of lines in 1860; 52,000 in 1870; 166,000 in 1890; and 242,000 in 1910. Beginning at first with the construction of lines between strategic centers like Boston and Albany, and Philadelphia and Reading, the leaders in this new enterprise grew more bold. They pushed rapidly into the West where there were no cities of magnitude and no prospect of developing a profitable business within the immediate future. Capital flowed into the railways like water; . . . and the whole West was aflame with dreams of a new Eldorado to be created by transportation systems. . . .

It must not be thought that this rapid railway expansion was due solely to private enterprise, for, as has been the standing custom in American politics, the cost of doubtful or profitless undertakings was thrown as far as possible upon the public treasury. Up to 1872, the federal government had granted in aid of railways 155,000,000 acres of land, an area estimated as "almost equal to the New England states, New York, and Pennsylvania combined; nineteen different states had voted sums aggregating two hundred million dollars for the same purpose; and municipalities and individuals had subscribed several hundred million dollars to help railway construction." To the Union Pacific concern alone the federal government had granted a free right of way through public lands, twenty sections[2] of land with each mile of railway, and a loan up to fifty million dollars secured by a second mortgage on the company's property. The Northern Pacific obtained lands which a railway official estimated to be worth enough "to build the entire railroad to Puget Sound, to fit out a fleet of sailing vessels and steamers for the China and India trade and leave a surplus that would roll up into the millions." Cities, townships, counties, and states voted bonds to help build railways within their limits or granted rights of way and lands, in addition, with a lavish hand.

The chronicle of all the frauds connected with the manipulation of land grants to railways and the shameless sale of legal privileges cannot be written, because in most instances no tangible records have been left. Perhaps the most notorious of all was the Crédit Mobilier scandal connected with the Union Pacific. The leading stockholders in that company determined to secure for themselves a large portion of the profits of construction, which were enormous on account of the prodigal waste; and they organized a sham concern known as the Crédit Mobilier in which they had full control and to which the construction profits went. Inasmuch as the federal government, through its grants and loans, was an interested party that might interfere at any time, the concern, through its agent in Congress, Oakes Ames, a representative from Massachusetts, distributed generous blocks of stock to "approachable" Senators and Representatives. News of the transaction leaked out, and a Congressional investigation in 1872 showed that a number of men of the highest standing,

[2] COMPILER'S NOTE: A section covers a square mile.

including Mr. Colfax, the Vice-President, were deeply implicated. Nothing was done, however; the leading conspirator, Ames, was merely censured by the House, and the booty, for the most part, remained in the hands of those connected with the scandal. When the road was complete, "it was saddled with interest payments on $27,000,-000 first mortgage bonds, $27,000,000 government bonds, $10,000,000 income bonds, $10,000,000 land grant bonds, and if anything were left, dividend payments on $36,000,-000 of stock."

It would be easy to multiply figures showing astounding gains in industry, business, foreign trade, and railways; or to multiply stories of scandalous and unfair practices on the part of financiers, but we are not primarily concerned here with the technique of inventions or the history of promotion.[3] The student of social and political evolution is concerned rather with the effect of such material changes upon the structure of society, that is, with the rearrangements of classes and the development of new groups of interests, which are brought about by altered methods of gaining a livelihood and accumulating fortunes. It is this social transformation that changes the relation of the individual to the state and brings new forces to play in the struggle for political power. The social transformation which followed the Civil War embraced the following elements.

In the first place, capital, as contrasted with agriculture, increased enormously in amount and in political influence. Great pecuniary accumulations were thenceforward made largely in business enterprise—including the work of the entrepreneur, financier, speculator, and manipulator under that general term. Inevitably, the most energetic and the keenest minds were attracted by the dominant mode of money-making. Agricultural regions were drained of large numbers of strenuous and efficient men, who would otherwise have been their natural leaders in politics. To these were added the energetic immigrants from the Old World. That forceful, pushing, dominating section of society historically known as the "natural aris-

[3] COMPILER'S NOTE: The footnote inserted here in the original text listed numerous inventions. It has been omitted.

tocracy" became the agent of capitalism. The scepter of power now passed definitely from the masters of slaves to the masters of "free laborers." The literary and professional dependents of the ruling groups naturally came to the defense of the new order.[4] The old contest between agrarianism and capitalism now took on a new vigor. . . .

. . . Senators of the old school, Clay, Webster, Calhoun, Roger Baldwin, John P. Hale, James Mason, and Jefferson Davis, were succeeded by the apostles of the new order: Roscoe Conkling and Thomas Platt, James Donald Cameron, Leland Stanford, George Hearst, Arthur P. Gorman, William D. Washburn, John R. McPherson, Henry B. Payne, Matthew S. Quay, Philetus Sawyer, John H. Mitchell, and James G. Blaine. The new Senate was composed of men of affairs—practical men, who organized gigantic enterprises, secured possession of natural resources and franchises, collected and applied capital on a large scale to new business undertakings, built railways, established cities with the advancing line of the western frontier—or represented such men as counsel in the courts of law. . . .

The political philosophy of this notable group of political leaders was that of their contemporaries in England, the Cobden-Bright school. They believed in the widest possible extension of the principle of private property, and the narrowest possible restriction of state interference, except to aid private property to increase its gains. They held that all of the natural resources of the country should be transferred to private hands as speedily as possible, at a nominal charge, or no charge at all, and developed with dashing rapidity. They also believed that the great intangible social property created by community life, such as franchises for street railways, gas, and electricity, should be transformed into private property. They supplemented their philosophy of property by a philosophy of law and politics, which looked upon state interference—except to preserve order, and aid railways and manufacturers in their enterprises—as an intrinsic evil to be resisted at every point, and they developed a system of jurisprudence which, as Senators having the confirming power in appointments

[4] For the keenest analysis of this social transformation, see Veblen, *Theory of the Leisure Class* and *Theory of Business Enterprise*.

and as counsel for corporations before the courts of the United States, they succeeded in transforming into judicial decisions. Some of them were doubtless corrupt, as was constantly charged, but the real explanation of their resistance to government intervention is to be found in their philosophy, which, although consonant with their private interests, they identified with public good. . . .

Inasmuch as the attacks on private rights in property, franchises, and corporate privileges came principally from the state legislatures, it was necessary to find some way to subject them to legal control—some juristic process for translating *laissez faire* into a real restraining force. . . .

The problem of how best to check the assaults of state legislatures on vested rights . . . was one of the first concerns of the Convention of 1787 which drafted the original Constitution of the United States, and it was thought by the framers that security had been attained by forbidding states to emit bills of credit and make laws impairing the obligation of contract. Under Chief Justice Marshall, these clauses were so generously interpreted as to repel almost any attack which a state legislature might make on acquired rights. However, in the closing years of Marshall's service, the Supreme Court, then passing into the hands of states'-rights justices, rendered an opinion in the case of Ogden *v.* Saunders, which clearly held that the contract clause did not prevent the legislature from stipulating that *future* contracts might be practically at its mercy. When a legislature provides by general law that all charters of corporations are subject to repeal and alteration, such provision becomes a part of all new contracts. Marshall delivered in this case a vigorous and cogent dissenting opinion in which he pointed out that the decision had in effect destroyed the virtue of the obligation of contract clause.

The case of Ogden *v.* Saunders was decided in 1827. Between that year and the Civil War the beginnings of corporate enterprise were securely laid in the United States; and the legislatures of the several states began the regulation of corporations from one motive or another, sometimes for the purpose of blackmailing them and sometimes for the laudable purpose of protecting public inter-

ests. At all events, large propertied concerns began to feel
that they could not have a free hand in developing their
enterprises or enjoy any genuine security unless the legislatures of the states were, by some constitutional provision,
brought again under strict federal judicial control.

The opportunity to secure this judicial control was afforded during the Civil War when the radical Republicans
were demanding federal protection for the newly emancipated slaves of the South. The drastic legislation relative
to Negroes adopted by the Southern states at the close of
the war showed that even in spite of the Thirteenth
Amendment a substantial bondage could be re-established
under the color of criminal, apprentice, and vagrant legislation. The friends of the Negroes, therefore, determined
to put the substantial rights of life, liberty, and property
beyond the interference of state legislatures forever, and
secure to all persons the equal protection of the law.

Accordingly, the Fourteenth Amendment was adopted,
enunciating the broad legal and political doctrine that no
state "shall abridge the privileges or immunities of citizens
of the United States; nor shall any state deprive any
person of life, liberty, or property without due process of
law; nor deny to any *person* within its jurisdiction the equal
protection of the law."

Here was a restriction laid upon state legislatures which
might be substantially limitless in its application, in the
hands of a judiciary wishing to place the broadest possible
interpretation upon it. What are privileges and immunities?
What are life, liberty, and property? What is due process
of law? What is the equal protection of the law? Does the
term "person" include not only natural persons but also
artificial persons, namely, corporations? That the reconstruction committee of Congress which framed the instrument intended to include within the scope of this generous
provision not only the Negro struggling upward from
bondage, but also corporations and business interests struggling for emancipation from legislative interference, has
been often asserted. In arguing before the Supreme Court
in the San Mateo County case, on December 19, 1882,
Mr. Roscoe Conkling, who had been a member of the
committee which drafted the Fourteenth Amendment, un-
folded for the first time the deep purpose of the commit-

tee, and showed from the journal of that committee that it was not their intention to confine the amendment merely to the protection of the colored race. In the course of his argument, Mr. Conkling remarked: "At the time the Fourteenth Amendment was ratified, as the records of the two Houses will show, individuals and joint-stock companies were appealing for congressional and administrative protection against invidious and discriminating state and local taxes. One instance was that of an express company, whose stock was owned largely by citizens of the State of New York, who came with petitions and bills seeking Acts of Congress to aid them in resisting what they deemed oppressive taxation in two states, and oppressive and ruinous rules of damages applied under state laws. That complaints of oppression in respect of property and other rights, made by citizens of Northern States who took up residence in the South, were rife, in and out of Congress, none of us can forget; that complaints of oppression in various forms, of white men in the South,—of 'Union men,'—were heard on every side, I need not remind the Court. The war and its results, the condition of the freedmen, and the manifest duty owed to them, no doubt brought on the occasion for constitutional amendment; but when the occasion came and men set themselves to the task, the accumulated evils falling within the purview of the work were the surrounding circumstances, in the light of which they strove to increase and strengthen the safeguards of the Constitution and laws." [5]

In spite of important testimony to the effect that those who drafted the Fourteenth Amendment really intended "to nationalize liberty," that is, *laissez faire,* against state legislatures, the Supreme Court at first refused to accept this broad interpretation, and it was not until after several of the judges of the old states'-rights school had been replaced by judges of the new school that the claims of Mr. Conkling's group as to the Fourteenth Amendment were embodied in copious judicial decisions.

. . . [No] layman can easily unravel the mysterious re-

[5] Taylor, *Origin and Growth of the American Constitution,* p. 355. As a matter of fact, Conkling, who was a member of the committee that drafted the Fourteenth Amendment, voted against these provisions in committee.

finements, distinctions, and logical subtleties by which the fact was finally established that property was to be free from all interference except such as might be allowed by the Supreme Court (or rather five judges of that Court) appointed by the President and Senate, thus removed as far as possible from the pressure of public sentiment. Had a bald veto power of this character been suddenly vested in any small group of persons, there can be no doubt that a political revolt would have speedily followed. But the power was built up by gradual accretions made by the Court under the stimulus of skillful counsel for private parties, and finally clothed in the majesty of settled law. It was a long time before the advocates of leveling democracy, leading an attack on corporate rights and privileges, discovered that the courts were the bulwarks of *laissez faire* and directed their popular battalions in that direction.

Those who undertake to criticize the Supreme Court for this assumption of power do not always distinguish between the power itself and the manner of its exercise. What would have happened if the state legislatures had been given a free hand to regulate, penalize, and blackmail corporations at will during the evolution of our national economic system may be left to the imagination of those who recall from their history the breezy days of "wild-cat" currency, repudiation, and broken faith which characterized the thirty years preceding the Civil War when the federal judiciary was under the dominance of the states'-rights school. The regulation of a national economic system by forty or more local legislatures would be nothing short of an attempt to combine economic unity with local anarchy. It is possible to hold that the Court has been too tender of corporate rights in assuming the power of judicial review, and at the same time recognize the fact that such a power, vested somewhere in the national government, is essential to the continuance of industries and commerce on a national scale. . . .

On the side of the masses involved in the transition . . . [the industrial] revolution meant an increasing proportion of wage workers as contrasted with agriculturalists, owning and operating their farms, and with handicraftsmen. . . .

This industrial development meant the transformation

of vast masses of the people into a proletariat, with all the term implies: an immense population housed in tenements and rented dwellings, the organization of the class into trades-unions, labor parties, and other groups; poverty and degradation on a large scale; strikes, lockouts, and social warfare; the employment of large numbers of women and children in factories; the demand for all kinds of legislation mitigating the evils of the capitalist process; and finally attacks upon the very basis of the industrial system itself.

This inevitable concomitant of the mechanical revolution, the industrial proletariat, began to make itself felt as a decided political and economic factor in the decade that followed the war. Between 1860 and 1870, the railway engineers, firemen, conductors, bricklayers, and cigarmakers had formed unions. In the campaign of 1872 a party of Labor Reformers appeared; and a few years later the Knights of Labor, a grand consolidated union of all trades and grades of workers, came into existence as an active force, conducting an agitation for labor bureaus, an eight-hour day, abolition of contract-labor systems, and other reforms, and at the same time engineering strikes.

In 1877 occurred the first of the great labor struggles in that long series of campaigns which have marked the relations of capitalists and workingmen during the past four decades. In that year, trouble began between the management of the Baltimore and Ohio railway and its employees over a threatened reduction in wages—the fourth within a period of seven years. From this starting point the contest spread throughout the East and Middle West, reaching as far as Texas. Inasmuch as there was already considerable unemployment, the strikers saw that only by violence and intimidation could they hope to prevent the companies from moving their trains. Troops were called out by the governors of several states and federal assistance was invoked. Pittsburgh fell almost completely into the hands of the strikers; railway buildings were burned and property to the value of more than ten million dollars destroyed. Everywhere the raw militia of the states was found to be inefficient for such a serious purpose, and the superior power of the federal government's regular troops was demonstrated. Where railways were in the hands of receivers, federal courts intervened by the use of injunctions and the first blood in the contest between the judiciary and labor was drawn. . . .

However, emphasis upon this great industrial revolution should not be allowed to obscure the no less remarkable development in agriculture. The acreage in improved farm lands rose from 113,032,614 in 1850 to 478,451,750 in 1910. In the same period the number of farms increased from 1,449,073 to 6,361,502. Notwithstanding the significant fact that "whereas the total population increased 21 per cent between 1900 and 1910, the urban population increased 34.8 per cent and the rural population 11.2 per cent," the broad basis of the population during the half a century here under consideration has remained agricultural, and in 1913 it was estimated that at the present rate of transformation "it will take a generation before the relative number of industrial wage workers will have reached half of all bread winners." . . .

Notwithstanding the prominence given to the Negro question during and after Reconstruction, the South had other problems no less grave in character to meet. Industry and agriculture were paralyzed by the devastations of the war. A vast amount of material capital—railways, wharves, bridges, and factories—had been destroyed during the conflict; and fluid capital seeking investment had been almost destroyed as well. The rich with ready money at their command had risked nearly all their store in Confederate securities or had lost their money loaned in other ways through the wreck of the currency. . . .

The very necessities of the South served to bind that section to the North in a new fashion. Fluid capital had to be secured, in part at least, from the North, and Northern enterprise found a new outlet in the reconstruction of the old, and the development of the new, industries in the region of the former Confederacy. . . . This [interest] was, in part, due to the abundance of water power in the hill regions, the cheap labor of women and children, the low cost of living, and the absence of labor laws interfering with the hours and conditions of work in the factories. . . .

The social effects which accompany capitalist development inevitably began to appear in the South. The industrial magnate began to contest with the old aristocracy of the soil for supremacy; many former slave owners and their descendants drifted into manufacturing . . . and energetic Northern businessmen were to be found in Southern market places vying with their no less enterprising Southern brethren. The men concerned in creating this new nexus of interest between the two regions naturally deprecated the perpetual agitation of sectional issues by the politicians, and particularly Northern interference in the Negro question. Business interest began to pour cold water on the hottest embers which the Civil War had left behind.

CHAPTER XVIII

THE GROWTH OF DISSENT [1]

ALTHOUGH the two historic parties commanded the allegiance of the mass of the people during the period just reviewed, there was always a dissenting element in each of them. In fact, every party is a more or less miscellaneous aggregation with a conservative right and a radical left, shading off into each other by imperceptible degrees. If a citizen does not approve the policies adopted by the party with which he is associated by birth or temper, he has three choices before him. He can stay within the party and work to secure the nomination of other men and the declaration of other principles. He can go over to another party which more nearly represents his idea about politics. Or he may leave his party and join others who are of a like mind in forming a new organization. Since the candidates and platforms of the major parties usually represent the middle average, the person of extreme views is likely to be disgruntled with them, especially in times when changing circumstances call for sweeping political adjustments. . . .

Naturally, the new conditions of American life forced to the front appropriate doctrines. As far as they involved radical changes, these doctrines usually found their first exponents in minor parties; and as the respective issues came within the range of practical politics, they were presented to the country in national campaigns by one or both of the two great parties. Accordingly, it is necessary to review briefly the minor parties since the Civil War, for, in spite of their apparent insignificance, they have been

[1] From Chapter VI of *The American Party Battle*, Macmillan (1928).

important factors in the American governing process. These parties fall readily into three groups: temperance, labor, and agrarian.

THE PROHIBITIONISTS

About the middle of the nineteenth century there arose a temperance movement which carried several states for absolute prohibition. A reaction, however, speedily set in, and the temperance question was overshadowed by the great slavery issue. After the Civil War, prohibitionists appeared once more upon the political scene. At a convention . . . in 1872, they nominated a presidential candidate and launched a national party. . . . [Their] influence exceeded their numerical strength. Moreover, the idea of prohibition was taken up by leaders in the old parties. . . . In the course of time, hundreds of localities and two-thirds of the states were made "dry" by referendum after referendum; finally the prohibition of intoxicating liquor as a beverage throughout the United States was incorporated in the Eighteenth Amendment to the Constitution, put into effect in January, 1920. . . .

LABOR AND SOCIALISM

Almost immediately after the Civil War, labor entered American politics as a separate and independent element. In 1872, a party known as the Labor Reformers held a national convention in Columbus, Ohio. . . . At that convention, the party declared in favor of Chinese exclusion, an eight-hour day in government employments, civil-service reform, one term for the President, restricting the sale of public lands to bona-fide homeseekers, the regulation of railway and telegraph rates, and the subjection of the military to civil authority.

For a time, the labor element seems to have been absorbed into the agrarian groups . . . but in 1888 a Union Labor party met in a national convention. . . . Although the American Federation of Labor was organized under its present name about this time, namely in 1886, it lent no countenance to the idea of a separate labor party. . . .

An avowed socialist organization appeared on the national stage in the campaign of 1892, when the Socialist Labor party held its first national convention in New York. This party made its appeal almost exclusively to the working class. . . .

Internal dissensions and the extreme views of the Socialist Labor leaders led to the organization of another radical group, known as the Socialist party, which held its first convention in 1900. At the presidential election of 1908 it polled 448,453 votes. . . . Four years later its vote rose almost to a million, and exerted a decided influence on the two major parties. . . . Though fairly united on domestic policy, the Socialist party split on foreign issues. . . . Extremists on the left wing, the Workers' party, declared in favor of communism, nominated a candidate, and polled about 36,000 votes in that year. . . .

LEFT-WING AGRARIANISM

Not long after the Civil War, a distinctly agrarian party, professing the principles of left-wing Democracy, challenged the right of the major parties to rule. With the rapid decline in the prices of agricultural produce, which accompanied the general collapse of the inflated war prices, the farmers began to grow bitter over their lot and to organize societies, known as granges. At length they came to believe that the railways, the corporations, and the financial policy of the federal government were principally responsible for the evils under which they labored. Working through the legislatures, especially in Illinois, Iowa, Wisconsin, and other Western states, they attempted to secure relief by means of laws regulating railway rates and warehousing.

In 1876, the discontented farmers entered politics as the Independent National, or "Greenback," party, and waged warfare especially on the Republicans, whom they charged with having brought about the decline in prices by placing the monetary system on a specie basis and contracting the currency. . . .

Although it gained in votes at first, the Greenback

party went to pieces completely after the campaign of 1884. Within a short time, however, restless agrarians formed a new association, known as the Farmers' Alliance, which, although it did not officially enter politics, was instrumental in creating the Populist party. This party drew together, in 1892, both agrarian and labor elements. At a national convention in Omaha, it put forth a radical program, demanding government ownership of railway, telegraph, and telephone lines, a graduated income tax, postal savings banks, and the free coinage of silver and gold at the legal ratio of 16 to 1.

On this platform the Populists went into the campaign of 1892, and polled more than a million votes, principally in the Western and Southern states. . . . Indeed, in 1896, the Populistic wing of the Democratic party captured the organization and tested its principles in the memorable campaign of that year. . . .

CHAPTER XIX

THE UPHEAVAL[1]

. . . [Slowly] through the decades, as we have just seen, a left-wing agrarian movement gathered strength; finally, in 1896, it overwhelmed the Democratic party and split the Republicans.

THE DEMOCRATIC PLATFORM OF 1896

Neither in principles nor in language did the Democratic platform of that year depart essentially from the traditions set by the agrarians in the days of Jackson, although, of course, new times had brought new devices for conquering the party of "wealth and talents." As of old, the currency question, with all its implications for the distribution of wealth, was a central issue of the battle. This time, however, the agrarian remedy was not more paper money issued by state banks, but an increase in the volume of the currency to be effected by the free coinage of silver on a ratio of sixteen units to one of gold. The practical purpose was the same, namely, to make it easier for debtors to pay and at the same time raise the price of farm produce.

In dealing with the second historic question, namely, the United States banking system, the Democratic platform of 1896 cited specifically the language of Andrew Jackson and denounced the issuance of notes by national banks as undesirable and unconstitutional. This was true to form.

[1] From Chapter VII of *The American Party Battle*, Macmillan (1928).

Equally direct was the plank on protection for American industries: "We hold that tariff duties should be levied for purposes of revenue . . . and not discriminate between class or section." John C. Calhoun could not have been more explicit.

An income tax was endorsed "to the end that wealth may bear its due proportion of the expenses of the Government." Besides levying on great riches, such a tax would afford revenue to make up for the reduction of protective duties on goods consumed by the masses.

Returning to a tradition temporarily weakened during their long tenure of power in the Middle Period, the Democrats in 1896 assailed the federal judiciary, this time for declaring null and void the income tax law of 1894. . . .

And what did labor—that other "humble order of society" dear to Andrew Jackson's heart—receive at the hands of the Democracy rampant? A plank denouncing the use of injunctions in industrial disputes and approving "trials by jury in certain cases of contempt."

Having made a platform in harmony with the traditions of the left wing, the Democrats proceeded to nominate William Jennings Bryan, aptly called "the Tiberius Gracchus of the West." There could be no doubt about his position with reference to the century-old battle. In his famous "Crown of Thorns [or "Cross of Gold] Speech" he placed himself on the side of the wage earner, the country lawyer, the crossroads merchant, the farmer, and the miner. He expressly named them as his friends and exclaimed: "It is for these that we speak." The great question, as he saw it, was: "Upon which side shall the Democratic party fight? Upon the side of the idle holders of idle capital, or upon the side of the struggling masses? . . . The sympathies of the Democratic party, as described by the platform, are on the side of the struggling masses, who have ever been the foundation of the Democratic party." No line could have been more clearly drawn.

On such principles, Bryan appealed to the country in 1896 and again in 1900, only to go down to defeat before William McKinley, a statesman of the Hamilton-Webster school. Again, in 1908, after attempting a conservative tack to the right under Alton B. Parker in 1904, the

Democrats swung back to Bryan, adopted a platform even more aggressive in tone, and were vanquished once more at the polls.

THE REPUBLICAN PROGRAM

On their side of the line, the Republicans were loyal to the Hamilton-Webster-Seward heritage. In not a single relation did they depart from the traditions of a hundred years.

In Hamilton's creed, protection for American industries was a leading article. On coming to power in 1897, the Republicans enacted the Dingley tariff bill which carried the duties, on the average, to a new high level. There were compromises in it, of course, but in the main manufacturers were delighted with it.

Of equal importance in the Hamilton creed were banking and currency. The Whigs and their successors in interest, the Republicans, knew this quite well. Having won a great victory over the easy-money party in 1896, Republicans proceeded as fast as circumstances would allow to give attention to that issue. To solidify the currency they enacted the gold-standard law of 1900, and, under the leadership of Senator Aldrich of Rhode Island, were preparing to revise the whole banking system, when they were ousted from power once more.

Especially did the Republicans attend to the development of the trading empire which Federalist legislation had favored, Webster had promoted, and Seward had advanced. In McKinley's first administration, they annexed the Hawaiian Islands, waged war on Spain, made Cuba a protectorate, added Porto Rico, Guam, and the Philippines to the American empire, and united with foreign powers in upholding their rights in China. Victorious every time the Democrats assailed them for "imperialism," the Republicans not unnaturally looked upon themselves as commissioned by the people to exploit the resources added to the country by arms and diplomacy.

THE RISE OF PROGRESSIVISM

Underneath the prosperity so vaunted in the age of the full dinner pail, rumblings of discontent on the left wing could be heard. . . . Although the makers of unrest, or the spokesmen of it, differed among themselves as to their remedies, they were all united in waging war on what they were fond of calling "government by a plutocracy." With some variations, they demanded an inflation of the currency either by the free coinage of silver or some form of paper, graduated income and inheritance taxes, a reduction of the tariff on goods consumed by the masses, stricter regulation of railways and trusts to cut down their revenues, aid to farmers in the shape of loans at low rates of interest, and laws designed to improve the status of industrial workers.

When the prosperity that followed the Spanish War declined, the agitations of the socialists and the agrarians became more vigorous than ever. After the enactment of the tariff law of 1909, the discontent of Western farmers began to make marked inroads upon the apparent solidarity of the Republican party. Indeed, a rift in that party had been in process since the accession of Theodore Roosevelt to the Presidency in 1901, for he soon aroused the distrust of the capitalistic wing by appealing to the populistic sentiments cherished in the agrarian wing. . . . He advocated income and inheritance taxes partly with a view to helping equalize fortunes; he recommended a stricter federal control of business corporations; and he advocated a few measures for the benefit of the working classes.

Discovering that his successor, President Taft, supported the conservative wing of the Republican party in Congress, Roosevelt, on the appeal of many followers, sought the Republican nomination at Chicago in 1912. Failing to secure it, he and a large portion of his adherents "bolted" and formed a new party, taking the name of "Progressive."

Encouraged by the split in the Republican ranks, the Democrats entered the campaign with great confidence, led by Governor Woodrow Wilson as their candidate. The conservatism of Cleveland and Parker they definitely abandoned.

Now, for the first time since its formation, the Republican party was confronted by an overwhelming combination that threatened it in the language of populism. The Progressive platform, on which Roosevelt ran for President, declared that both the old parties had become "tools of corrupt interests" and that "to dissolve the unholy alliance between corrupt business and corrupt politics is the first task of the statesmanship of the day." The Democratic candidate asserted in similar language that "the government of the United States at present is a foster child of the special interests," meaning thereby "the big bankers, the big manufacturers, the big masters of commerce, the heads of railroad corporations and of steamship corporations."

As the Republican party was shattered by the Progressive defection, Wilson was easily elected President, although his popular vote was more than two million below the total poll of the opposing candidates.

Within a little more than a year after Wilson's inauguration, the European war broke in upon the peace of the world. American industry and agriculture were made prosperous again by the extraordinary demands of the European belligerents, especially the Entente powers. Social questions which had emerged in 1912 were thrust into the background, and the campaign of 1916, waged while the war was still raging, naturally took on the color of that conflict. . . . Rejecting Progressive overtures, the Republicans selected as their standard-bearer Justice Charles E. Hughes. . . . In their platform, the Republicans favored maintaining "a straight and honest neutrality between the belligerents in Europe" and the protection of American rights. The Democrats renominated President Wilson and based their appeal mainly on his record of achievement and on the fact that he had kept us out of war.

THE PROGRAM OF THE NEW FREEDOM

Although the clangor of the European war made more headlines for the newspapers, as a matter of fact there was enacted during the eight years of President Wilson's administration the most remarkable program of legislation passed since the Civil War. And it is to be noted that this legislation merely expressed in legal letter the spirit of the Democratic platform of 1912.

In the third paragraph, that platform declared that "the high Republican tariff is the principal cause of the unequal distribution of wealth; it is a system of taxation which makes the rich richer and the poor poorer; under its operations the American farmer and laboring man are the chief sufferers." Jacksonian Democracy was never more precise. The platform also condemned the "so-called Aldrich bill or the establishment of a central bank" and advocated "such a systematic revision of our banking laws as will render temporary relief in localities where such relief is needed, with protection from control or domination by what is known as the 'money trust.' " It asserted that "of equal importance with the question of currency reform is the question of rural credits or agricultural finance." The suppression of "gambling in agricultural products by organized exchanges and others" was also promised as a part of a program "to improve the conditions of trade in farm products." Recalling the previous pledges of the party to organized labor, it promised trial by jury in cases of indirect contempt and the relief of trade unions from prosecution as illegal combinations in restraint of trade.

With a fidelity to promises not always observed in American politics, the Democrats under the leadership of President Wilson passed a series of laws that squared fairly well with the historic principles of the Jefferson-Jackson-Bryan heritage.

First of all, the tariff was materially reduced in 1913—for the first time since 1857—and in the revision agricultural interests received a consideration which was more than friendly.

Currency and banking questions were attacked in the Federal Reserve Act. As if to recall the tussle of Jackson with an independent corporation, this Act put the control of the new banking system in the hands of a political board appointed entirely by the President and Senate. Bryan had declared that gold was too narrow a basis for the currency: the Federal Reserve Act provided for the issue of money on prime commercial paper—in practical operation going far beyond the gold foundation. Bryan had been accused of demanding a fifty-cent dollar for debtors and farmers: the country lived to see a dollar worth less than fifty cents in the market place. Jacksonian Democracy had feared a centralized "money power": the Federal Reserve Act attempted to distribute that power throughout the whole country by creating twelve separate banking districts.

In keeping with their professions, the Democrats, while framing their revenue program, resorted to the income tax —that old device of the Populists, now made constitutional by the Sixteenth Amendment. To render it quite palatable to the left wing, they placed the exemptions at a good figure and made it progressive, increasing the rates as riches mounted upward. Under the financial stress of the World War, the income tax, individual and corporate, rose to percentages in the higher brackets that fairly staggered the possessors of great fortunes. Besides being besieged to give to war charities "until it hurts," they were compelled to pay taxes until it caused positive anguish of spirit and a serious depletion of purse. Nothing like it had occurred during the Republican administration of the Civil War.

"Big Business," so called—the concentration of "wealth and talents"—was attacked by the Clayton Anti-Trust Act of 1914, designed to break up monopolistic undertakings and force price reductions by competition. In line with this measure was another law creating the Federal Trade Commission and endowing it with power to force the adoption of "fair practices" by business concerns in various relations.

Besides the pleasures and advantages conferred by these laws, such as they were, farmers and planters received aid through the Farm Loan Act which enabled them to keep money in their pockets by borrowing at a lower rate of interest than had been customary, especially in the West and South.

Labor, that powerful ally of Jacksonian Democracy, was not forgotten in the program of the New Freedom. It secured so many lines in the Clayton Anti-Trust Act that Samuel Gompers called the law "The Magna Carta of Labor." It is true that most of the gifts turned to ashes in the fire of judicial interpretation, but labor did not blame the Democratic party for this untoward outcome of its efforts on behalf of the "plain people."

If, as may be surmised, this program of laws did not re-store farmers, planters, and mechanics to the position they had enjoyed in the days of Andrew Jackson, it certainly was conceived with reference to their state of mind rather than to the "special interests" so vigorously attacked by Wilson in his presidential campaign. Without question, there would have been a square alignment on this legislation in 1916 if the World War—so profitable to both American business and agriculture—had not intervened and obscured somewhat the ancient political division. If there was any doubt on this point at the time, it must have been cleared in the very first presidential campaign waged after the conclusion of the War.

In the sphere of imperial and foreign affairs, the Democrats certainly made movements in the direction of re-trenchment. Their platform of 1900 denounced the "greedy commercialism which dictated the Philippine policy of the Republican administration . . . and the war of 'criminal aggression' against the Filipinos." "We assert," ran the document, "that no nation can long endure half republic and half empire, and we warn the American people that imperialism abroad will lead quickly and inevitably to despotism at home."

True to their tradition, the Democrats did not oppose expansion, "when it takes in desirable territory which can be erected into states in the Union and whose people are willing and fit to become American citizens." But they were against the imperialism of commerce—[the] absorbing [of] subject races and the development of trade and invest-ment opportunities through military power. Again and again, the Democrats repeated this profession of faith. In 1912, for example, they declared: "We condemn the exper-iment in imperialism as an inexcusable blunder."

When in a position to give effect to their creed, the Democrats naturally spoke more softly, but they did not overlook their pledges. They gave more self-government to Porto Rico and the Philippines, promising the latter in-dependence sometime in the future. In dealing with the Far East, President Wilson looked coldly upon the devices of "vigorous diplomacy." He at first declined to lend his sanction to projects of international bankers, known as the consortium, for lending money to China and introducing a certain administrative control over her finances. He refused to utter any threats against Japan, even when she made the "twenty-one demands" upon China, and he so neglected American interests in the latter country that his own minister at Peking threw up his office in disgust.

Nearer home, however, especially in the Caribbean, President Wilson continued the strong policy which had been inaugurated under Republican auspices. It is true, he promised the Latin Americans freedom from intervention on behalf of economic interests in the United States but for one reason or another was unable to carry out his pledges.

Nevertheless, when he entered the World War, he condemned imperialism in terms almost savage and at the Paris peace table he sought no material advantages for the United States in the distribution of the spoils of victory. Moreover, he proposed a League of Nations which seemed to threaten some kind of international control over undeveloped races, some limitations on the exploitation of the backward countries by powerful peoples, and the possible interference of a super-state with the ordinary processes of imperial expansion. At all events, statesmen of the McKinley school did not believe that Wilsonian doctrines expressed in the League Covenant squared with the traditions which their party had followed since the days of Webster and Seward.

CHAPTER XX

RESTORATION AND HEALING [1]

"AMERICA'S PRESENT NEED is not heroics but healing; not nostrums but normalcy," exclaimed Senator Warren Gamaliel Harding in an address delivered to Boston businessmen in the spring of 1920. . . . He was himself of the McKinley school and knew very well that for nearly two decades the course of business enterprise had been disturbed; first by Roosevelt and then by Wilson.

Strictly speaking, both of them could be regarded as "political accidents." Roosevelt had been elevated to the Presidency by the assassination of McKinley. Wilson had slipped into that high office during a scrimmage in the Republican camp. All the while the number of people engaged in business enterprise, as distinguished from agriculture, and the amount of capital employed in that branch of economy had been increasing. There was some justification for believing that the clock started by Alexander Hamilton could not be set back.

If Wilson's legislation was directed to farmers, planters, trade unionists, and the lower middle classes, it certainly did not seriously cripple industrial undertakings, perhaps because the demand of the warriors in Europe more than made up for losses in the domestic market. At all events, the World War made several thousand millionaires in the United States, thereby adding strength to the Republican, rather than the Democratic, side of the political alignment.

With fitting propriety, the Republicans nominated as their candidate for President, in 1920, the maker of the

[1] From Chapter VIII of *The American Party Battle*, Macmillan (1928).

captivating slogan, "normalcy." . . . In the campaign which followed, it was made perfectly clear that normalcy meant a return to a high protective tariff, a reduction in income and inheritance taxes, less "government interference with business," vigorous naval and diplomatic support for foreign commerce, and a resort to "firm policies" in the Philippines and the Far East. Against this program, the Democrats offered the record of the Wilson administrations and the League of Nations.

. . . On the whole, the Republican leaders of practical experience were against the League. They knew that the United States now had a good navy and were convinced that the development of the commercial empire, especially in the Caribbean and the Far East, could be more effectively managed if they were free from formal international scrutiny and control. On the other hand, the Democrats had repeatedly condemned imperialism. President Wilson had denounced it in strong language and frankly offered the League as a kind of remedy for the wars in which commercial rivalry had so often involved the great powers. With the issues fairly joined, the Democrats went down to the most terrible defeat ever suffered in the long history of their party.

Before President Harding had gone very far on the way back to normalcy, death cut short his career, leaving his high office to the Vice-President, Calvin Coolidge, of Webster's state, a competent political leader even more determined, if possible, to effect the restoration which his predecessor craved. . . . Nominated for the Presidency by the Republicans in 1924, Coolidge easily overcame John W. Davis, the Democratic candidate, and Robert M. La Follette, the candidate of independent progressives and socialists. . . .

Concerning the significance of this triumph there could be no doubt. The philosophy of Coolidge was well known. He had once said emphatically that "the driving force of American progress has been her industries. They have created the wealth that has wrought our national development. . . . Without them the great force of agriculture would now be where it was in the eighteenth century." Nor was there any confusion in his concept of the party alignment. He regarded himself as the heir of William

McKinley, and McKinley, he said, had taken up "the work of Hamilton and Clay . . . reëstablished their principles."

During the years of Republican administration under Harding and Coolidge, long-standing policies of the party were put into effect:

1. In harmony with the doctrines of Hamilton, Webster, and McKinley, the Republicans raised the protective tariff which the Democrats had reduced under the leadership of Wilson.

2. Although President Wilson had kept the Federal Reserve Bank out of the hands of Bryan agrarians, its administration was not quite to the liking of his successor. Under Harding, the high control was moved over to the right—so far in fact that the left-wing Republicans insisted on having a "dirt farmer" added to the Board in Washington.

3. Roosevelt had given pain to the conservative wing of his party by appointing Oliver Wendell Holmes to the Supreme Court and Wilson had positively scandalized the same group by selecting Louis D. Brandeis for that high tribunal. Though these liberals were somewhat offset by appointments of another kind, their dissenting opinions on occasion were not pleasing to the normalists. Hence, under the renewed Republican régime, William Howard Taft, whose conservative political views were well known, was elevated to the post of Chief Justice, and other selections were made from the same school. Very soon jurisprudence registered a turn in the direction of Marshall's Federalism.

4. For businessmen eager to develop the natural resources of the country, the Harding administration made the way smooth by a leasing policy none too strict in its terms. In fact, in this connection there occurred certain scandals which recalled the misadventures of the Grant administration some fifty years before.

5. Income, excess profit, and inheritance taxes were materially reduced, particularly with reference to the heaviest burden bearers.

6. Foreign commerce was promoted with all the engines of the federal government, the Secretary of Commerce, Herbert Hoover, taking the active lead in this operation, with the general support of the State and Navy Departments. In 1928, a carefully conceived scheme for sub-

sidizing the merchant marine was embodied in the Jones-White Act.

7. The commercial empire was renewed in spirit. In the Philippines the strong hand was restored. Firm warnings were issued to Japan, calling attention to American interests in China and indicating that trespasses would not be permitted.

8. As a corollary, perhaps, of foreign and imperial policies, the League of Nations was utterly rejected by the Republican administration and direct support was given to the advance guard of American businessmen wherever engaged on the frontiers of enterprise.

Beyond cavil, the return to normalcy brought with it prosperity to the industrial world. But . . . farmers and cotton planters . . . received low prices for their produce, suffered from a heavy burden of debts, and eagerly pressed for relief at the hands of Congress.

As of yore, agrarian discontent appeared in the left wing of the Republican party—the party formed by the union of industrialists and farmers at Chicago in 1860. Indeed, as the Democratic party became more urban in tone and direction, the Republican agricultural group steadily developed in strength. . . .

As time passed, three features of the century-old contest between agriculture and capitalism became increasingly evident. First of all, the gravity of the agricultural problem was now dimly appreciated in circles accustomed to crying down the farmers as "crazy populists." Since tenancy was rising, the question was asked by responsible statesmen: "Are American farmers to sink down into a semi-servile condition akin to that of the Roman *coloni*? If so, what bearing does this have on the future of American civilization?" Even manufacturers, alarmed at the development of foreign competition under the direction of American investment bankers, began to take a more serious interest in the fate of their best customers—the farmers.

In the second place, the farmers were no longer content with classical remedies for agrarian distress, such as currency inflation. They now demanded a kind of socialization of their industry, with government assistance, and the fixing of prices by elaborate agencies. . . . As stanch individualists, farmers could never effect by private arrangement an organization comparable to that brought about among capitalists and fix their prices at dinner conferences. Hence they demanded that the government undertake the task. Moreover, the experiment was to be expensive, not as costly as the additions to the navy made necessary by the commercial empire, but still very costly, entailing perhaps a long continuance of income and inheritance taxes.

In the third place, the agrarian group now had leaders quite different from Bryan of 1896—men like Frank O. Lowden, for example, who besides being capitalists in their own right, stood firmly on the contention that the future of America was really at stake, that the fundamental question of maintaining a balanced economy of manufacturing and farming was actually involved, and that a decision in favor of unfettered capitalism would be ruinous in its consequences. . . . But in 1928 the Republican and Democratic parties both refused to take the drastic steps demanded by the agrarians; the age of Jackson and Bryan had come to a close.

BY WAY OF SUMMARY

Reviewing this long political conflict certain conclusions seem to emerge.

Political Federalism of the Hamilton type has practically disappeared. No responsible statesman now speaks of the masses in the fearsome and contemptuous language used by eighteenth-century leaders, such, for example, as John Adams and Gouverneur Morris. The idea of giving property a strategic frontier by qualifications on the right to vote and hold office is no longer ardently championed. Political democracy, subject to some limitations, has become accepted. . . .

Economic federalism of the Hamilton type . . . has continued steadily to the present time. It was and is primarily the working philosophy of business enterprise. It holds that the wealth, the comfort, and the mechanical, scientific, and commercial advance of America are essentially due to business enterprise and that the policies of government associated with it are necessary to its operations and expansion. In an unbroken line, the economic principles of Hamilton were carried forward by Webster, Lincoln, McKinley, and Coolidge. The only noteworthy departure in appeal during the nineteenth century was the open partnership made with the Western farmers in 1860, which gave the party of Hamilton a strange agrarian tinge, particularly in times of distress in the wheat and corn belts.

On the other side has been the frank alignment of agricultural interests made by Jefferson, continued by Jackson (who added an army of mechanics), solidified by the slave-owning planters, and marshaled anew by Bryan after division in the Civil War. In this party also, except when it swung too violently to the left, were to be found many importing merchants and other capitalists (with their professional associates) whose undertakings were injured or at least not benefited by Federalist-Whig-Republican adventures in political economy. As time went on and the country became increasingly industrial and urban, the capitalistic wing of the Democratic party acquired a power fairly proportioned to its economic strength. . . .

To some extent, it is evident from the story, the long political battle has involved the distribution of wealth directly. It is true that the party of Hamilton, Webster, McKinley, and Coolidge never admitted that it was attempting to divert goods from the agricultural to the industrial class. . . . But the leaders of the Republican party have more than once asserted that the left-wing agrarians were "assaulting accumulated wealth"—bluntly attempting to take goods from the rich—by currency, banking, and taxing measures.

The latter, the agrarians, have been equally sure that the Hamilton-Webster-McKinley-Coolidge wing has been engaged in enriching capitalistic classes at the expense of the masses. They have often been frank in declaring their purpose to make a diversion of wealth to their side by currency, banking, and taxing measures.

Whatever the truth in the case as far as economic substance is concerned, in fact leaders in both historic parties have believed that their operations involved a contest over the distribution of goods, sometimes subtle, sometimes crude, but always very real in character. In politics it is beliefs that count. In that great game, opinion and conflict have evolved together. It is impossible to discover to what extent the one is due to the other, although we may suspect with the poet that in the beginning was the deed.

Among the instrumentalities employed by the two parties in this contest over the distribution of wealth, the tariff, currency, banking, and taxation have been constant factors from the beginning. As time has gone on, however, the conflict has become more complex. Today the agrarian interests have abandoned currency inflation as a method of farm relief and, like the capitalists, are demanding positive measures of government intervention calculated to raise the prices of their products, that is, to affect the distribution of wealth by political action.

When charged with abandoning the ancient creed promulgated by Jefferson respecting "the less government the better," the agrarians either ignore the indictment or point out the forms of government intervention employed by industrialists to keep up the prices of manufactured goods. Discrimination in this relation is difficult.

If either party to the struggle has ever sacrificed a substantial interest to consistency in political theory, history gives no record. Democrats, in 1850, were willing to make a drastic use of government engines to secure the return of property in runaway slaves. Forty years later Republicans, who had professed a liberal view of the Constitution with respect to the things they favored, vigorously denounced the income tax as a violation of that fundamental law, even though a similar tax had been imposed by a Republican administration to finance its war for the Union. At the opening of the new century, President Coolidge, heir to Federalist traditions, finding Congress inclined to make experiments in social legislation for ends not like those of protective tariffs, made strong speeches on behalf of "states' rights."

Surely no one who has examined the relation of constitutional and political theory to practical ends or observed the use of it by both parties can conclude that it is a determining factor in driving men into one party or the other. Indeed this type of speculation, if examined closely, looks more akin to protective coloration than to causation.

A similar conclusion has been reached by some historians after studying the evolution of theory respecting the judiciary. When the Jeffersonian Republicans were being baffled by the decisions of the Federalist Chief Justice, John Marshall, they were highly critical in their attitude toward the federal judiciary. When the same Supreme Court, under the direction of a Democratic Justice, Roger B. Taney, upheld slavery in two ringing decisions, Jeffersonian Democrats, then led by planters, called for loyalty, and criticism came from the other side of the line. Within forty years the tables were reversed and Democrats were assailing the judiciary for its income tax and labor opinions. Still, on the whole, it must be said that the Hamilton-Webster-McKinley-Coolidge party has maintained a more friendly attitude toward the federal judiciary and has had good reasons for so doing.

Now we come to expansion and commercial empire. Jefferson's agricultural party has been fairly consistent in its attitude toward the acquisition of land—for the use of planters and farmers. There is not much mystery about this. Under the auspices of that party, Louisiana was purchased, Florida acquired, Texas annexed, and an empire wrested from Mexico. In waging war on the imperialism of the McKinley epoch, the Democrats made it clear that they did not object to expansion provided it took in desirable territory and people "willing and fit to become American citizens." On the other side, the Federalists generally opposed western expansion on the ground that it would enable the farming population to overbalance, that is, outvote the commercial sections.

With equal attention to substantial matters, the Federalist-Whig-Republican party supported commercial empire, first by legislation, then by active naval interposition, and finally by war. It was under the auspices of this party that favors and bounties were given to shipping, formal relations with China were begun, Japan was opened, Hawaii acquired, and Porto Rico, Guam, the Philippines, and other territories added to the American heritage. Opposition to such enterprises, such as it was, came mainly from the agrarian party.

In this conflict between agriculture and capitalism, which has been at the heart of the American party battle, is to be found some clue, at least, to the existence of two parties in the United States as distinguished from the multiple-party system of Europe. American society has been simpler from the beginning than European society. There have been here no racial minorities with historic roots and special territorial interests, such as once furnished the Polish party for Germany and now supplies the Alsatian party for France. The army of the United States has been small, for obvious reasons, and has never constituted a great separate class in the American social system. The various churches, while undoubtedly powerful in influence, have never possessed large landed property or high offices in the state. Hence there has been no practical nutriment for clerical and anti-clerical parties. So the conflict between agriculture and capitalism has not been confused by collateral issues. Moreover the size of party machines and the expense of maintaining them work against the rise of small parties in the United States. It is usually easier for a person with a new idea—if it is not too radical—to get a hearing in one of the major parties than to attract a following by pursuing an independent course of action.

WHERE ARE WE GOING?

At the end of such speculations one cannot help asking: "To what extent have the political parties controlled the development of the country and to what extent have they merely reflected movements and groupings derived from economic activities of the people?" This is an old question. A similar problem puzzled the Greeks and nobody has ever been able to solve it.

Two or three times in the history of the United States, political decisions, seemingly momentous in consequence, have been made. One was in 1787–88 when the federal Constitution was adopted, giving an immense impetus to business enterprise. Another was in 1800 when the agricultural party was put into power and proceeded to acquire all the land between the Mississippi River and the Pacific. A third was in 1860 when, as a result of the election of Lincoln, the planters were unhorsed and subjugated to businessmen and farmers.

From all this we may conclude that politics is not mere

sound and fury, a futile game in which the prime consideration is to get the right man and the right slogan. Certainly from the beginning to the end, economic realities as substantial as capitalism and agriculture have been behind the party battle. It can hardly be denied that the center of gravity in accumulated capital has been on the Hamilton-Webster-McKinley-Coolidge side of the contest, although it has been strongly supported by freehold farmers, north and west, since the formation of the union of hearts at Chicago in 1860 on the basis of reciprocal concessions. Neither can it be denied that the Jefferson-Jackson-Bryan array was essentially agrarian in its economic philosophy and practical measures—with an active mechanic-labor wing after the upheaval of 1828.

But it is difficult to believe that the election of Blaine instead of Cleveland in 1884 or Parker instead of Roosevelt in 1904 would have made much difference in the economy, social life, or general culture of the American people. Indeed, it may be said that, given a vigorous, ingenious race endowed with marvelous natural resources, the final triumph of business enterprise was as inevitable as the movement of the suns. As far as the great body of social legislation enacted during the last thirty years is concerned, it must be confessed that it sprang from movements of opinion quite outside the range of political orthodoxy, that is, from the agitations of minorities winning concessions from the major parties.

To some extent, certainly, the conflict between these two parties has been an emotional antagonism arising from divergent economic situations. The same violent outbursts of temper have appeared on both sides—the superior education of the rich making little impression on the verbal patterns employed to express their passions. Yet to some extent also, the party antagonism has been due to a difference of opinion with respect to the values of agriculture and capitalism.

Jefferson certainly had a very clear-cut ideal for the nation—one thoroughly "reasoned" although perhaps the materialist might wish to point out that it was an agriculturalist's praise of agriculture. But it was not a slave owner's concept, and Jefferson was a slave owner. On the contrary, it was a freeholder's ideal. The Republic of which

Jefferson dreamed was to be composed principally of freehold farmers owning the soil they tilled. There were to be towns and villages, of course, but they were to be small and their prime function was to supply the wants of farmers. Great cities of capitalists and "mobs" of artisans were to be avoided like poison; factories were to be kept in Europe. A complete system of education from the primary school to the university was to open careers to talent, to furnish abilities for the state, and to promote culture for society. A simple government, inexpensive to operate, owing its authority to popular majorities, was to maintain order and defend the heritage. Peace with all mankind was to be a fixed policy, so that this Utopia might be continued indefinitely.

Whether this dream could have been realized, if Jefferson's party had labored at the task night and day with all the engines of government in their hands, affords an interesting, perhaps a melancholy, subject for speculation. But all members of Jefferson's party did not always labor under the spell of this fixed vision. Neither did Jefferson as a practical politician. Yet to a certain extent it was realized, more on account of the immense area of free land available than on account of the political measures adopted by Democratic administrations.

Nevertheless, it is no longer the dream of the Democratic party with its huge urban membership. In fact, with the growth of the industrial population, the center of gravity in the Democratic party is passing, has already passed, from the open country to the cities. The mechanical wing, originally annexed by Jackson, probably outnumbers the freehold section, and there are enough capitalists not engaged in protected industries to furnish the sinews of war for a considerable party campaign. For example, from the public utilities operating in cities controlled by the Democrats handsome contributions and inside tips for political managers are available to promote candidacies and party enterprises. Contracts and public works likewise yield magnificent political returns. On the other hand, the power of the cotton planters sinks relatively in the scale. Chained to the Democratic party by their antagonism to the Negro, they cannot force concessions by threats of desertion and retaliation.

It is perhaps no exaggeration to say that the Democratic party, founded by Jefferson to represent the agricultural interest, has become the organ of "the mobs of the great cities" which he feared and despised, thus to a large extent the organ of industrial masses of alien origin or immediate alien descent. As the party accustomed to pummeling the people of "wealth and talents," the Democrats also draw to their ranks recruits from the lower middle classes. Indeed, if the statement of the party ideal made by President Wilson in *The New Freedom* is authoritative, utopia is the land which offers abundant opportunity for the poor boy to rise into the heaven of the middle class by building "a small but independent business" of his own.

On the other side of the battle-line, the utopia to be won by political action has never been so perfectly sketched by leading participants. Hamilton's ideal, no doubt, was a society in which the rich and well-born governed without any questions from below, industries flourished, and the poor, though compelled to work, were not unprosperous. During the middle period, Hamilton's spiritual heirs spoke of developing manufacturing to such a point that it would supply an adequate market for farm produce.

McKinley did not go far beyond this concept in choosing the full dinner pail for his symbol. None of the men busily engaged in promoting machine industry seem to have conceived of the day when capitalism would be dominant beyond all dispute, when three-fourths or nine-tenths of the people would be dwellers in cities, when the export of manufactured commodities would be deemed vital to our very existence, when the United States would be the first naval power in the world, when the members of the industrial army would outnumber freehold farmers five or six to one.

At all events, few of them took the trouble to work out any kind of ideal goal for machine industry, offering peace and security to labor such as Jefferson conceived for the farmer. The nearest attempt on that side was, perhaps, the Progressive platform of 1912, which indeed summed up all the newer social tendencies of the age. Only socialists have taken the philosophy of the machine at face value and dreamed of carrying manufacturing economy over into a sort of utopia for the industrial masses.

It is doubtless for this reason that individualists of the Democratic school are wont to speak of Socialists and masters of business enterprise as "allies"—unwitting allies perhaps—in destroying the heritage handed down from the days of Jefferson. But this is all speculation and falls outside the province of history.

CHAPTER XXI

AMERICA AND THE BALANCE OF POWER [1]

[COMPILER'S NOTE: In the lecture presented in this chapter, printed in 1922, Beard said "the menaces that confront the United States today are not European. As President Harding has said, they are in the Pacific . . . we want markets in China in which to sell goods . . . that means intense and active rivalry with England, France, and Japan in the Far East." In February, 1935, *Scribner's Magazine* carried a statement by Beard that: "Confronted by the difficulties of a deepening domestic crisis and by the comparative ease of a foreign war, what will President Roosevelt do? Judging by the past history of American politicians, he will choose the latter, or, perhaps it would be more accurate to say, amid powerful conflicting emotions he will 'stumble into' the latter. The Jeffersonian [now Democratic] party gave the nation the War of 1812, the Mexican War, and its participation in the World War. The Pacific war awaits."

Two years later, Japan began an invasion of the Chinese mainland and proceeded to restrict the commercial activities of Americans in the area. On November 26, 1941, after a secret understanding with the British, the United States government plunged into a touchy situation by officially calling upon Japan to withdraw "all military, naval, air and police forces from China and from Indochina" and to respect the open-door program, thereby giving American businessmen access once more to the trade

[1] From *Cross Currents in Europe To-Day*, Marshall Jones Co. (1922).

of China's teeming millions. To have complied would have meant the abrupt reversal of the whole direction of Japanese economic imperialism, which was then trying to "solve" the problems of overcrowded islands at home by bursting forth on the great plains of Asia. A few days later, as is a matter of common knowledge, the Japanese, instead of retiring quietly to their homeland, opened fire on American installations at Pearl Harbor. Under the terms of the Axis agreement for mutual security, this act of war soon carried Germany and Italy into formal armed conflict with the United States.

Given this sequence, Beard's analysis of the economic aspects of American imperialism in the Orient, and its potential outcome, as phrased in 1922, should be of considerable retrospective interest.]

"In the beginning was the deed," wrote the wise poet. Activity yet remains the essential thing in the life of mankind. Political speeches, addresses on foreign policies, and Fourth of July orations exert little influence on the course of human affairs, save occasionally in time of a crisis when the spoken word indicates a line of action to be followed. The fate of a nation—its destiny—lies not in words but in deeds. The nation lives by work, not by rhetoric. It is no detraction from the high honor rightly ascribed to the Fathers of this Republic to say that, well as they built, they alone did not make America. Our America was made by the pioneers, men and women, who leveled the forests, laid out the roads, tilled the fields, and carried American life to the Pacific, and by the capitalists and laborers who constructed and operated the steel mills with their roaring furnaces and the spinning mills with their flying spindles. I do not mean to say that concepts of life and duty do not underlie this fabric of human endeavor, but merely that the majestic signs of power are the outcome of activity.

So, whoever fain would divine the fate of a nation must ponder deeply its activity. It is not what we say about the sea that counts; it is what our sailors do upon the seas. It is not our academic theories about finance that carry weight in the councils of nations; it is our dollars and our cents that imperatively command the attention and wholesome respect of those engaged in the counting houses of the earth's great cities. It is not what President Harding thinks about China or what John Hay has written about China that will shape the coming fateful years in the Pacific; it is what our merchants, our capitalists, our railway builders, and our moneylenders do in China that will set the problem for the rising generation.

Now America is primarily an industrial and a trading nation. Its prime activities are connected with the production and sale of goods. It has no landed nobility to cultivate the graces of leisure. It has no military aristocracy devoted to the exercise of arms. Napoleon once sneered at the nation of shopkeepers, but it was the sneer of jealousy, and the Anglo-Saxon is proud of the term of contempt thus flung at him. Whether this pride is warranted or not, whether the virtues of trade—those bourgeois virtues so scorned of the emancipated—are really virtues, is a matter for the theologian and the ethical teacher. The fact remains. America is an industrial and trading nation. Our activities at home and abroad are mainly related to these essential elements in our national life. Here then is the key to our domestic history and to our future foreign policies. Our empire of trade extends to the four corners of the world. It stretches out under many flags and many governments. Those working at its periphery, under the pressure of economic laws, make the conditions with which American foreign policy must deal. They create the stern and solemn facts with which statesmen and politicians must reckon.

Moreover, recent circumstances have given a new turn to the significance of business. Many nations of antiquity in the course of their history came to rely upon the food supplies brought from distant lands. Rome in her imperial days was fed by wheat carried from her uttermost provinces; when this supply was cut off and the fields of Italy failed to make good the shortage, the staff of life failed. The new nations and new states that rose upon the foundations of Rome were almost self-sufficing. At all events they could feed their population by food grown within their own borders. With the advent of the machine age, this fortunate condition was lost by the leaders in invention and manufacture. In 1914 neither England nor Germany could maintain a standard of living for the laboring population without drawing heavily upon the granaries of America and Russia. The huge populations, called into being by the opportunities of industry, constituted a growing pressure upon the agencies of business and of government, compelling them to extend and maintain foreign markets. This naturally drove the seekers for markets into the backward places of the earth where industry had not penetrated or had made little advance. For nearly a century England had no formidable rival in this imperial enterprise, then one after another competitors appeared upon the world stage—Germany, Japan, Italy, France, and the United States. Even in China and India the whir of the spindle and the clank of the loom were heard ringing out the fate of Lancashire cotton mills. Here were the roots of imperialism, armaments, and warfare. Those who asked where this all would finally lead and what would be the outcome when every nation became industrial were silenced by the inexorable demands of current business. After us the deluge!

In this swiftly drifting world economy, the United States occupies a peculiar position. From one point of view it is very fortunate. It can feed its immense population with almost every kind of product from oranges and sugar to wheat and bacon. It can clothe its people with the cotton of the South and, did exigencies again demand, with wool from the sheep ranges. Considered abstractly it could be a self-sufficing nation. But considered practically, it is, as things now stand, dependent upon foreign trade, if not for a livelihood, at least for what is called "prosperity." It is the city populations of England and Germany that must have markets abroad and import food supplies. In the United States, the wheat and corn grower of the West, the cotton grower of the South, as well as the maker of silks in Paterson, or the manufacturer of steel in Pittsburgh, all depend upon foreign business for that margin of trade which spells prosperity. In short, having an endowment of agricultural resources beyond the strength of our domestic markets for the produce, we must perforce sell the foreigner foodstuffs as well as boots and clothes. Here is a paradox which seems to have received small attention from professional economists.

In every respect, the World War [I] has increased the·

dependence of the United States upon world markets even for the profitable disposal of its surplus capital. It has discharged a very large portion of its indebtedness abroad and has become an insistent moneylender itself. In 1915, European capitalists held $2,704,000,000 worth of American railway stocks and securities; two years later more than half of these holdings had been transferred to America; and the stream still continues to flow westward. In 1914 more than one-fourth of the stocks of the United States Steel Corporation were held in Europe; today less than one-tenth are in foreign hands. The crisis induced in London, long the money center of the world, by the exigencies of the war, led to the phenomenal rise of New York. To sustain their credit here for huge borrowings, England and France opened their strongboxes and sent across the sea the very finest of their gilt-edge securities. As a keen French economist puts it: "One fact dominates all others: the rise of the United States to world hegemony. Lord Robert Cecil has compared the position of the United States after the Great War with that of Great Britain after the Napoleonic wars. That comparison is not quite exact; because the British hegemony was then essentially European while that of the United States today is universal. An immense reservoir of raw materials, of manufactured products, and of capital, the United States has become an economic centre and financial centre in connection with which all the world must work and trade." Fact, stern and tremendous, as Carlyle might say, indubitable and fateful. Beside it all rhetoric fails. The loom on which is woven the texture of world politics has been brought across the sea and the picks of its flashing shuttle can be counted in the financial columns of any great New York daily.

The United States has, therefore, entered upon the role long played by England and France as an international banker and money lender. The visible signs of these new activities are the numerous American banking houses which are to be found in the principal streets and squares of European cities. The Morgan House and the Bankers Trust Company look upon the monument erected to Napoleon's glories in Place Vendôme. If you will turn to the financial section of such a metropolitan paper as *The New York Times,* you will see the statistical record of

American operations in foreign finance. Only recently the transactions in foreign government bonds upon the Stock Exchange have become so great as to require a separate section of the daily statement. Often such transactions occupy one-fourth of the space given to the day's record. The list of bonds bought and sold on a single day is both interesting and full of meaning. The list includes Argentine [Government], Chinese Railway, City of Berne, Bordeaux, Christiania, Copenhagen, Lyons, Marseilles, Rio de Janeiro, Tokyo, Zürich, Danish Municipalities, Department of the Seine, Dominican Republic, Dominion of Canada, Dutch East Indies, French Government, Japanese Government, Belgium, Denmark, Italy, Sweden, Chile, Cuba, Uruguay, San Paulo, Queensland, Rio Grande do Sul, Swiss Confederation, United Kingdom of Great Britain and Ireland, Brazil, and Haiti, not to mention the defaulted securities of Russia and Mexico. When to the sales of these government bonds are added the transactions in the currency and bonds of Central and Eastern European powers and the transactions in the stocks and obligations of foreign industrial corporations, it becomes apparent that American investors are deeply involved in the fate of governments and enterprises in all parts of the world. Almost every week records the floating of a new loan to some foreign city or country or railway already staggering under a burden of debt. The rates are high, the commissions enormous, and the risks correspondingly great.

In accordance with a custom, consecrated by time, the bondholders, whenever a disturbance is threatened or a default is at hand, look eagerly to the government at Washington to support their interests diplomatically if not more vigorously. The genial American public, that takes up millions of oil stocks every year, seizes eagerly at the opportunity to get seven and eight per cent on the bonds of foreign countries, and so every new loan is received with enthusiasm. Let this process go on for fifty years, and the people of the United States will have reconditioned Europe and Asia, and at the same time created an interest obligation that will either flood our markets with European goods by way of repayment, or raise the dollar to a ruinous height in the exchanges of the world. They will also have incurred a gigantic financial risk which a new war or a social revolution in Europe would transform into widespread ruin with its corresponding effects on our political issues. In short, the United States, through the investment of capital, has become a silent partner in the fate of every established order in the world. Unless we are to assume on the basis of the experience of the past three hundred years that there will be no more World Wars or social cataclysms, it is safe to conjecture that days of greater trouble are ahead, whether we enter the League of Nations or stay out of it. Once a great European war merely deranged our foreign trade; in the future it will disturb every investor in every village Main Street. Entangling political alliances may be pieces of paper, as the past has shown, but the texture of the economic alliance is woven of tougher materials. Politics comes after the fact. The gilt-edged pieces of parchment handed out to American investors will speak louder than the silver tongues of professional orators.

In industry, as in finance, the upward swing of the United States after 1914 was incredible in its swiftness and majestic in its range. Our old competitors in Europe were not only paralyzed by war activities; they clamored louder and louder for the products of American mills, mines, and factories. Measured in tons of steel, pounds of copper, and bolts of cloth, the sales of the United States abroad between 1914 and 1918 were nothing short of staggering. We supplied not only belligerents in Europe but their former customers in South America, Asia, and the islands of the seas. Colossal factories sprang up on our soil. Old plants were enlarged and extended. Thousands of new workers were drawn into the cities from the countryside, especially as immigration fell off. American capital was amassed in stupendous quantities and preparations were made to seize the empire of world trade. Having an immense home market with the corresponding advantages of large-scale production, American businessmen prepared to lead the world in industry and finance. They were even able to induce a Democratic Congress, in spite of its inveterate suspicion, to enact the Webb law authorizing the formation of gigantic combinations to develop and exploit foreign markets.

In the normal course of things, if the history of England

and Germany is our guide, a merchant marine and sea power follow the growth of foreign business. In this sphere also the trend of American economic development is true to form. On the eve of the World War [I], the American merchant marine was an almost negligible factor upon the high seas. It is true that long ago our wooden ships were upon every ocean and our sailors rivaled in skill and daring the best upon the wave; but the glory of our enterprise upon the waters vanished during the Civil War. After 1865 the record of nearly every year showed a decline. In 1861 American ships brought to our shores more than one-half, in values, of all the goods imported; in 1913 they carried only about eleven per cent of the values. Meanwhile the tonnage of ships for oceanic trade fell from 2,547,000 to 1,928,999, reducing the United States to a position below that of England, Germany, and Norway. During the same period the proportion of exports carried from our shores in American ships dropped from seventy-two per cent in values to nine per cent. Americans, busy with the development of their continent, and content with their lake and coastwise trade, let foreign ships carry their exports and imports. The planters and farmers of the country rejected every proposal to build a merchant marine by national subsidies—the only device which American capitalists could offer as a means of bringing the ocean carrying trade into American hands.

So things stood in 1914 when the war drove the German merchant marine from the seas and compelled the other belligerents to commandeer ships for military purposes. Then the United States found itself in the presence of a crisis similar to that induced by the Napoleonic wars. One hundred years before, cotton, tobacco, corn, and bacon from American plantations and farms lay wasting at the docks for want of ships to carry them abroad. In 1914 the owners of vast masses of manufactured goods as well as the owners of farm produce clamored for ships. Thus it happened that the Democratic party, which many years before had withdrawn subsidies from the American marine, found itself confronted by a trying situation. The cry for ships went up on every hand. It was no longer the steel-makers and the owners of shipyards alone that were heard in the lobbies of Congress. The munition-makers needed ships. The farmers and planters needed them. So the Democratic party, the party of the less government the better, like all parties, laid aside theories in the presence of compelling facts and set about creating an American marine. Without utterly repudiating the teachings of half a century, it could not openly resort to the subsidies and bounties it had so long and so passionately denounced. But the ships had to be built. There was another alternative. The government itself could go into shipbuilding. In 1916, the Shipping Board was created for that purpose. Soon the war came to America. Then with lavish grants from the public treasury ships were built with a speed that astonished the world.

Thanks to what appears to be a historical accident, the United States has now become one of the great oceanic carrying powers. In 1914 our shipyards turned out 200,000 tons of shipping while those of Great Britain turned out 1,683,000 tons. In 1918, our yards launched 3,000,000 tons while the English yards set afloat 1,348,000 tons. All around our long coast-lines American ingenuity was applied with astounding zeal and marvelous results. The experiment was costly, for money was spent like water, but "the goods were delivered." Within the course of five years the American flag was restored to its old pre-eminence on the high seas. In the Atlantic and the Pacific new steamship lines made their appearance bidding for freight and passenger business. New shipping offices were opened in all the chief ports of the world. An ever increasing proportion of our exports and imports was carried in American bottoms. The steamship companies of Europe found themselves face to face with a new and formidable competitor. In 1920 the total number of American vessels, registered as engaged in foreign trade and whale fishing, showed a tonnage of 9,928,595, to say nothing of the 6,395,429 tons engaged in coastwise and internal trade. In 1918 the entire merchant marine of the United Kingdom amounted to 10,000,000 tons in round numbers. Thus it happened when the war stopped that the world was overstocked with merchant vessels and in every harbor steamers and sailing ships lay rusting and rotting. Then the great cry went up that the government which by lavish expenditures had built the ships should subsidize those into whose hands they passed at a nominal cost. With the economics of this great transaction, we are not concerned. The striking fact is established that the United States has become within six years one of the first oceanic carriers of the world, a formidable competitor of all the maritime nations.

Coincident with this growth in the merchant marine was a tremendous stride forward in battleship construction. Until the Spanish War, America was not reckoned among the great sea powers, although her sailors had given a good account of themselves in many contests upon the ocean. After Manila Bay and Santiago, however, increasing attention was given to the navy, and in 1914 the United States ranked third in naval strength. Then began a period of feverish activity marked by constantly increasing acceleration. In 1920 the Navy General Board reported its grand designs: "A navy second to none recommended by the General Board in 1915 is still required today. But in addition the great war has shown the importance of unimpeded ocean transportation for commerce. If either belligerent loses the control of the sea, the national fighting power and endurance are greatly affected. In time of peace a great and developing country needs a proportionately great merchant fleet of its own to insure its markets and preserve its commerce from subservience to rival nations and their business." That report struck home and its spirit was reflected in the new building program. So rapid was American progress that experts were able to calculate that by 1926 the fighting power of the United States on the sea would surpass that of Great Britain. The long supremacy inaugurated in the defeat of the *Armada* was on the verge of passing to America when the Washington conference called a halt in competitive armaments.

So out of the World War [I] emerged a new America, first among the investing, industrial, commercial, maritime, and naval powers of the earth—a country endowed with an immense productive equipment and ready to penetrate the most inaccessible markets of the most distant lands. At the same time, a paralysis of Europe cut down the demand for American agricultural produce and manufactured goods, and the destruction of the Russian and German empires gave a new and startling turn to events in the Orient, leaving Japan without the support of any great power save England. It was inevitable, amid these circumstances, that we should witness a burst of American activity in the Far East.

This is of course a new emphasis rather than a new factor, for Oriental trade had been an important element in American economy and politics since the maturity of the Pacific seaboard states, especially since the acquisition of the Philippines and the opening of the Panama Canal. The Pacific has become the new theater. It has been said that the drama of antiquity was played on the shores of the Mediterranean and that the drama of the modern world has been enacted on the shores of the Atlantic. The drama of the future is preparing on a more majestic stage where teeming millions stand ready to take part in it. The curtain has risen upon this new drama. The actors are in their places, but no living mind can divine even the first act, to say nothing of the denouement. Asia is old, wise, fertile in ideas and rich in potential resources. It had its empires, its religions and philosophies long before the geese cackled on the banks of the Tiber. Many conquerors have tried their fortunes there. England has brought the vast southern peninsula under her imperial dominion, but her subjects stir ominously and the solid structure may in time dissolve. Japan, aroused from her lethargy by Yankee enterprise, is equipped in wealth, industrial power, and military strength to extend and defend her mighty hegemony. China, huge, amorphous, beset by a thousand ills, threatened with dissolution, and restless under the influence of western ideas, lies prostrate, but, having survived a hundred conquests and conquerors, may yet smile in her enigmatic way upon the Lilliputians who assail her. Russia, at present broken and powerless, seems out of the play, but that is an illusion except to those who reckon human affairs in terms of flags and states. The Russian people multiply with the passing years and they push out upon the Asiatic plains with the relentless force of an Alpine glacier. Those who occupy the earth and till the soil at their feet will in the long run possess it. Russia, the land of Tolstoi and Lenin and Sazonov and Nicholas Romanov, still lives and will again play a leading part in the drama that unrolls in the Pacific basin.

The first speeches of the American actors have already been delivered. The policy of "the Open Door" has been announced. It has an immense advantage. It has an ethical ring. It respects the integrity, sovereignty, and territory of the Chinese nation. It contemplates no military aggression, no forcible annexations, no political power. It merely asks that all nations have equal rights to go and come, buy and sell, invest and collect in China. In theory it corresponds to the modern ideal of free commerce, though it may mean that in practice immense monopolies may be built up, monopolies such as have arisen in Europe and the United States out of the same freedom of commerce. In theory it meets the approval of China, for China, naturally anxious to preserve her territorial unity against foreign domination, welcomes assistance. While thus corresponding to China's immediate desires and expressing an ethical doctrine, the open-door policy also satisfies the practical interests of the United States, at present. The seizure and government of Chinese territory would involve difficulties, financial and administrative; if opportunities of trade may be secured without this hazard, territorial annexations would be exercises in foolhardiness.

The belief in our own disinterestedness in the pursuit of the open-door policy is so widespread that any opposition to it on the part of other countries concerned in the Orient is viewed as a manifestation of unwarranted ill-will. Undoubtedly American policy offers a striking contrast to the policy of penetration and aggression followed by many other powers. Nevertheless, it does not appear to be entirely benevolent to the seasoned diplomats of the Old World, as the papers recently published from the Russian archives show. In these papers, the American State Department is represented as aiding vigorously in the economic penetration of China and as supporting American banks with interests hostile to those of the other powers. It is not necessary to accept these criticisms at face value or on the basis of them to entertain doubts as to the correctness of American diplomacy. That is not the point. The heart of the matter is that neither Europeans nor the Japanese look upon American imperial methods in the Orient as different in any essential respect from those of other powers. The American goal, they say, is the same, namely, opportunities for profitable trade and investment, and, as the Philippines bear witness, territorial expansion is not avoided when it becomes necessary. The spirit of cynicism and doubt as to the ultimate intentions of America in the East, though we may vigorously condemn it, must nevertheless be understood if we are to gauge correctly forces of the future. Nowhere is this spirit more accurately reflected than in an article by an eminent French publicist, in the *Mercure de France* for January, 1922. This single passage gives the heart of the matter:

"The realist, the positive, and especially the financial, mentality which is the true characteristic of the Yankee and his raison d'être has been profoundly stirred by the situation created in the United States during and after the war—a situation which he had not foreseen and which is presented under the form of a genuine paradox. Enriched in that conflict to the point of securing almost all the gold of the world, North America nevertheless is passing through a crisis of appalling proportions; unemployment, a paralysis of the export trade, and all the economic calamities, now oppressing American citizens, fell upon them at the same time as an exceptionally favorable state of exchange and an unexpected abundance of treasure. It occurred at once to the minds of these practical men that it was necessary henceforward to secure a market other than that afforded by Europe, a field of action in which their preponderant or semi-sovereign influence will permit them to sell their products and their primary materials under conditions of exchange which they will regulate themselves. Thus they will avoid as far as possible the economic laws which, in their operation, have become so dangerous for them in Europe. Since they were powerless in Europe to regulate the value of money which depends upon a number of circumstances—upon a state of affairs peculiar to the Old World and beyond their control,—it was urgent that they should have at their disposal an Asiatic country where they could act, direct, and organize at their pleasure and where their commerce would not encounter the same perils as among their old customers. China is there, immense and ready, they think, to receive all authorities, and so disorganized that she is ready to accept anything they wish to impose upon her. Hence there were, even during the war, missions of all sorts, economic, financial, religious, educational, and recreational sailing from Frisco to the Middle Kingdom.

"At that moment, Japan began to be disturbed. For other reasons than the United States, even for opposite reasons, Japan felt the need of extending her influence over the great Yellow Republic; above all for reasons connected with natural resources. Wanting in coal and iron, Japan must of necessity possess these things without depending upon any powerful nation. Moreover her seventy-seven million people are crowded into a country about as large as France and at any price it was necessary to search for an outlet for emigrants. In short, with the United States established in China, there was at her gate an enemy which had shown a tenacious hatred for her and an unchanging contempt for the yellow race, since, according to the Yankee conception of things, the yellow man, who is only a charming being when one visits him to get his money, becomes intolerable when he asks for simple reciprocity. . . . Mr. Hughes has proposed that the American republic should dominate the Pacific—twenty-eight million more inhabitants than Japan to undertake the economic conquest of China, eight super-battleships more than the Mikado possesses to curb his desires—there are the powerful trump cards, and if America succeeds in making them serve her purpose, she will have a beautiful party. Although officially disinterested for the moment in the affairs of Europe, she sees that they are being reintegrated secretly in general policy through financiers who meet in their private chambers and associate with themselves at the council table some Anglo-Saxon business men and some Germans who more than ever divide the world." Such is a view of American policy now, by an eminent French publicist. How much untruth there is in it each may decide for himself according to his knowledge. Now that we have set out upon the way it is wise to see ourselves as our critics see us, for it is our critics, not our friends, who will make trouble for us.

Whether we accept or reject the criticisms of the French observer, we cannot overlook the fact that the widely heralded Washington conference was related mainly, even almost exclusively, to Pacific, not European, problems.

Though associated in the minds of some with various world enterprises such as the League of Nations, it was in fact confined in its chief activities to the practical adjustment of Pacific matters in such a way as to facilitate the prosperity of American trade. When the conference was first called, many enthusiasts began to see visions of general disarmament and universal peace, but President Harding sharply reminded them that nothing of the sort was contemplated. He had in view reducing the cost of warlike preparations in time of peace, to the great relief of the burdened taxpayers, and settling certain specific matters likely to cause friction among the powers concerned. The two projects were closely knit in the realm of fact. As President Harding said in his address to the Senate on February 9, 1922, in submitting the results of the conference to that body: "Much as it was desirable to lift the burdens of naval armament and strike at the menace of competitive construction and consequent expenditures, the Executive branch of the Government, which must be watchful for the Nation's safety, was unwilling to covenant a reduction of armament until there could be plighted new guarantees of peace, until there could be removed probable menaces of conflict." After this plain declaration of prosaic fact, President Harding went to the heart of the matter. "We have seen the eyes of the world," he said, "turned to the Pacific. With Europe prostrate and penitent, none feared the likelihood of early conflict there. But the Pacific had its menaces and they deeply concerned us. Our territorial interests are larger there. Its waters are not strange seas to us, its farther shores not unknown to our citizens. . . . We covet the possessions of no other power in the Far East and we know for ourselves that we crave no further or greater governmental or territorial responsibilities there. Contemplating what is admittedly ours, and mindful of a long-time and reciprocal friendship with China, we do wish the opportunity to continue the development of our trade peacefully and on equality with other nations." When all the rhetoric, ceremonials, and formalities are laid aside, there is the sum and substance of the whole business. "The Pacific had its menaces and they deeply concerned us."

What were those menaces in fact and deed? Who made

those menaces? No informed person is under any delusions on this matter. Russia, long the aggressor and high chief engineer of intrigues against Chinese territory, is paralyzed and powerless for the present and the indefinite future. France, though possessed of a huge Indochinese empire, offers no serious challenge. Germany is bankrupt in military power and can do no more than make commercial gestures. There remain England and Japan. They are the only powers in a position to encroach upon Chinese territorial integrity, and in 1921 these two powers were bound by an alliance. "The Pacific had its menaces." They were real; they were twofold; they were united, and the United States at the same time had no intention of surrendering any of the opportunities of American merchants, manufacturers, and financiers in China.

Thus it happened that the desires of the taxpayers for relief and the pacific aspirations of the American people, coincided with a genuine crisis in the Far Eastern relations of the American government. For eight years conditions had been abnormal. President Wilson, as the spokesman of planters, farmers, and trade unions, did not continue the aggressive policy pursued by the Secretary of State, Philander Knox, in the advancement of American trading and investing interests in the East. Moreover the war had dislocated forces, engaged the energies of England, paralyzed Russia, eliminated Germany, and given Japan a free hand. In fact, between the retirement of President Taft and the inauguration of President Harding, Japan had made immense strides in the extension of her hegemony over China. At first she operated in conjunction with Russia, with the consent of England. Then, in the midst of the war, Japan made her famous Twenty-one Demands, which in effect promised to destroy the remnants of Chinese sovereignty. Mr. Wilson, so zealous in the interest of universal peace and the League of Nations, approved the Lansing-Ishii doctrine, let Shantung go to Japan, and neglected Yap.

It is in the light of these things that the results of the Washington conference must be examined. First, there is the naval holiday and the Four Power treaty. As all conversant with naval affairs know, by 1924 or 1926 at the latest, according to the prevalent rate of construction, the

United States would have been supreme at sea over Great Britain in fighting units and weight of metal. But Great Britain was united to Japan by a treaty of alliance and the two constituted a formidable power. By offering debt-burdened Britain a relief in naval construction the United States induced her to cut loose from a separate alliance with Japan. Hence the naval holiday. It is an immense gain to the taxpayers. It gives experts time to study the whole question of sea fighting in view of the great probability that dreadnoughts and super-dreadnoughts are as obsolete as wooden walls.

The accompanying Four Power treaty is likewise susceptible of many interpretations as to origin, purpose, and implications. The terms of the instrument are very general. The high contracting parties agree to respect one another's insular possessions in the Pacific and to enter into communication in case any disturbance arises in that connection. On its face that declaration appears to be a truism. President Harding informed the Senate and the country that "nothing in any of these treaties commits the United States or any other power to any kind of alliance, entanglement or envolvement." But, as if baffled by his own statement, he added: "It has been said, if this be true, these are meaningless treaties and therefore valueless. Let us accept no such doctrine of despair as that." It has been stated, but not officially, that the purpose of the Four Power treaty was to destroy the Anglo-Japanese alliance and if this is true the somewhat uncertain terms become full of meaning. At all events the way is made clear for the pursuit of the open-door trading policy in China.

More precise is the treaty laying down the principles to be pursued with regard to China. The high contracting parties once more proclaim the sovereignty, the independence, the territorial and administrative integrity of China, and free and equal opportunity for commerce and industry. They agree that they will not seek or support their nationals in seeking: (a) any arrangement which might purport to establish in favor of their interests any general superiority of right with respect to commercial or economic development in any designated regions of China; (b) any such monopoly or preference as would deprive the nationals of any other power of the right of undertaking any legitimate trade or industry in China or of participating with the Chinese government or with any local authority in any category of public enterprise, or which by reason of its scope, duration, or geographical extent is calculated to frustrate the practical application of the principle of equal opportunity.

Two things are to be noted about this treaty. The language, though perhaps as specific as circumstances admitted, is nevertheless general in character. It is open to a variety of interpretations in the application. It is less specific and pointed than the language of the famous Algeciras compact which was supposed to put an end to friction among the powers in Morocco. It does not contain the detailed provisions, limitations, prohibitions, and specifications laid down in 1906 for the conduct of the Sultan's estate. That is the first point to be noted. The second is that it is, like the Algeciras compact, applicable to a country in disorder and revolution, to a rapidly changing situation, not to a settled society like the United States or England where commerce can be carried on without recourse to armed force. When France was reproached with having torn up the compact of Algeciras, she could with justice reply that local conditions were such that its application, according to the ordinary norms of legal procedure, was impossible. So it was.

CONCLUSIONS

Anyone who has given two or three years to the study of the course of affairs in Europe since 1918 will hesitate to advance with firm assurance very many "conclusions." The pages which follow should really be entitled "A Few General and Tentative Reflections." Europe is in an unstable equilibrium and serious changes may take place any moment. Generalizations are dangerous. Prophecy is more dangerous. But the human mind longs for something more positive than a glimpse at a swirling tide. Hence these last words.

The first reflection is perhaps the easiest to formulate. There are many signs of European recovery in the realm of fact. The reconstruction work in France has been truly marvelous. The basic industry, agriculture, though disturbed by agrarian changes in Eastern Europe, is being restored and a decided turn upward may be expected shortly. The quarrels among the new nationalities are being allayed by negotiations and treaties and new bonds of trade and intercourse are taking the place of those snapped by the war. In this sphere time will bring healing.

Secondly, finance and industry in Europe are in a state of chaos and conditions are growing worse rather than better. If the analysis [in another volume] . . . is sound, it is difficult to see how business can be brought to its old course without reducing reparations and inter-allied debts, scaling down domestic debts, and restoring the currency to a gold basis. Europe must soon choose between some kind of a general economic constitution and a realignment of powers for more costly and deadly conflicts.

Thirdly, the principle of conscious and systematic support for commercial enterprise has been adopted by England, France, Germany, and Italy, and the capitalists of these countries are driving forward to the conquest of new markets with a greater zeal than in the days before the war. There is this difference: they are more effectively organized within their respective countries and more vigorously supported by their respective governments. The restoration of Europe without a constitution designed to mitigate these rivalries will mean a return to secret diplomacy and the armed peace, preparatory to a re-enactment of the great drama which we have just witnessed. What would be left of European civilization after several repetitions of this cycle may be left to the imagination. But if Europe cannot learn from experience, it is hardly probable that more pronunciamentos from Washington will have any effect upon the course of events there.

Fourthly, there seem to be only two policies open to the United States. The first is to enter into a general European council and attempt by international pressure to compel a readjustment of indemnities, debts, tariffs, and currencies; that is, to join in forcing the various nations to do what they must do before the course of business is returned to a pre-war basis. If anyone will read the European press closely, he will see what grave complications this would involve, what new hatreds, what new discords. In my opinion it would be unwise for the United States to attempt to play the part of a general receiver or a big brother for Europe tortured by the inevitable after-war hatreds. This is not because we are wanting in the spirit of helpfulness, but because in this case intermeddling is likely to do more harm than good. The other course is that now pursued, except as far as Russia is concerned. It is the course of allowing Europe to set its own house in order under the stress of its own necessities and experiences. Its statesmen know little enough, perhaps, but they know Europe better than any agents sent out from Washington.

Fifthly, if the United States leaves Europe to its own devices in recovering its economic prosperity, then logic as well as common decency requires our government to refrain from publishing periodical homilies on the place of Russia in Europe's affairs.

Sixthly, new loans to European countries by American banking houses, though they yield high commissions and high interest rates at present, merely add to the burdens and confusion of Europe and help postpone the day of fiscal reckoning which all continental countries must face sooner or later. Indeed these very loans may involve us, in spite of ourselves, in grave problems of readjustment now facing European statesmen.

Finally, the menaces that confront the United States today are not European. As President Harding has said, they are in the Pacific. What does that mean? What does it imply in terms of American policy and of obligations for American citizens? President Harding has given us the key. He says that we do not want any more territory in the Pacific, but that we want trade. That means, in plain English, that we want markets in China in which to sell goods; we want opportunities to invest money with good commissions and high rates of interest; and we want concessions to build railways, exploit natural resources, and develop Chinese industries to our profit. Assuming that the open door is really open, that means intense and active rivalry with England, France, and Japan in the Far East. So the great question is: "Shall the government follow trade and investments?"

That is the crucial question. It is a question fraught with momentous significance for this country. Behind all the notes, treaties, speeches, and declarations, that is the one great issue in foreign affairs before the people of this country. It must be considered without bitterness or partisan rancor in the light of national interests and national destiny. There must be no sneering criticism of our manufacturers and bankers. They are following economic opportunities as other men do. Nothing short of the interest of the whole nation should come into the decisions upon policy.

At this fateful juncture in American history, there are three courses open to those who fain would mold the world to their hearts' desires. There is, first, the policy of positive imperialism, naked and unashamed. Under it, our government would give vigorous support to merchants, bankers, and manufacturers in all parts of the earth in their search for trade and investment opportunities. It presupposes armies and navies adequate to all exigencies and strong enough to compel respect for all decisions taken in behalf of national economic interests. The Department of State, operating mainly in secret through a corps of consuls and diplomats, would become the adjunct to industrial and investment interests. A merchant marine would be subsidized, and government support given to the prosecution of commercial advantages. Discriminatory and preferential tariffs would be constructed with reference to the promotion of American industries.

This policy is commonly defended on two grounds. Some say that it is the natural, inevitable, and irresistible development of an imperial race—the manifest destiny of every nation to expand, conquer, and dominate. Possibly it is the decree of fate. If so, then all arguments for and against it are equally futile and irrelevant.

Others, brushing aside such philosophy, say that imperialism is necessary to American prosperity, that we must sell more and more manufactured goods every year or perish. Let us examine briefly that hypothesis in operation. More billions in trade means bringing more business to American manufacturing industries and drawing more millions of people from Europe and from our own countryside into mines, mills, and factories. It means more billions in stocks and bonds in strongboxes, and more millions of men, women, and children in industrial cities—a vaster aristocracy of wealth and a huger proletariat. Whoever can contemplate the possibility of a hundred years of that development without thought of consequences lying beyond, deserves to wear the badge of courage. Still the policy involved in it may be pursued without regard to the long future.

Imperialism is not new. It offers no novel features to the adventurous spirit of man. The past affords ample records for the study of its processes, operations, and consequences. It cannot however be pursued today under the conditions of the past three hundred years. The experience of the British Empire is no guide to us now. The backward places of the earth are all staked out and in the possession of powers bent upon the kind of commercial and financial imperialism that is recommended to us. Imperialism of the future will involve competitive risks far more dangerous than the risks of Pitt, Disraeli, and Sir Edward Grey. Still the policy is an intelligible one and is defended by some of the ablest minds of our generation. Ample support for it is to be found in the voluminous literature of the late German Empire.

There is before us, possibly, a second policy. It is covered by that term of opprobrium hurled at it by the devotees of imperialism, namely, "Little Americanism." Its implications are likewise clear. Let us examine them. According to this philosophy, the government of the United States would not lend diplomatic or any other kind of support to investment bankers placing loans abroad, [whether] in making them, collecting the interest, or insuring the principal. It would not use the army or the navy in the collection of debts due to private citizens. The government would feel under no greater obligation to a banker who made a bad loan in Guatemala than it would to a banker who made a bad guess in lending money to a dry-goods merchant in Des Moines, Iowa. It would not seize any more territory. It would discontinue the policy of annexing spheres in the Caribbean and would invite the Latin American countries into a co-operative system for settling all disputes in this hemisphere. It would give independence to the Philippines and draw back upon the Hawaiian base. It would maintain an army and a navy adequate for the defense of our territories, by universal service if necessary, and perhaps preferably. It might possibly contemplate entering a League of Nations, provided all other countries were prepared to adopt a similar domestic policy. It would bend all national energies and all national genius upon the creation of a civilization which, in power and glory and noble living, would rise above all the achievements of the past. This policy, whatever may be said against it, has on its side at least the advantage and interest of novelty. The great power that pursued it might, indeed, sink down into dust like the empires of Tamerlane or Augustus, but at least the world's experiences would be enriched.

There is finally another alternative, that of no policy at all, save the policy of drift and muddle. It would support our capitalists and merchants abroad, but not adequately. It would encourage them to pursue their economic interests and then fail to sustain them in a crucial hour. It would create, inadvertently, situations calling for imperial military and naval forces, but would not have the forces ready on the fateful day. It would follow in the paths of Alexander and Cæsar but would be content with the philosophy of Buncombe County. Yet, under Providence many things might be accomplished by this policy. It might land the nation at the gates of destruction; but that can be said of the imperial policy pursued by Rome and Germany. As in individual life we find our little plans and purposes but frail reeds in our hands, so in national life, the wisdom, understanding, and penetration of the best and most practical statesmen often prove to be in the test of time and circumstance the weirdest of delusions.

Here I take leave of the subject, saying with Bossuet, the good bishop: "All those who are engaged in the work of government are subject to a higher power. They always do more or less than they intend and their counsels have never failed to produce unforeseen effects. They are not the masters of the turn given to affairs by the ages past. Neither can they foresee the course the future will take. Far less can they force it." Still, who would not rather have the heritage of Athens than the legacy of Cæsar?

INDEX

THE TEXT of this book was set in Linotype TIMES ROMAN, designed by Stanley Morison for *The Times* (London), and first introduced by that newspaper in 1932. The book was composed, printed, and bound by THE COLONIAL PRESS INC., Clinton, Massachusetts. Paper manufactured by S. D. WARREN COMPANY, Boston, Massachusetts. Cover design by HARRY FORD.

Vintage Books

Vintage Books